TE TAIAO
MĀORI
AND THE NATURAL WORLD

BATEMAN BOOKS

Te Manatū Taonga
Ministry for Culture & Heritage

TeAra.govt.nz
The Encyclopedia of New Zealand

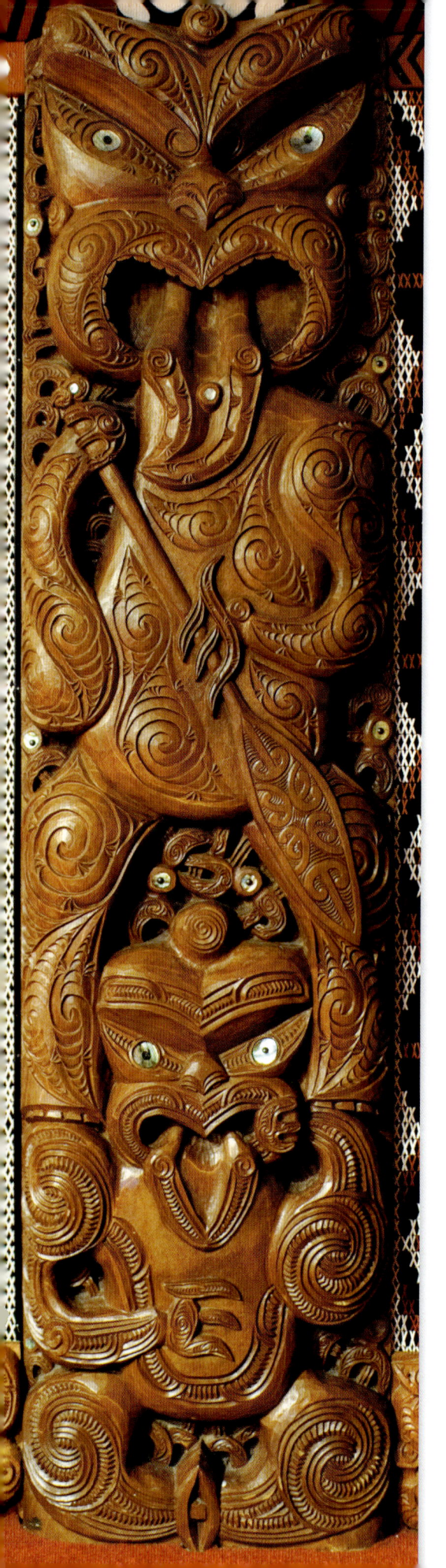

Copyright © Crown copyright, 2010
Copyright © in typography and design David Bateman Ltd, 2010

Copyright in the illustrations not attributed to Te Ara – the Encyclopedia of New Zealand is held by the individual owners of the illustrations.

Published 2010 by David Bateman Ltd,
Unit 2/5 Workspace Drive, Hobsonville, Auckland, New Zealand
www.batemanbooks.co.nz

Reprinted 2016, 2020

ISBN 978-1-86953-775-3

This book is copyright. Except for the purpose of fair review, no part may be stored or transmitted in any form or by any means, electronic or mechanical, including recording or storage in any information retrieval systems, without permission in writing from the publisher. No reproduction may be made, whether by photocopying or by any other means, unless a licence has been obtained from the publisher or its agent.

Book design: Alice Bell
Printed in China through Colorcraft Ltd, Hong Kong

Tamatea, Te Herenga Waka marae.

Contents

Te Ara Wānanga / The Te Ara team **4**

Foreword **5**

Introduction Te ao mārama *the natural world* **6**

Part I   Ranginui *the sky*
    Ranginui *the sky* **12**
    Maramataka *the lunar calendar* **18**
    Matariki *Māori New Year* **22**
    Tāwhirimātea *the weather* **26**

Part II   Papatūānuku *the land*
    Papatūānuku *the land* **40**
    Whenua *how the land was shaped* **48**
    Ngā waewae tapu *Māori exploration* **56**

Part III   Tangaroa *the sea*
    Tangaroa *the sea* **72**
    Te whānau puha *whales* **78**
    Taniwha **84**
    Ngārara *reptiles* **94**

Part IV   Te Waonui-a-Tāne *the forest*
    Te Waonui-a-Tāne *forest mythology* **100**
    Te ngahere *forest lore* **106**
    Ngā manu *birds* **116**
    Te aitanga pepeke *the insect world* **126**
    Patupaiarehe **132**

Part V   Te mahinga kai *food gathering*
    Te hī ika *Māori fishing* **138**
    Mātaitai *shellfish gathering* **144**
    Te tāhere manu *bird catching* **152**
    Te hopu tuna *eeling* **162**
    Ngā tupu mai i Hawaiki *plants from Polynesia* **170**
    Kiore *Pacific rats* **174**
    Kurī *Polynesian dogs* **178**

Kaitiakitanga **182**

Glossary of Māori words **184**

Glossary of species names **185**

Endnotes **187**

Bibliography **187**

Picture credits **189**

Index **191**

Te Ara Wānanga

Ranginui Walker (Te Whakatōhea), chair
Mason Durie (Rangitāne)
Edward Ellison (Ngāi Tahu)
Ngapare Hopa (Tainui)
Keri Kaa (Ngāti Porou)
Wharehuia Milroy (Ngāi Tūhoe)
Te Ahukaramū Charles Royal (Ngāti Raukawa)
Hone Sadler (Ngāpuhi)
Piri Sciascia (Ngāti Kahungunu)
Monty Soutar (Ngāti Porou)
Rāwiri Taonui (Te Hikutu, Ngāti Rora, Te Kapotai)
Mere Whaanga (Ngāti Rongomaiwahine, Ngāti Kahungunu)
Martin Wikaira (Ngāti Tūwharetoa)

The Te Ara team

GENERAL EDITOR: Jock Phillips

EDITOR MĀORI THEME: Basil Keane (Ngāti Kahungunu, Ngāpuhi, Rangitāne)

THEME EDITORS: Allan Gillingham (The Settled Landscape), Simon Nathan (The Bush; Earth, Sea and Sky)

WRITERS: Gerard Hutching, Nancy Swarbrick (managing editor), Christina Troup, Carl Walrond, Maggy Wassilieff

TRANSLATORS: Rangi McGarvey (Ngāi Tūhoe), Tamahou McGarvey (Ngāi Tūhoe)

PRODUCTION EDITORS: Tessa Copland, Jennifer Garlick, Fiona Oliver, Helen Rickerby, Ross Somerville (production manager), Caren Wilton

RESOURCE RESEARCHERS: Emma Dewson, Janine Faulknor (team leader), Marguerite Hill, Melanie Lovell-Smith (senior researcher), Alastair McLean, Leanne Tamaki (Ngāi Tūhoe, Ngāti Maniapoto), Emily Tutaki (Ngāti Kahungunu), Shirley Williams (team leader)

RIGHTS ADMINISTRATORS: Philothea Flynn (Ngāti Kahungunu, Ngāti Porou), Andy Palmer

DESIGNERS: Helene Coulson (lead designer), Kristy Mayes, Gareth Railton, Heath Sadlier (lead designer), Julia Vodanovich

ADMINISTRATORS: Angela Mitchell (Te Whānau-ā-Apanui, Ngāti Porou, Te Arawa, Ngāi Tahu), Olivia Walley

Varieties of pounamu

Foreword

Kotahi anō te tupuna o te tangata Māori, ko Ranginui e tū nei, ko Papatūānuku e takoto nei.

From the millions of stars which glide across the night sky, to ocean pathways navigated using currents, winds and the movement of constellations, to forests and wetlands rich in bird life, and coastal fisheries and rivers full of fish, Māori wove stories and genealogies which connected celestial beings to all living things.

At the first human footprint on Aotearoa, explorers began to name places and strange new plants and birds, relating them to their whakapapa. Ranginui the sky was separated from Papatūānuku the earth by Tāne the god of the forest. Tawhirimātea the god of weather laid siege on Tāne for this act of treachery. Tāne shaped the first person out of the earth and breathed life into her, and he was the ancestor of all the trees and creatures of the forest. Tangaroa was god of the vast Pacific Ocean, navigated by intrepid ancestors, bringing seeds and tubers and animals to their cold new land.

This relationship between the universe and all living things provided guidelines for daily life and gathering food – fish and shellfish, birds and eels, kūmara and other plants from Polynesia grown in well kept gardens, and the kiore (rats) and kurī (dogs) from faraway tropical islands.

These are the stories which are to be found in this book. Its contents are drawn from Te Ara, the Encyclopedia of New Zealand, a free online reference work. Te Ara will be a complete encyclopedia of New Zealand. It is being prepared by a team at Te Manatū Taonga – the Ministry for Culture and Heritage.

The entries included in *Te taiao* come from three of the seven themes published so far: from Earth, Sea and Sky/Te Rangi, te Whenua me te Moana; The Bush/Te Ngahere; and The Settled Landscape/Te Whenua Nōhia. They draw on material written about Māori ways of viewing the natural world, its origins, and how Māori exploited its resources.

These entries have Māori-language versions online, and are enriched with multimedia resources and many more images, including maps, diagrams, interactives, film and audio, found at www.TeAra.govt.nz.

Some entries in the book omit material found online, to avoid repetition. *Te taiao* was edited by Jennifer Garlick and Basil Keane from Te Ara, and Tracey Borgfeldt of David Bateman Ltd.

INTRODUCTION

Te ao mārama
the natural world

Taharoa, Kāwhia

Te ao mārama *the natural world*
Te Ahukaramū Charles Royal

The natural world forms a cosmic family, in the traditional Māori view. The weather, birds, fish and trees, sun and moon are related to each other, and to the people of the land.

In traditional Māori knowledge, as in many cultures, everything in the world is believed to be related. This linking was explained in tātai (genealogies) and kōrero (stories), collectively termed whakapapa (meaning to make a foundation, to place in layers). Experts recited the whakapapa of people, living things, the heavens or the weather to explain the relationships between all things and thus to place themselves within the world. This helped people to understand the world, and how to act within these relationships.

The entire world was seen as a vast and complex whānau (family). In the Māori story of creation, the earth and sky came together and gave birth to some 70 children, who eventually thrust apart their parents and populated the world. Each of the children became the god of a particular domain of the natural world. Their children and grandchildren then became ancestors in that domain. For example, Tangaroa, god of the sea, had a son called Punga. Punga then had two children: Ikatere, who became the ancestor of the fish of the sea, and Tūtewehiwehi, who became the ancestor of the fish and amphibious lizards of inland waterways.

Whakapapa express our need for kinship with the world. They describe the relationships between humans and the rest of nature. In one tradition, some tribal groups and the fish of the sea claim descent from Tangaroa. Whakapapa also explain the origins of animals, plants and features of the landscape. To tell a story about the origin of a bird, for example, is to invoke its true essence or character.

Although many of the stories are myths, they also have a practical function. They can pass on knowledge about the natural world, such as where to find kererū, New Zealand pigeon, and how to harvest them.

Although science is another way of understanding the natural world, the traditional principle of interconnectedness is still important and meaningful to Māori. For example, the genealogy of fish and sea animals makes clear their kinship to people and other creatures. It also points out values that guide people's interaction with other species, teaching respect and correct conduct.

Carvings on either side of this woven panel depict Papatūānuku (the earth mother, top left) and Ranginui (the sky father, top right), with their children beneath. Below Papatūānuku are Tānemahuta, deity of forests, and Haumiatiketike, deity of uncultivated foods. Below Ranginui are Tangaroa, who ruled the oceans, and Rongo, god of peace and cultivated foods. These poupou (carved posts) were made by master carver Rangi Hetet of the Ngāti Tūwharetoa and Ngāti Maniapoto tribes. Two of his daughters wove the tukutuku panel.

Harakeke, flax, features in a saying about the sanctity of human life, where a human is likened to the central shoot of the bush:
   Unuhia te rito o te harakeke, kei hea te kōmako e kō?
   Ui mai ki ahau, 'He aha te mea nui o te Ao?'
   Māku e kī atu,
   'He tangata, he tangata, he tangata.'
   If you remove the central shoot of the flaxbush, where will the bellbird find rest?
   If you were to ask me, 'What is the most important thing in the world?'
   I would reply,
   'It is people, it is people, it is people.'
Harakeke also represents the world of families within families.

The importance of the land

Until the arrival of Europeans in the late 1700s, Māori held a world view that originated in their Polynesian homeland. This grew and changed according to life in the new land.

Some iwi (tribes) hold that their ancestors did not come from over the sea, but sprang from the New Zealand landscape. For example, the Ngāi Tūhoe people claim that their ancestor is Hinepūkohurangi, the mist that dwells in the valleys of the Urewera ranges. Similarly, Ngāti Whātua tradition states that their ancestor, Tuputupu-whenua, came up from beneath the ground. Some Whanganui traditions speak of the inland mountains as their place of birth.

TANGATA WHENUA PEOPLE OF THE LAND

The world is a vast family, and humans are children of the earth and sky, and cousins to all living things. Such unity means that nature is the ultimate teacher about life.

Traditional knowledge is inspired by heritage, passed down the generations by word of mouth. There is no alternative – to ensure success in fishing, long journeys, or handling life's challenges, you have to trust your ancestors, who include the entire natural world.

Humans are born of the earth and achieve fulfilment when the earth speaks through the human community. True tangata whenua can speak authoritatively about the world they inhabit – the animals, plants, weather patterns and natural rhythms of life. Tangata whenua are descendants of other tangata whenua, and know the histories of their forebears and how life spoke through them.

According to this world view, when people are asked about their identity, they do not mention themselves directly. They refer to their mountain, their river and their esteemed ancestor. For example, a Ngāti Tūwharetoa person from the Taupō region would respond in this way:
   Ko Tongariro te maunga
   Ko Taupō te moana
   Ko Te Heuheu te tangata.
   Tongariro is the mountain
   Taupō is the waterway
   Te Heuheu is the person.

PART I

Ranginui
the sky

Rangitātā, Canterbury

Lake Wānaka

Ranginui *the sky*
Rāwiri Taonui

Ranginui, the sky father, was torn away from Papatūānuku, the earth mother, and formed the vault of the heavens. When Māori looked up at the sky they saw the sun god, Te Rā, whose journey was slowed by the legendary Māui. At night, they sometimes saw Rona, who had been pulled up from Earth by the Moon. These live among a vast family of celestial bodies, all encompassed within Ranginui.

Māori mythology personified the heavens as a sky father, naming him variously Rangi (heavens), Ranginui (great heavens), Rangiroa (expansive heavens), or Te Ranginui-e-tū-nei (the great-standing heavens). He was also called Te Rangiātea, which referred to the great breadth of the heavens, or Te Rangitiketike and Te Rangipāmamao, which denoted loftiness and remoteness. The names Te Rangiwhakataka and Te Rangitakataka describe how the heavens reach down to the horizon to meet Papatūānuku, the earth mother.

The term Rangi-tūhāhā comes from the Māori conception of the heavens comprising 10 or sometimes 12 layers, with Rangi being the closest to the earth.

Creation of the heavens

In myths about the creation of the world, the union of Ranginui and Papatūānuku led to Te Pō (darkness, the night). In an account given by Wiremu Maihi Te Rangikāheke of Te Arawa, these primal parents gave birth to several anthropomorphic gods, including Tāwhirimātea (god of the winds), Tāne (forests), Tangaroa (seas), Rongo (kūmara, cultivated foods and peace), Haumia (fern root and uncultivated foods) and Tūmatauenga (humankind and war). These gods dwelt in darkness between their parents, until Tāne and several others decided to separate them. Rongo, Tangaroa, Haumia and Tūmatauenga all tried unsuccessfully to drive Ranginui and Papatūānuku apart. Then Tāne lay on his back and pushed with his arms and legs, while the others severed the limbs of their parents, breaking their last grasp. Tāne planted posts to keep his parents apart, which is why he is also known as Tāne-tokotoko-o-ngā-rangi (Tāne of the posts that hold the heavens aloft).

Ranginui and Papatūānuku are celebrated in whakataukī (aphorisms), waiata (songs) and whaikōrero (speech making):

E mihi atu ki Te Matua, ki a Ranginui, ki a Rangiroa,
Tāwhirirangi, Te Hauwhakaora, Te Hau e pāngia ngā kiri o te tangata.
E mihi atu ki a Papatūānuku, ki a Papatūārangi
Te Papa i takatakahia e ngā mātua tūpuna, te papa i waihotia
    e rātou mā
Te Papa e maroro ki te itinga, e maroro ki te opunga
Te Papa-awhi, e awhi ana i a tātou, o tēnā, o tēnā, o tēnā o ngā
    whakatupuranga e tupu ake nei.
Te Ūkaipō, Te Ūkaiao o tātou katoa.

Greetings to the sky father, the great heavens, the expansive heavens,
The heavenly winds, the life-giving winds, the winds that caress
    the skin of all people.
Greetings to the earth mother, extending beyond the visible land
    and beyond the visible heavens.
The earth mother trampled by our ancestors, the earth mother
    left in heritage by the ancient ones
The earth mother that stretches unto the sunrise, that stretches
    unto the sunset
The embracing earth mother, which embraces each of us from
    all generations sustained by her grace.
She that sustains us night and day.

This carving of the god Tāne is part of a larger work by Cliff Whiting, called 'Te wehenga o Rangi rāua ko Papa'. Tāne is shown separating his parents, Ranginui and Papatūānuku, by standing on his head and pushing up with his feet.

On this postage stamp, Tāne is separating his parents, Ranginui, the sky father, and Papatūānuku, the earth mother.

Ranginui as knowledge and life

Human life and knowledge were said to originate in the realm of Ranginui, the sky father. In one tradition, the god Tāne climbed to the citadel Te Tihi-o-Manono, in the highest of the 12 heavens, known as Te Toi-o-ngā-rangi. There he retrieved three baskets of knowledge: te kete-tuatea (basket of light), te kete-tuauri (basket of darkness) and te kete-aronui (basket of pursuit). There are several interpretations of what each basket represents. The scholar Māori Marsden has suggested that the basket of light is present knowledge, the basket of darkness things unknown, and the basket of pursuit is the knowledge humans currently seek.

Tāne, imbued with te ira atua (godly life force), also obtained te ira tangata (the human aspect) from the heavens before creating and implanting both aspects within Hineahuone, the first woman. She in turn gave birth to humankind, which accounts for the belief that people possess both a human and spiritual nature.

Tāne's famous journey to the heavens is remembered in the following ritual chant:

> Tēnei au te hōkai nei o taku tapuwae
> Ko te hōkai nuku ko te hōkai rangi
> Ko te hōkai a tō tupuna a Tānenui-a-rangi
> Ka pikitia ai ki te rangi tūhāhā ki te Tihi-o-Manono
> Ka rokohina atu rā ko Io Matua-kore anake
> Ka tīkina mai ngā kete o te wānanga
> Ko te kete-tuauri
> Ko te kete-tuatea
> Ko te kete-aronui
> Ka tiritiria ka poupoua
> Ka puta mai iho ko te ira tangata
> Ki te wheiao ki te ao mārama
> Tihei-mauri ora!

Carved by Jim Wiki of Te Aupōuri in Ōamaru stone, 'Ngā kete o te wānanga' represents the ascent of Tāne into the twelfth heaven to gain the three baskets of knowledge. From this deed Tāne gained one of his many names, Tānenuiarangi (Tāne who ascended the heavens).

This is the journey of sacred footsteps
Journeyed about the earth, journeyed about the heavens
The journey of the ancestral god Tānenuiarangi
Who ascended into the heavens to Te Tihi-o-Manono
Where he found the parentless source
From there he retrieved the baskets of knowledge
Te kete-tuauri
Te kete-tuatea
Te kete-aronui
These were distributed and implanted about the earth
From which came human life
Growing from dim light to full light
There was life.

RANGINUI | THE SKY

Te Rā *the sun*

Te Rā was the main deity of the heavens. During winter he was known as Te Rā-tūoi (the lean sun) and during summer Te Rā-kura (the red sun). Midday was Te Poupoutanga-o-te-rā (the post of the sun) or Te Pou-tū-a-tamanui-te-rā (the standing post of the sun). Dawn and sunset were called Te Tamanui-te-rā-kā (the burning sun). The flight of the sun across the sky was described as Te Manu-i-te-rā (the bird of the sun).

Māori mythology says that after the world's creation the sun moved across the sky so rapidly that night and day were very short; there was not enough time for people to perform daily tasks or get sufficient sleep. One of Māori mythology's most important ancestors was the demigod Māui, who devised a plan to slow the sun. He and his brothers made several strong ropes and journeyed to where the sun rises from the underworld.

TE WHĀNAU MĀRAMA THE FAMILY OF LIGHT

According to Māori myth, Ranginui played a pivotal role in the birth of the sun, moon, planets, stars and constellations – collectively called Te Whānau Mārama. One version told by Hāmiora Pio of Ngāti Awa is that Tangotango (blackness of the heavenly night) and Wainui (the ocean) – two children of Ranginui and Papatūānuku – produced offspring: Te Rā (the sun), Te Marama (the moon), Ngā Whetū (the stars) and Te Hinātore (moonlight). The god Tāne took these offspring and placed them in their abodes in the sky.

A Ngāti Kahungunu version of this tradition says that Kewa, also a child of Ranginui and Papatūānuku, went to the peak of Te Maunganui (the great mountain), where he fetched te whānau mārama (the children of light) from the celestial guardian Te Āhuru. Kewa carried the astronomical bodies in sacred baskets, planting them in the heavens. The basket holding the sun was named Rauru-rangi, the basket carrying the moon was Te Kauhanga, and the basket containing the stars was Te Ikaroa (the Milky Way). Some stars such as Atutahi (Canopus) were put in baskets which hung to one side of Te Ikaroa.

15

The Southern Cross is at the centre of this photograph, just above and to the right of a dark region of the galaxy, where few stars are visible. The two bright pointer stars are on the left.

RONA – THE WOMAN ON THE MOON

One night a woman named Rona went to fetch water in her hue (gourd). As she walked, the moon went behind a cloud, causing her to stumble in the dark. In her anger she cursed the moon. To counter, the moon came down to Earth to grab her. She grasped a tree, but was pulled up together with her gourd and the tree. They can all be seen on the surface of the full moon.

They built a low wall to hide behind, and laid out their ropes as nooses. When the sun appeared, the brothers leapt out from their hiding place, threw the ropes over the sun, and ensnared it. Their quarry securely held, Māui leapt up and beat the sun until it cried for mercy. Today Māori believe that the rays of the sun are the remnants of the ropes used to slow its path.

Te Marama *the moon*

Marama, ahoroa, māhina and atarau are common names for the moon. The moon has important symbolic meaning for Māori and is strongly associated with women and the menstrual cycle, as in many cultures. The moon as Hineteiwaiwa is associated with fertility and the cycle of life. The terms Hina-te-ao (female light), Hina-keha (pale moon), Hina-te-pō (female dark) and Hinauri (dark moon) refer to the waxing and waning moon respectively. Its cycle was likened to the opening and closing of a portal through which departed spirits returned to the origin of life. The moon was also used as a guide for planting and fishing (see pages 20–21).

Ngā Whetū *the stars*

The stars were used by Polynesians in canoe navigation. The rising and setting points of the brightest and most distinctive stars and planets were gauged with the help of sophisticated star compasses, and then memorised. Compasses were also used to chart the winds.

Navigators steered their canoes toward a star on the horizon. When that star rose too high in the sky or set beneath the horizon, another would be chosen, and so on through the night. Seven to 12 stars were sufficient for one night's navigation, and the moon and bright planets such as Kōpū (Venus) and Pareārau (Jupiter) were also useful. At daybreak, navigators noted the position of the canoe in relation to the rising sun. As the sun got higher in the sky, they looked to where it would set in the evening.

Several hundred Māori star names survive from the time before Europeans arrived in New Zealand. Unfortunately, apart from the more prominent stars – Takurua (Sirius), Tautoru (Orion's Belt), Ruawāhia (Arcturus), Matariki (the Pleiades), Whānui (Vega), Puanga (Rigel), Rehua (Antares), Atuatahi, Atutahi, Autahi (Canopus) – we no longer know with any certainty which stars many of the names refer to.

However, we do know that different tribes celebrated the rising of certain stars to mark the seasons. Tribes in different parts of the country also identified what we now call the Māori New Year (see page 22) by the dawn rising of one or more of Matariki, Puanga, Takurua and/or Atutahi.

Other members of the family of light
Planets

Māori had a sophisticated understanding of the movement of the planets and held particular regard for Kōpū (Venus), Pareārau (Jupiter), Matawhero (Mars) and Whiro (Mercury).

Venus, which is only seen on the horizon before dawn or after the sun sets, was also known as Tāwera, whose name refers to the way it appeared to be burned up on the eastern horizon by the rising sun, and Meremere-tū-ahiahi (to stand out on the western horizon after the sun sets).

Rangiwhakaoma (Castlepoint)

Jupiter was a female entity, known as Pareārau (Pare of a hundred lovers) or Hine-tiweka (wayward Hine). These names come from the observation that at certain times, Jupiter and Venus sit together on the horizon, but that over subsequent nights Jupiter appears to wander away. Jupiter is interpreted as the wife of Venus, leaving her husband at home while she has affairs with other stars.

Comets

Auahiroa and auahitūroa, meaning 'long smoke trails', and ūpokoroa, were common names for comets. One tradition from the Mātaatua tribes in the Bay of Plenty says that Te Rā sent his son Auahi-tūroa, a comet, to give fire to humankind. Auahi-tūroa married Mahuika, who bore five children, Te Tokorima (the five fingers): Takonui, Takoroa, Māpere, Manawa and Toiti. Another account says that Māui retrieved fire from the fingernails of Mahuika, his grandmother, and planted it in trees such as kaikōmako, rimu and tōtara, which were used in traditional fire-making. Fire is often known as Tama-a-Auahi-tūroa (son of Auahi-tūroa).

Meteors

Meteors, or shooting stars, are called matakōkiri, tūmatakōkiri, kōtiri and kōtiritiri. Māori interpreted them in several ways – they were thought to convey fire to Earth, or to be stars that the sun or moon had struck down. Bright meteors were taken as a good omen, indicating future action. Duller ones were bad omens. Meteors also augured the death of great leaders and the rise of new ones.

Auahiroa and auahitūroa, meaning 'long smoke trails', were two names for comets. In this 1882 photograph, a comet's trail can be seen over Mt Taranaki (Egmont) and the village of Parihaka.

RANGINUI | THE SKY

Maramataka *the lunar calendar*
Paul Meredith

According to the maramataka, or Māori lunar calendar, the winter month of Hereturi-kōkā is so cold that 'the scorching effect of fire is seen on the knees of man.' But as the moon continues to wax and wane, the earth warms up and by the summer month of Kohi-tātea, fruit hangs ripe on the trees.

Lunar months

The maramataka divided the traditional Māori year into 12 lunar months. The word marama means both the moon and the lunar month – a lunar month is the 29 and a half days between successive new moons, and normally straddles two calendar months.

Māori needed a system that matched lunar months with the solar year – a lunar year is around 11 days shorter. Some tribes listed 13 months in their lunar year, indicating that one month was occasionally added to account for the extra period of time. Those tribes which had only 12 months would have used a different system to account for the extra time.

The months were commonly listed numerically: May–June was Te Tahi (the first), June–July was Te Rua (the second), and so on. Each month also had its own name, which sometimes varied between tribes. Over 100 years ago, Tūtakangahau of Maungapōhatu, a member of Ngāi Tūhoe, provided the ethnographer Elsdon Best with these names and descriptions:

Poutū-te-rangi (February–March) was the time to harvest kūmara, shown here being collected in flax baskets.

Cold weather in the month of Hongonui (or Hōngongoi, June–July) prompted people to light fires. Fire was generated using a fire plough, pictured here. The kaurima (fire stick) was rubbed against the kaunoti (grooved batten) to make sawdust and heat. When smoke appeared, the sawdust was placed on kindling and blown until the wood ignited.

RANGINUI | THE SKY

Different types of food were collected according to the time of year; however, aruhe (fern root), shown piled up, was a reliable year-round staple.

1. Pipiri (May–June).
   All things on Earth are contracted because of the cold; likewise man.
2. Hongonui (or Hōngongoi, June–July).
   Man is now extremely cold and kindles fires before which he basks.
3. Here-turi-kōkā (July–August).
   The scorching effect of fire is seen on the knees of man.
4. Mahuru (August–September).
   The earth has now acquired warmth, as have vegetation and trees.
5. Whiringa-ā-nuku (September–October).
   The earth has now become quite warm.
6. Whiringa-ā-rangi (October–November).
   It has now become summer, and the sun has acquired strength.
7. Hakihea (November–December).
   Birds are now sitting in their nests.
8. Kohi-tātea (December–January).
   Fruits are now ripe, and man eats of the new food of the season.
9. Hui-tanguru (January–February).
   The foot of Rūhī (a summer star) now rests upon the earth.
10. Poutū-te-rangi (February–March).
    The crops are now harvested.
11. Paenga-whāwhā (March–April).
    All straw is now stacked at the borders of the plantations.
12. Haratua (April–May).
    Crops are now stored in pits. The tasks of man are finished.[1]

Each month was represented by a star or stars. According to one Ngāti Kahungunu authority, 'without exception, stars were the ariki (controllers, heads) of these months'.[2]

A 10-MONTH YEAR?

The Māori calendar is sometimes referred to as 'ten plus two'. Poutū-te-rangi (February–March) is the tenth month, during which the star of the same name (Altair in English) could be seen in the night sky. It was a month of harvest, and another two months would pass before planting began again. These interim two months were considered to be of no significance, which is why some Māori calendars have only 10 months.

The maramataka was revived in 1990 by Te Taura Whiri i te Reo Māori (the Māori Language Commission). Instead of using transliterations of the English names, such as Hānuere for January and Mei for May, they promoted the traditional names cited by Tūtakangahau. However, lunar months were dropped in favour of calendar months, so that, for example, Pipiri became June.

The most important function of the Māori lunar calendar was to regulate planting and harvesting, fishing and hunting. The four seasons – raumati (summer), ngahuru (autumn), kōanga (spring) and takurua (winter) – called forth a series of activities to do with procuring food. These tended to vary among tribes, depending on where they lived, local climate, and the availability of edible plants, birds and seafood.

RANGINUI | THE SKY

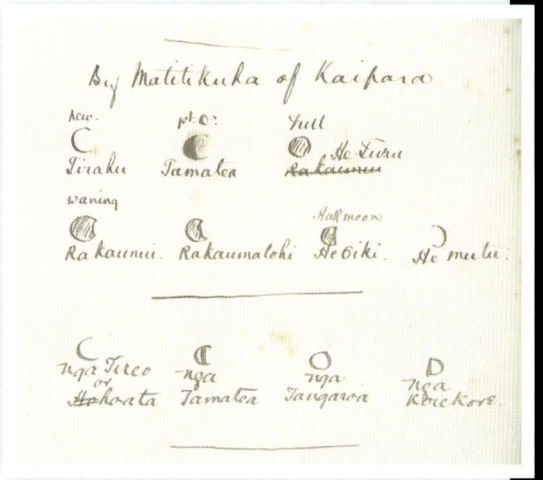

Each night of the month had a name and a specific characteristic. This handwritten chart shows some of the key phases of the moon as described by Matiti Kūhā of Kaipara. Some nights were considered unlucky for planting and fishing, while others were favourable. The moon was also known as the true husband of women.

Yellow-eyed mullet

Nights of the month

The new moon determined the start of the lunar month. Rather than referring to the days of the month, Māori spoke of nights, and each night had its own name. Generally, Whiro was the first night of the new moon and Mutuwhenua was the last. Some nights were considered unlucky for planting and fishing, while others were favourable.

There are a number of tribal variations relating to the nights of the moon. The following list has been adapted from the names and observations made by members of Ngāti Kahungunu:

Whiro	An unpleasant day, the new moon appears.
Tirea	The moon is very small.
Hoata	A pleasing day, the moon is still small.
Ōuenuku	Get to work! A good night for eeling.
Ōkoro	A pleasing day in the afternoon; good for eeling at night.
Tamat[e]a-ngana	Unpleasant weather, the sea is rough.
Tamatea-kai-ariki	The weather improves.
Huna	Bad weather, food products suffer.
Ari-roa	Favourable for spearing eels.
Maure	A fine, desirable day.
Māwharu	Crayfish are taken on this day.
Ōhua	A good day for working.

20

RANGINUI | THE SKY

According to the maramataka there were a number of nights favourable for catching eels. Some nights were good for all aspects of eeling, while others indicated specific methods, such as spearing or setting traps. This group is at Lake Forsyth (Wairewa) in the South Island, a traditional Ngāi Tahu eeling ground. The men skin and dry the eels, while the women make flax baskets to transport them.

TIME FOR PLANTING

Māori farmers planted kūmara on the nights called Ōuenuku, Ari, Rākau-nui, Rākau-matohi, Takirau and Ōrongonui, which were the 4th, 9th, 16th, 17th, 18th and 27th nights of the lunar month. No planting was done during full moon or on Korekore days (the 20th, 21st and 22nd nights). The planting months were in spring: September, October and November. By the early 2000s there was renewed interest in the maramataka, and it was used by some Māori for planting and fishing. Many fishermen believe that they catch more fish on a day deemed favourable by the calendar. In an example where Māori knowledge and science come together, a group of researchers at Massey University in Palmerston North have planted 25 varieties of taewa (potato) according to the Māori lunar calendar, with the dual aim of preserving traditional knowledge and establishing the crop commercially.

Hotu	An unpleasant day, the sea is rough.
Atua	An abominable day.
Turu	A day to collect food from the sea.
Rākau-nui	The moon is filled out, produce from the sea is the staple food.
Rākau-matohi	A fine day, the moon now wanes.
Takirau	Fine weather during the morning.
Oike	The afternoon is favourable.
Korekore-te-whiwhia	A bad day.
Korekore-te-rawea	A bad day.
Korekore-hahani	A fairly good day.
Tangaroa-ā-mua	A good day for fishing.
Tangaroa-ā-roto	A good day for fishing.
Tangaroa-kiokio	An excellent day for fishing, a misty aspect prevails on land.
Ōtāne	A good day, and a good night for eeling.
Ōrongonui	A desirable day, the īnanga (whitebait) migrate.
Mauri	The morning is fine, the moon has now darkened.
Ōmutu	A bad day.
Mutuwhenua	An exceedingly bad day, the moon has expired.[3]

Matariki *Māori New Year*
Paul Meredith

Once a year, twinkling in the winter sky just before dawn, Matariki (the Pleiades) signals the Māori New Year. Traditionally, it was a time for remembering the dead, and celebrating new life. In the 21st century, observing Matariki has become popular again. Heaven-bound kites, hot-air balloons and fireworks help mark the occasion.

Matariki is the Māori name for the small cluster of stars also known as the Pleiades or the Seven Sisters, in the Taurus constellation. In New Zealand it comes into view low on the north-eastern horizon, appearing in the tail of the Milky Way in the last days of May or in early June, just before dawn. This heralds the Māori New Year.

Various Māori tribes celebrated Matariki at different times. Some held festivities when Matariki was first seen in the dawn sky; others celebrated after the full moon rose or at the beginning of the next new moon.

For all tribes, the importance of Matariki has been captured in proverbs and songs, which link it with the bright star Whānui (Vega):

Ka puta Matariki ka rere Whānui.
Ko te tohu tēnā o te tau e!
Matariki re-appears, Whānui starts its flight.
Being the sign of the [new] year!

Matariki is also associated with the winter solstice, which in the southern hemisphere is 21 June. It appears when the sun, drifting north on the shortest day in winter, reaches the north-eastern end of the horizon. The sun then turns around and begins its journey south.

RANGINUI | THE SKY

Matariki is the Māori name for the cluster of stars known as the Pleiades. When it rises in the north-eastern skies in late May or early June, it signals to Māori that the New Year will begin.

SAYINGS

Matariki has given rise to a number of sayings. 'Matariki kāinga kore' (homeless Matariki) refers to the star cluster's constant travel – disappearing from the sky only once a year, when it pauses to rest in May when the moon wanes. The association of Matariki with crops has given rise to the saying: 'Matariki ahunga nui' (Matariki provider of plentiful food). Because it appears in the season when game had been caught and preserved, there is the saying: 'Ka kitea a Matariki, kua maoka te hinu' (When Matariki is seen, then game is preserved).

Legends

Matariki literally means the 'eyes of god' (mata ariki) or 'little eyes' (mata riki). Some say that when Ranginui and Papatūānuku were separated by their offspring, the god of the winds, Tāwhirimātea, became angry, tearing out his eyes and hurling them into the heavens. Others say Matariki is the mother surrounded by her six daughters, Tupu-ā-nuku, Tupu-ā-rangi, Waitī, Waitā, Waipuna-ā-rangi and Ururangi. One account explains that Matariki and her daughters appear to assist the sun, Te Rā, whose winter journey from the north has left him weakened.

Matariki and Puanga

Some Māori tribes believed that it was the rising of the star Puanga (Rigel in Orion) which heralded the new year, not Matariki. Hence the saying: 'Puanga kai rau' (Puanga of abundant food). This divergence was explained to the scholar Elsdon Best by a Māori elder: 'The task of Puanga is to strive with Matariki (the Pleiades) that he may gain possession of the year.'[4]

Cycles of life and death

Traditionally, Māori were keen observers of the night sky, determining from the stars the time and seasons, and using them to navigate the oceans. Lookouts would watch for the rise of Matariki just before dawn. For Māori, this time signified remembrance, fertility and celebration.

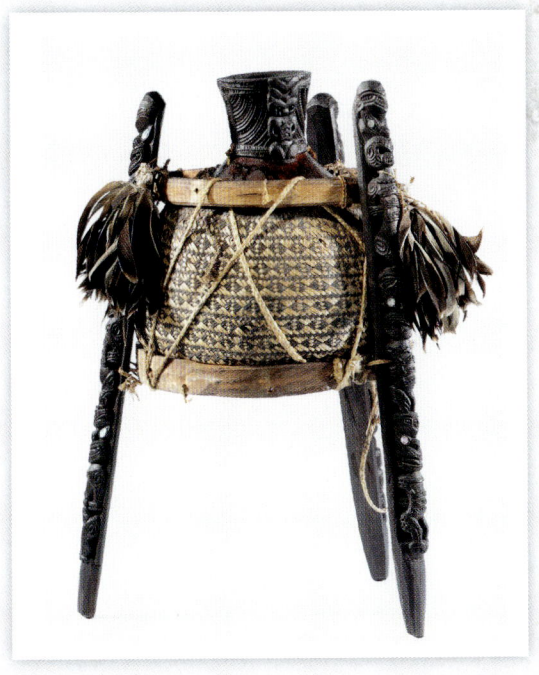

Matariki was associated not only with planting and harvesting, but also with the plentiful supply of game. Often birds would be preserved in their own fat in a gourd like the tahā huahua pictured here.

Amongst other stars and star clusters can be seen Matariki and Puanga (Rigel in Orion). For some Māori tribes, it was the rising of Puanga that signalled the new year rather than Matariki. Whichever the sign, for all Māori it was a time to celebrate seasonal fertility and remember those who had passed.

MATARIKI IN GREEK MYTH

According to Greek myth, the Pleiades are the seven daughters of Pleione and Atlas – Electra, Maia, Taygete, Alcyone, Celaeno, Asterope and Merope. While wandering through the woods one day, they were spied by Orion, who gave chase. To save them from Orion's dishonorable intentions, Zeus transformed them into stars and placed them in the sky. A number of ancient temples on the Acropolis in Athens face the direction where the Pleiades rise.

Remembrance

Haere atu rā e koro ki te paepae o Matariki, o Rehua. Haere atu rā.
Farewell old man, go to the threshold of Matariki, of Rehua. Farewell.

In times of old, the sighting of Matariki was greeted with expressions of grief for those who had died since its last appearance. Some said the stars housed the souls of those departed. Rangihuna Pire, in his 70s, remembered how as a child he was taken by his grandparents to watch for Matariki in mid-winter at Kaūpokonui, South Taranaki:

The old people might wait up several nights before the stars rose. They would make a small hāngī. When they saw the stars, they would weep and tell Matariki the names of those who had gone since the stars set, then the oven would be uncovered so the scent of the food would rise and strengthen the stars, for they were weak and cold.[5]

Planting crops

Matariki atua ka eke mai i te rangi e roa,
E whāngainga iho ki te mata o te tau e roa e.
Divine Matariki come forth from the far-off heaven,
Bestow the first fruits of the year upon us.

The coming season's crops were planted according to the portents read in the Matariki star cluster. If the stars were clear and bright, it was a sign that a favourable and productive season lay ahead, and planting would begin in September. If the stars appeared hazy and closely bunched together, a cold winter was in store and planting was put off until October.

RANGINUI | THE SKY

Traditionally, kites were flown as part of Māori New Year celebrations.

Making and flying kites has played a part in a number of recent celebrations. Te Rangi Huata included fireworks, shown here, and hot-air balloons at his Matariki festival in Hawke's Bay. He considered these a more modern way to reach for the stars.

MODERN MATARIKI

Matariki celebrations were popular before the arrival of Europeans in New Zealand, and they continued into the 1900s. Gradually they dwindled, with one of the last traditional festivals recorded in the 1940s. At the beginning of the 21st century Matariki celebrations were revived. Their increasing popularity has led some to suggest that Matariki should replace the Queen's birthday, the celebration of which is also in June, as a national holiday. The revival of Matariki has also played a part in the increasing popularity of the traditional Māori kite. Hekenukumai Busby, an expert in traditional Māori navigation, has said that the ancestors of Māori, including the Polynesians of ancient history, welcomed Matariki by flying kites.

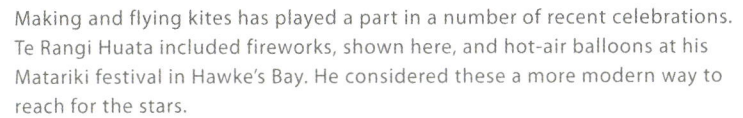

Harvest

Ngā kai a Matariki, nāna i ao ake ki runga.
The foods of Matariki, by her scooped up.

Matariki happened at the end of harvesting, when food stores were plentiful. The variety of food which had been gathered and preserved ensured an abundant supply for feasting – Matariki was an important time for festivity. Women rejoiced, sang and danced to celebrate the change of season and new beginnings. Often kites (pākau) were flown – they were thought to get close to the stars.

25

Tāwhirimātea – the weather
Basil Keane

New Zealand's rapid weather changes, frequent rain, distinctive cloud patterns and strong winds all had a huge influence on the daily life of Māori. Each region developed a rich store of words, sayings and traditions relating to the domain of Tāwhirimātea – god of the weather.

This akeake tree is bent by the powerful winds on the Chatham Islands. The fierce assault brings to mind the attack by Tāwhirimātea against Tāne Mahuta, god of the forest, for his role in separating Ranginui and Papatūānuku.

Tāwhirimātea

While the Māori word for weather is rangi (also meaning sky), in Māori tradition the deity who controls the weather is Tāwhirimātea.

In the creation story, the children of Ranginui and Papatūānuku wished to separate their parents so that light could come into the world. The only brother who did not agree to this was Tāwhirimātea, the god of wind and storms. When Ranginui and Papatūānuku were separated, he ascended to the sky to be with his father. Together they plotted revenge against the other brothers.

At this time Tāwhirimātea began to produce his numerous offspring. They included the four winds, and Tāwhirimātea sent away his wind children: one to the north (Tūāraki), one to the south (Tonga), one to the east (Marangai) and one to the west (Hauāuru). The direction to which each child was sent became the name of that wind.

Tāwhirimātea then sent forth a variety of clouds, including Aonui (dense clouds), Aopōuri (dark clouds), Aowhētuma (fiery clouds), Aowhēkere (clouds which precede hurricanes), Aokanapanapa (clouds reflecting glowing red light), Aopakakina (clouds wildly drifting from all quarters and wildly bursting), Aopakarea (clouds of thunderstorms) and Aotakawe (clouds hurriedly flying).

To take revenge on his brothers, Tāwhirimātea first attacked Tāne Mahuta – the god of the forest, who had separated Rangi and Papa. The mighty trees of Tāne's domain were snapped in the middle and fell to the ground. Then Tāwhirimātea attacked Tangaroa, the god of the sea, causing the waves to grow as tall as mountains. After this he turned on Rongomātāne, whose domain was cultivated food and the kūmara, and Haumia-tikitiki, god of fern root and uncultivated food. To escape, they hid within their mother Papatūānuku. That is why kūmara and fern root burrow into the earth.

During this time, Tāwhirimātea also released Uanui (terrible rain), Uaroa (long continued rain) and Uawhatu (fierce hail-storms). Their offspring were Haumaringi (mist), Haumarotoroto (heavy dew), and Tōmairangi (light dew).

Tāwhirimātea finally attacked Tūmatauenga, the god of war and of humans. Tūmatauenga stood firm and endured the fierce weather his brother sent. He developed incantations to cause favourable winds, and tūā (charms or spells) to bring fair weather to the heavens. But because neither brother can win, Tāwhirimātea continues to attack people in storms and hurricanes, trying to destroy them on sea and land.

RANGINUI | THE SKY

This mural by Cliff Whiting depicts the struggle of Tāwhirimātea to control his children, the wind and weather (the blue spiral forms). Tāwhirimātea sent forth the clouds, winds and storms as part of his war against his brothers. It was a punishment for separating their parents, Ranginui and Papatūānuku.

RANGINUI | THE SKY

The seasons

Spring
Kōanga is the Māori word for spring (September to November). It includes the word 'kō', a digging implement: spring was the time for digging the soil. 'Takē Kōanga, whakapiri Ngahuru' (absent at planting time, close by at harvest) refers to people who disappear during the hard work of planting in spring, but show up when food is abundant at the autumn harvest. Light spring showers were known as 'ua kōwhai' or kōwhai showers, referring to the September bloom of yellow flowers on the kōwhai tree.

Summer
Summer, from December to February, is known as raumati. One tradition holds that Te Rā (the sun) and Hine Raumati (the summer maid) had a child, Tānerore. The saying, 'Te haka a Tānerore' (Tānerore's war dance) refers to the shimmering of the hot air during summer. In other traditions, Parearohi, the wife of the star Rehua (Antares), personifies heat-shimmer. When she dances around the margins of the forests, summer is approaching.

A tūī sits in a kōwhai tree, whose beautiful blossom heralds the arrival of spring. Light showers during spring were known as 'ua kōwhai' (kōwhai rain), referring to the flowering of the tree at this time.

RANGINUI | THE SKY

Members of Ngāti Tūwharetoa perform a peruperu (a dance with weapons) on Waitangi Day (6 February), 1934. The shimmering air seen in summer is sometimes likened to the way the air quivers during such a performance.

Summer and Rehua

Antares is one of the brightest stars in the night sky. Known to Māori as Rehua, it was closely linked with summer, when it became visible. There is a saying, 'Te tātarakihi, te pihareinga; ko ngā manu ēnā o Rēhua' (the locust and the cricket are Rehua's song birds) because these creatures sing when the heat of summer has arrived.

The flying kēkerewai or green mānuka beetle was also known as 'Rehua's bird'. Plentiful in summer, the beetle was harvested for food when it became trapped in mud around streams and lakes. Similarly, 'Ngā pōtiki a Rēhua' (Rehua's infants) were the fish maomao and moki, which ran in large shoals during summer.

The cicada or kihikihi conjures up images of hot summer days. The cicada and cricket were described as the song birds of the 'summer' star Rehua because their song heralded the arrival of warmer weather.

The trials of summer

Māori often expressed a negative attitude towards the arrival of summer. 'Rehua whakaruhi tangata' meant Rehua the weakener, and referred to the exhaustion which summer could bring about. 'Ngā te rā o te waru' ('the days of the eighth month', in the traditional lunar calendar) meant the height of summer, when food was often scarce. 'Rehua pona nui' (Rehua of the big joints) referred to how the summer heat could make people lose weight and their joints appear larger.

Autumn

The name for autumn was ngahuru, an archaic word for ten. This was because autumn started during the tenth month (February–March) in the traditional calendar. Ngahuru was also the name for harvest, which occurred at this time. The saying 'Ngahuru, kura kai, kura tangata' (harvest-time, wealth of food, the wealth of people) indicated that food was plentiful in autumn.

Winter

Hōtoke and makariri were two words for winter (from June to August) and for cold. Winter was associated with the star Sirius or Takurua – another word for winter. People would say, 'Takurua hūpē nui' (winter, when your nose runs).

WEATHER REPORTS

Days of good and bad weather were compared to the birthdays of good-natured or unpleasant ancestors. On a beautiful day people would say, 'Mehemea ko te rangi i whānau ai a Te Rangitauarire' – 'It's like the day when Te Rangitauarire was born'. On a stormy, miserable day, they would say, 'Mehemea ko te rangi i whānau ai a Te Tuarariri' – 'It's like the day when Te Tuarariri was born'.

RANGINUI | THE SKY

Māori likened this cloud pattern to planted rows of kūmara and called it te māra kūmara a Ngātoroirangi, meaning 'the kūmara garden of Ngātoroirangi' – an important ancestor.

This cirrus cloud lies above Sealy Range, near Aoraki Mt Cook in the South Island. Pūrehurehu was one Māori word for this type of cloud.

The Māori name for these cirrus clouds is iorangi, meaning strips (io) in the sky (rangi). The word 'cirrus' is derived from a Latin word meaning 'wisp of hair', and another meaning of the 'io' is 'lock of hair'. In English the clouds are known as mares' tails.

Clouds

There are many words for clouds, but the most common is kapua. Another word, ao, is used in the Māori name for New Zealand: Aotearoa – long white cloud. In one tradition, Kuramārōtini, the wife of Polynesian explorer Kupe, named New Zealand after the cloud stretching over the land.

While there are still many names relating to clouds and cloud formations, some have fallen out of use. These include:
- Pīpipi for cirro-stratus clouds, which are high sheets of ice crystals. They are relatively transparent, and the sun or moon can easily be seen through them. At times the only sign of their presence is a halo around the sun or moon. Māori knew the halo around the sun as 'Kura hau awatea' and that around the moon as 'Kura hau pō'.
- Pūtahi means long stratus clouds and Pūrehurehu describes cirrus.
- Taipua describes the way cumulus clouds bunch together in rounded masses.
- Okewa is the nimbus or rain cloud.

There were a number of metaphors for cloud formations. Clouds in layers were known as 'te kupenga a Tara-mainuku' (the net of Tara-mainuku). 'A mackerel sky' is a European metaphor, likening the clouds to the markings on a fish. However, Māori saw in this pattern the raised beds of kūmara and named it 'te māra kūmara a Ngātoroirangi' (the kūmara gardens of Ngātoroirangi). Mares' tails (high, wispy clouds) were known as iorangi (strips in the sky).

Horizontal cloud bands were like a belt. Red clouds at sunset were 'te tātua o Te Kaha' (the belt of Te Kaha). A bank of clouds in the west, lit by the setting sun, was known as te tātua o Te Kahu (the belt of Te Kahu), and a clear band near the horizon was 'te Tātua o Kahu' (the belt of Kahu).

RANGINUI | THE SKY

Cumulus clouds gather in the sky above the Waimakariri River, in Canterbury. The Māori term 'taipua' refers to the way these clouds bunch together in rounded masses.

READING THE CLOUDS

An East Coast elder explained how to read a cloud that had sharply defined points, known as 'pīpipi o te rangi' (pīpipi means 'the wind will come'). The points indicated the direction from which the wind would arrive. If the cloud was red, rain would also arrive. If it was pale, only wind would come. If yellow, a gentle wind and fine weather would follow. If it projected upwards and was pale, there would be a long storm. If it was dark, the storm was near.

Predicting the weather

Certain types of clouds were used to predict the weather or certain events:
- Layers of cloud above the horizon, known as rangi mātāhauariki, were the forerunner of the cold south wind Tutakangahau.
- Atiru clouds threatened rain and wind.
- Titi taranaki (radiating streaks) were a sign of bad weather.
- A bank of clouds, 'he whare hau' (a house of wind), indicated coming wind.
- Kaiwaka were threatening clouds on the horizon, and a sign of misfortune. Cloud (or mist) uniformly covering the sky was papanui, and people would say, 'He papanui tōna tohu he āio āpōpō' (the clouds signal that it will be calm tomorrow).

Rain

Te Ihorangi is the god who personifies rain, while Hinewai is the female personification of light misty rain.

The word for rain is ua, but a drop of rain is kōpata. Whakataritari ua is the name for weather leading up to rain, while taru whakaru is damp, cloudy weather. Maomao is the moment when rain stops. Māwake rangitahi refers to a sudden short squall, and māwake pā roa to a continuing rainstorm. A day's rain is called koripo marama.

When it came to distinguishing different types of rain, Māori had a remarkable range of descriptive words.

Clouds are lit by the setting sun at Karekare, west of Auckland. Red

Rain clouds loom over the Mackenzie Basin, in the South Island. This kind of weather is called whakataritari ua – weather leading up to rain. Taru whakaru refers to damp, cloudy weather.

- Light rain was described variously as: uapūkohukohu – misty rain; ua koehuehu – light mist falling in small drops; uwhiuwhi taua – a shower; and tarariki – persistent showers.
- Heavy rain was described as: pūroro – driving rain; pōua – a rain squall; and ua kōpiro – drenching rain.

Rain and death

Many tribes interpreted rain or a storm as an expression of grief at a funeral, as at the burial of Te Puea Hērangi (a Waikato leader and granddaughter of King Tāwhiao): 'as the cortege approached Taupiri mountain, fierce rain began to fall. All the Māori kings were, it is said, buried in heavy rain, but no rain could have been more violent and powerful than it was on this occasion. It was the heavens weeping.' [6]

Tribal laments sometimes compare the rain to their tears falling when they mourn. This is an extract from the lament, 'E pā tō hau', for Te Wano of the Ngāti Apakura tribe:

E ua e te ua e taheke
Koe i runga rā
Ko au ki raro nei riringi ai
Te ua i aku kamo.
Come then, O rain, pour down
Steadily from above
While I here below pour forth
A deluge from mine eyes.[7]

A RAIN CHARM

This charm was intended to stop rain falling, and was known as 'he tūā i te rangi' (weather charm). It was documented from Tuta Nihoniho, a 19th-century Ngāti Porou leader.

E ua, e te uaua; e mao, e te maomao!
Tihore mai i runga, tihore mai i raro,
Koi mate nga tamariki a te ika nui
E kiko! E kiko e.
Rain, O rain,
cease raining, fair sky!
Clear away from above,
clear away from below,
Lest the offspring of
te ika nui be distressed
Bring about a blue,
unclouded sky.[8]

RANGINUI | THE SKY

In the traditions of the South Island tribe of Ngāi Tahu, Tiu was the northerly wind, the child of the winds known as Rakamaomao. The hot, dry nor'wester is a common wind in the region. This dust storm is in Avoca, a river valley in the high country.

TOLAGA BAY

On his first voyage to New Zealand in 1769, Captain James Cook arrived at a spot on the East Coast of the North Island, and named it Tolaga Bay. He believed that this was the Māori name. But Rēweti Kōhere of Ngāti Porou has noted that the name was actually Ūawa. Māori who met Cook thought he was asking what the name of the wind was, and so they said Tāraki (north wind). Tolaga is a corruption of Tāraki.

Te whānau puhi

Te whānau puhi, the wind family, comprises many different winds. The common word for wind is hau. Hauraro is the north wind, or wind from below. Tonga is the south wind, and Hauāuru the west. There are numerous tribal names for winds.

The east wind is known as Marangai, also meaning a storm, or bad weather. However, in some districts, marangai means the north wind. It is likely that its meaning depended on the quarter from which bad weather tended to come in that district. Similarly, ori means wind from a bad quarter and can be north-west, or north-east to south-east, depending on the locality.

Local wind names

Particular districts had specific names for winds:
- Ōkiwa is the wind that blows down the valley of Whakatāne.
- Pāwhare is the north–northeast wind in Hawke's Bay.
- In Taranaki pieke means the east wind with rain.
- To the Ngāi Tahu people, Rakamaomao is the group of winds that blow from the south and north. Within this group, Te Pūnui o Te Toka was the southerly and Rakamaomao's child Tiu was the northern wind.
- To Ngāti Porou, tonga huruhuru is the south–southeast wind.

Raising the wind

It was thought that tohunga (priests) were able to bring winds that would favour their own people, or upset the enemy. They used prayers known as whakaarahau. Pururangi, or tūāumuiterangi, were the incantations that deprived winds of their power – for instance, to bring about calm weather for a fishing trip.

RANGINUI | THE SKY

Lightning flashes across the night sky at Lake Alexandrina, in the Mackenzie Country. Uira is the term for ordinary lightning, kohara refers to zigzag flashes, and kapo is a flash here and there, all around the horizon.

Storms
Āwhā, tūpuhi and marangai are all storms. A rōpu is a squall and a taupoki is a hurricane. The saying, 'Ngā uaua o te whitu rāua ko te ono' (meaning 'the strenuous times of the sixth and seventh months' in the traditional calendar) referred to the gales and extreme weather that could begin in the warmer months of November and December.

Thunder
Whaitiri or Hinewhaitiri is the goddess of thunder. Papaki whaititiri is a clap of thunder, while paoro is the moment when thunder crashes.

Aputahi a pawa was both the personification of thunder and a single peal. Ngaruru mai rangi describes a low, continued, rumbling thunder. Tangi pōhutu is a loud peal of thunder. Oho rangi was a rite that was believed to cause thunder.

Lightning
Tamateuira is the god who personifies lightning, and the ancestor Tāwhaki was also associated with lightning. The Moriori people of the Chatham Islands linked Tāwhaki with both lightning and thunder.

In the early 1900s Hōne Taare Tikao, a Ngāi Tahu elder, described three types of lightning. He said uira was ordinary lightning, kohara was the zigzag flashes of lightning across the sky, and kapo was an occasional flash all round the horizon, which he believed was a sign of wind.

Lightning and death
The association between lightning and death was described by the Ngāti Porou leader Tuta Nihoniho:

Kia ata titiro ki te hiko, haunga ia te uira me te kanapu, ko te hiko hiko he toto rangatira e hinga i te parekura, i te waka tahuri, i te whare wera ranei, i te mate tupapaku ranei.

Look carefully at the distant lightning, and disregard the ordinary lightning and the gleaming electric lightning at the horizon. Distant lightning predicts the death of chiefs in battle, or an overturned canoe, or a fire, or a natural death.

SIGNS ON THE MOUNTAIN

A rua kōhā or rua kanapu was a place, usually a mountain top, where lightning was seen. A double flash is particularly dramatic on a mountain, and was seen as a sign that an important member of the tribe had passed away, or might soon do so. There are frequent references in tribal laments to lightning flashing over important mountains.

The connection with death is also made in a lament for Te Huhu, a chief of Te Rarawa:

Terā te uira e hiko i te rangi
E wāhi rua ana rā runga o
  Tauwhare
Kāore ia nei ko te tohu
  o te mate.
*The lightning flashes in
  the sky
Splitting in twain over the
  sacred hill Tauwhare
Assuredly a token of death.*[9]

35

RANGINUI | THE SKY

In some traditions, sleet and drifting snow were seen as the children of the mountains Pīhanga and Tongariro, in the central North Island, as they were often covered in snow.

One word for dew is haukū. In the Māori story of the creation, dew is the tears of Ranginui, mourning his separation from Papatūānuku. The tears fall on her breast, as dew settles on the land. A saying among people of the moist, fertile lands of Hawke's Bay is 'Heretaunga haukū nui' (Heretaunga the dew-covered land).

Snow, hail and frost

Snow is known as huka or hukarere. Hail is either ua whatu (rain stones) or huka-ā-whatu (stone-like snow). Hukapapa is ice or frost, while hukapiri refers to hard frost. Upokomārō refers both to hard frost and the frozen ground.

The Ngāi Tahu people believed snow was the offspring of the deity Whēkoi. When it snowed they would say, 'Kai te rere te tama a Whēkoi' (the son of Whēkoi is falling). Others saw ice and snow as the children of Whaitiri (goddess of thunder), or described them as 'the fish of Whaitiri'. In other traditions, sleet and drifting snow were the children of the mountains Tongariro and Pīhanga, no doubt because these were often covered in snow.

RANGINUI | THE SKY

Mist

Pūkohu is the word for mist. Mist uniformly covering the sky is papanui, said to be a sign of calm the next day. In one tradition, mist is said to be the soft, warm sighs rising from the mountains and valleys – the earth mother Papatūānuku. This was a sign of her love for Ranginui, who was separated from her.

To the Tūhoe people of the Urewera mountains, Hine-pūkohu-rangi is the personification of mist and fog. According to tradition, Tūhoe are the descendants of the mist maiden and Te Maunga (the mountain). The tribe is often known as 'Ngā tamariki a te Kohu' – the children of the mist.

There are a number of names for the rainbow, the most common being āniwaniwa. The phenomenon was sometimes described as atua piko, a curved deity. The personified forms of the rainbow are Kahukura, Uenuku and Haere, and there are other minor names. In tradition, Kahukura appears in the heavens in the form of a double bow. The red lower bow is a female known as Pu-te-aniwaniwa, while the upper, which is darker-hued, is a male known as Kahukurapango.

PART II

Papatūānuku
the land

Mt Hikurangi

Papatūānuku *the land*

Te Ahukaramū Charles Royal

In the Māori world view, land gives birth to all things, including humankind, and provides the physical and spiritual basis for life. Papatūānuku, the land, is a powerful mother earth figure who gives many blessings to her children.

In the creation tradition, Papatūānuku (earth mother) and Ranginui (sky father) were locked in an embrace, and were later separated by their children. This lintel, carved in the Bay of Plenty in the 1850s, depicts Papatūānuku and Ranginui during the creation period. The spirals show light coming into the world.

The importance of Papatūānuku

In Māori tradition and history, Papatūānuku is profoundly important. Papatūānuku is the land, an earth mother who gives birth to all things of the world and imparts many blessings to her children. She is seen as the birthplace of all things and the place to which they return, and is considered a foundation for human action. Papatūānuku is the first kaupapa (platform) in the traditional world view.

In many Māori creation traditions, Papatūānuku emerged from under water. This reflects the experience of island peoples living within the vast expanse of the Pacific Ocean. A similar theme is expressed in the stories of the legendary trickster and demigod Māui fishing up various islands of Polynesia.

After the earth emerged from water, it gave birth to all life. Trees, birds and humans emerge from the land and are nourished by it. Figuratively, humans are born from the womb of Papatūānuku, and return there after death. People's emotional, intellectual and spiritual selves are born daily from the land, and thought itself is seen as coming from the land.

For an island people, land is hugely important. The traditional Māori world view is based in early Polynesian experience, where whole islands were sometimes lost beneath the sea. The world seemed unstable, as it consisted mainly of water. Land could not be taken for granted.

A person's search for their own foundation, values and principles is compared to a journeying canoe looking for land. An island comes as relief to the weary ocean traveller.

Papatūānuku is a powerful figure, as she represents the generative foundation of all life. All things are born from her and nurtured by her, including humankind. Many tribal traditions discuss the birth of humans from the earth. In the Hineahuone tradition, the first woman was formed from clay at Kurawaka by Tāne, a son of Ranginui and Papatūānuku. Her name, Hineahuone, means earth-formed woman. In a Northland tribal tradition, the ancestor Tuputupu-whenua emerged from the ground.

South of Te Mata Peak, Hawke's Bay. The often mountainous New Zealand landscape played an important role in the Māori world view. The land is seen as Papatūānuku, the earth mother. Mountain ranges are conceptualised as representing the goddess lying prone.

This whakapapa shows some of the children of Papatūānuku and Ranginui. They were the ancestors of all parts of nature, including people, birds, forests, fish, winds, and water.

			Ranginui — Papatūānuku			
Tūmatauenga	Tāwhirimātea	Tāne-mahuta	Tangaroa	Rongomātāne	Haumietiketike
People, war	Wind, weather	Forests, birds	Sea, fish	Cultivated food	Uncultivated food

In this artwork by John Bevan Ford, an amokura (red-tailed tropic bird) soars over Maungatautari, the traditional mountain of the Ngāti Raukawa tribe. Waitohi, a sister of Ngāti Toa chief Te Rauparaha, urged Ngāti Raukawa leaders to return to the mountain, near the present-day town of Cambridge, and convince their people to migrate south. The tribe moved south to the Kapiti Coast, showing the mana (status) of this important woman. When the chief Te Whatanui was asked to return to Maungatautari for good, he described it as Te Kura-a-Tauninihi (the sacred treasure of Tauninihi). This refers to the amokura's sacred feathers, brought to New Zealand on the *Tainui* migratory canoe.

There is an oft-quoted saying:
  Mā te wahine, mā te whenua, ka ngaro te tangata.
  By women and land do men perish.

Women and land

Traditional Māori culture aligns women with the land, because the land gives birth to humankind just as women do. As the world was born from Papatūānuku, so humankind is born from women. A woman's womb, called te whare tangata (the house of humanity), is seen as the same as the womb of the earth.

In tribal history, individual women had authority over, and embodied, particular areas of land. Ruawehea, a high-born woman of the Ngāti Hako tribe, had particular authority in the Hauraki region. Visitors are welcomed with the following expression:

Haere mai, nau mai
Haere mai, kuhu noa mai ki ngā hūhā o Ruawehea.
Come forth, welcome
Come forth and enter the thighs of Ruawehea.[1]

This saying recognises Ruawehea as the doorway to the land, and as being one with the land.

Women also exhorted men to act, to fight to secure land, or to express a particular kaupapa (plan or proposal). Women played an important role in keeping issues alive and resolving grievances and problems. Waitohi, a sister of the Ngāti Toa chief Te Rauparaha, was instrumental in convincing Ngāti Raukawa leaders to migrate south with their people. She said:

Ngāti Raukawa, e hoki ki Maungatautari! Mā wai o koutou e mau mai aku werewere hei noho mai i runga i te whenua i haha nei?[2]

Ngāti Raukawa, return to Maungatautari! Who of you will bring my barnacles here to settle upon these lands that have been procured?

Traditionally, a chief is likened to a mighty whale. A whale's barnacles can only move when the whale does, and similarly, the people would only

PAPATŪĀNUKU | THE LAND

A chief of the Ngāti Hikairo people welcomes Governor General Sir William Jervois and his party at Kāwhia in 1884. In the pōwhiri (formal welcome), the tangata whenua welcome visitors onto their marae.

TANGATA WHENUA

Tangata whenua – literally, people of the land – are those who have authority in a particular place. This is based on their deep relationship with that place, through their births and their ancestors' births. As tangata whenua express themselves in that place, they gain the authority and confidence to project themselves into the world. This idea, in turn, underpins the notion of mana whenua – spiritual authority in a given area.

move if the chief did. This powerful metaphor bore fruit when the Ngāti Raukawa chief Hūkiki Te Ahukaramū replied that he would bring the barnacles on the broad back of the whale. It was accepted that those who migrated did so because of Waitohi's invitation.

Whenua *the placenta*

The Māori word for land, whenua, also means placenta. All life is seen as being born from the womb of Papatūānuku, under the sea. The lands that appear above water are placentas from her womb. They float, forming islands.

In another perspective, all life takes place within the womb of the world. In that womb, preparations are being made for a new world. We are children within the womb of the world, soon to be born into another reality.

Burying a placenta

Traditionally, the whenua and pito (umbilical cord) of newborn babies are buried in a significant place. The placenta is placed in a specially prepared receptacle and buried in a particular location. This practice reinforces the relationship between the newborn child and the land of their birth.

The place where one's umbilical cord was severed is called 'te wāhi i kotia ai te pito'. This is a place of special importance for each person. It is their place of first emergence into the world, of first maturation and foundation.

Māori traditionally bury the placenta of a newborn baby in a special place. This was often done in vessels called ipu whenua, which were originally made from gourds. This replica ipu whenua was carved by Jacob Heberley of Te Āti Awa from tōtara wood.

PAPATŪĀNUKU | THE LAND

This wharenui (meeting house) is at Tūrangawaewae marae, at Ngāruawāhia. When the marae was established, it fulfilled a saying from Tāwhiao, the second Māori king. The king had described Ngāruawāhia as his tūrangawaewae (footstool). Since then, this idea has been expanded, and people from many tribes speak of their marae as their tūrangawaewae, meaning a place to stand.

Tūrangawaewae *a place to stand*

Tūrangawaewae is one of the most well-known and powerful Māori concepts. Literally tūranga (standing place), waewae (feet), it is often translated as 'a place to stand'. Tūrangawaewae are places where we feel especially empowered and connected. They are our foundation, our place in the world, our home.

Tāwhiao's tūrangawaewae

Tāwhiao, the second Māori king, referred to tūrangawaewae in a saying:

Ko Arekahānara tōku haona kaha
Ko Kemureti tōku oko horoi
Ko Ngāruawāhia tōku tūrangawaewae.
Alexandra [Pirongia township] will ever be a symbol of my strength of character
Cambridge a symbol of my wash bowl of sorrow
And Ngāruawāhia my footstool.[3]

King Tāwhiao's granddaughter, Te Puea Hērangi, fulfilled this saying when she established Tūrangawaewae marae at Ngāruawāhia. A person's marae (tribal forum for social life) is often seen as their tūrangawaewae. For each person, the marae is the place where their ancestors are present, where they spend their formative years and learn important lessons. They gain the right to stand upon their marae and proclaim their views about the world and life.

Tūrangawaewae can include other places as well. Many tribes identify themselves in terms of their mountains, waterways and important ancestors. When Ngāti Porou introduce themselves, they say:

Ko Hikurangi te maunga
Ko Waiapu te awa
Ko Ngāti Porou te iwi.
Hikurangi is the mountain
Waiapu is the river
Ngāti Porou is the tribe.

BIRTH FROM THE EARTH – BEING INDIGENOUS

To be indigenous is to be born from the land where you live, and continually born and reborn through an intimate relationship with earth, sea and sky. There are tribal stories of humans born from the land, and some tribes see themselves as descended from environmental phenomena; for instance, the Tūhoe people say they arose from the mist that surrounds their mountains.

44

PAPATŪĀNUKU | THE LAND

The metaphorical union between people and the land, Papatūānuku, is seen in places named after parts of the human body. The Tararua Range was named Te Tuarātapu-o-Te Rangihaeata (the sacred back of Te Rangihaeata) after an important Ngāti Toa chief, Te Rangihaeata, to commemorate a peace arrangement between the Ngāti Toa and Ngāti Kahungunu tribes. The range became a dividing line between Ngāti Toa on the west side and Ngāti Kahungunu on the east.

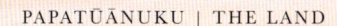

In the concept of tūrangawaewae, the external world is a reflection of an inner sense of security and foundation. The mountains, rivers and waterways to which one can claim a relationship also express this internal sense of foundation.

Place names and the human body

The human body and the physical landscape were metaphorically united when the Ngāti Toa people named the Tararua Range as Te Tuarātapu-o-Te Rangihaeata – the sacred back of Te Rangihaeata (a Ngāti Toa leader). The naming followed a peace pact between Ngāti Toa on one side of the range and Ngāti Kahungunu on the other.

When the *Te Arawa* voyaging canoe arrived from Polynesia, crew members laid claim to pieces of land by naming them after parts of their body. This is known as taunaha whenua. The Ōkūrei peninsula at Maketū in the Bay of Plenty was called Te Kūreitanga-o-te-ihu-o-Tamatekapua (the bridge of Tamatekapua's nose). A small hill nearby was named Te Takapū-o-Tapuika (Tapuika's belly). A large piece of land was called Te Takapū-o-Waitaha (Waitaha's belly).

This whare rūnanga (meeting house) at Ōhinemutu, Rotorua, is named after Te Arawa ancestor Tamatekapua.

PAPATŪĀNUKU | THE LAND

Many tribal traditions explain the origins of landforms with stories about ancestors. In the South Island, the Waitaha ancestor Rākaihautū created lakes by carving them out with his digging stick. Te Waihora (Lake Ellesmere) is known as Te Keteika-a-Rākaihautū – Rākaihautū's fishing basket.

Many place names come from stories of tribal ancestors. Rangitoto Island's full name is Te Rangi-i-totongia-ai-te-ihu-o-Tamatekapua (the day that Tamatekapua had a bloody nose). It was named after a fight between Tamatekapua, captain of the *Te Arawa* voyaging canoe, and the *Tainui* canoe captain, Hoturoa.

Stories of people and land

The idea of being born from the earth is the foundation for kinship between earth and humankind. There are many tribal stories about the relationship between a people and their land. These stories capture every corner of the New Zealand landscape in some way. The South Island's lakes are referred to as Ngā puna karikari a Rākaihautū – the springs dug out by Rākaihautū (a founding ancestor of the Waitaha tribe). Each lake has a particular story, and these are woven into a larger narrative. Te Waihora (Lake Ellesmere), for example, is called Te Keteika-a-Rākaihautū (Rākaihautū's fishing basket) referring to its importance as a rich food resource.

There are many stories about the North Island's Volcanic Plateau, which stretches from Whakaari (White Island) to Tongariro. The various geysers and 'hot spots' in between are said to have been created by Te Hoata and Te Pupū, the sisters of the priest Ngātoroirangi.

Tamatekapua of the Te Arawa people also left his name at many locations. Rangitoto Island in the Waitematā Harbour is known as Te Rangi-i-totongia-ai-te-ihu-o-Tamatekapua (the day that Tamatekapua had a bloody nose). Moehau mountain on the Coromandel Peninsula is called Te Moengahau-o-Tamatekapua (Tamatekapua's windy sleeping place). Tamatekapua is buried at the peak of the mountain.

Rongokako was the grandfather of Kahungunu, the founding ancestor of the Ngāti Kahungunu people. Rongokako was said to be able to take giant strides, and he left footprints at a place known as Te Tapuwae-o-Rongokako (Rongokako's footprint), near Whāngārā. Te Mata Peak in Hawke's Bay is known as his final resting place. It is said his form can be seen in the adjacent hills.

Rongokako's son (Kahungunu's father) was Tamatea-pōkaiwhenua. He is mentioned in a place name said to be the world's longest: Taumata-whakatangihanga-kōauau-o-Tamatea-turi-pūkaka-piki-maunga-horonuku-pōkai-whenua-ki-tāna-tahu. Near Pōrangahau in Hawke's Bay, it means 'the place where Tamatea, the man with the big knees, who slid, climbed and swallowed mountains, known as landeater, played his flute to his loved one'.

Whakapapa and kaupapa

Traditional Māori knowledge includes elaborate genealogies about the world. There are various classifications of species of flora and fauna, rocks, fish and so on. These interlink to form a grand fabric, in which all things are interrelated, and all are descended from the children of Ranginui and Papatūānuku. The genealogies form a framework which is 'clothed' in a vast array of stories and traditions. These explain the essential character and features of those in the genealogies. For example, a genealogy of relationships between bird species included stories about the birds themselves. One such story tells how the legendary hero Māui was turned into a kererū (wood pigeon) while holding his mother's colourful clothes. Genealogies and stories together make up whakapapa, a body of knowledge about the nature of the world.

'Whakapapa' describes the actions of creating a foundation, and layering and adding to that foundation. This is done by reciting genealogies (tātai) and stories, and through ritual. Whakapapa allows people to locate themselves in the world, both figuratively and in relation to their human ancestors. It links them to ancestors whose dramas played out on the land and invested it with meaning. By recalling these events, people layer meaning and experience onto the land.

Kaupapa is a plan, a set of principles and ideas that inform behaviour and customs. Mana whenua (authority in the land) is achieved when a person's inward kaupapa is aligned with the outward land. When the relationship with the land is lost, people's inner sense of security and foundation may be lost too.

A group waits for a Native Land Court hearing in the Whanganui area, in the late 1860s. Such hearings were part of a process which led to the loss of much tribal land. This loss of land destabilised Māori society, which relied on Papatūānuku (earth mother) as a foundation.

LOSS OF LAND

Much tribal land was lost in the 19th century. While some tribes willingly released some land, much was taken against their will. The New Zealand wars were followed by land confiscations, and the Native Land Court facilitated the sale of land by transferring land titles from tribes to individuals. Iwi made many attempts to halt this loss. The felling of forests and loss of land were a catastrophe for their traditional world view. The trees were a model for the tikanga or behaviour of a people, so their destruction was a calamity. The widespread loss of land meant the loss of foundation and stability, and of the centring, nurturing principle of Papatūānuku.

The desperation felt is captured by Wi Naihera of Ngāi Tahu:

> When the waves rolled in upon us from England, first one post was covered, then another till at last the water neared us and we tried to erect barriers to protect ourselves. That is we entered into agreement with those who purchased our lands from the Queen, but when the flood tide from England set in our barriers were cast down, and that is why you find us now, clinging to the tops of these rocks, called Native Reserves, which alone remain above water.[4]

He likened the loss of land to its disappearance under the sea, an echo of the old mythological idea of land rising up from the sea.

PAPATŪĀNUKU | THE LAND

> When Māui fished up the North Island, he is said to have used a hook made from the jawbone of his grandmother, Murirangawhenua. The curve of Cape Kidnappers represents the hook, and is known as Te Matau-a-Māui (Māui's fish hook).

Whenua *how the land was shaped*
Te Ahukaramū Charles Royal

New Zealand's dramatic and varied landscape sparked the Māori imagination. Their stories tell of giants digging out the South Island lakes, water creatures rising up to form tracts of land, and rival mountains moving in a battle for the affections of the beautiful Mt Pīhanga.

Just as iwi traditions contain stories and genealogies about the creation of the world, they also explain how the world, once created, was shaped.

Some tribal traditions speak of fantastic and powerful presences in the earth itself, and of characters who sculpted and arranged the world as we see it. They lived on mountain tops or in the depths of lakes, and scoured out rivers and gorges. Giant ancestors dug out the lakes, and the mountains moved. The stories about the forces that have shaped the land are a combination of explanation and metaphor.

Stories about the land were part of an oral tradition, and could function like maps. By likening the North Island to a fish – usually a stingray – people could remember its shape and various important locations. Likening the South Island to a canoe served the same purpose.

Accounts of the formation of river beds mapped the paths taken by various rivers. Stories about the major mountains detailed the distinctive topographical features that had been observed by local tribes. The maps could also record the locations of geothermal areas.

PAPATŪĀNUKU | THE LAND

A number of New Zealand places are named after the story of Māui fishing up the North Island, with the South Island as his canoe and Stewart Island its anchor. This map is oriented as Māori traditionally perceived the country, with the North Island below the South Island.

The North and South islands

One of the greatest stories of Māori literature recounts the fishing up of the North Island. It begins with Māui and his brothers setting off on a fishing expedition. The elder brothers did not want to take Māui, so he hid in the canoe and did not reveal himself until they were out at sea. When he emerged he managed to convince his brothers to row out to the deepest part of the ocean, where he cast a fish hook made from his grandmother's jawbone. It sank below the waves and fastened to the underwater house of Tonganui, the grandson of Tangaroa, god of the sea. Māui hauled up his catch above the water. The land, the North Island, became known as Te Ika-a-Māui (the fish of Māui).

Te Rangihaeata of the Ngāti Toarangatira tribe dictated this version of how the North Island got its shape after it was pulled from the sea:

Māui left his brothers and returned home. He said to his older brothers, 'After I leave, please do not partake of the fish ... Do not cut up our fish.' However, [after he left] they did not do what he said. They began to cut it up and eat it ... When he returned Māui became enraged ... He was greatly distressed as they cut the head, the tail, the gills and the fins ... This is why this land lies unevenly – there are mountains, plains, valleys and cliffs. If they had not fought over the fish, then the land would have retained its fish shape.[5]

In some traditions the fish is said to be a pātiki (flounder); in others it is a whai (stingray). The head of the fish lies at the south of the North Island, at present-day Wellington, and its tail is the Northland region. The barb at the base of the tail is the Coromandel Peninsula. The pākau (fins) are Taranaki and the East Coast, and the backbone runs between Taupō and Rotorua. The heart is at Maungapōhatu, in the Urewera district.

The stern of Māui's canoe is the southern tip of the South Island, and the prow is the north. When Māui hauled up his great catch he stood on the Kaikōura Peninsula, which is called Te Taumanu-o-te-waka (the thwart or seat of the canoe). Stewart Island is believed to be the anchor.

MĀUI AND NUKUTAIMEMEHA

It is often said that the North Island is Māui's fish and the South Island his canoe, but the East Coast tribe, Ngāti Porou, believe the canoe ended up somewhere else. They say that the first part of the fish to emerge from the water was their sacred mountain, Hikurangi. Māui's canoe, *Nukutaimemeha*, became stranded on it, and is still there in petrified form.

According to tradition the Southern Alps, reflected here in the Ōkarito Lagoon, were formed when the *Ārai-te-uru* canoe arrived from Hawaiki. As it travelled down the coast of the South Island, more than 150 passengers leapt ashore and became mountains. In one version of the story, Aoraki (Mt Cook) was a small boy carried on a relative's shoulders, which is why that mountain is taller than all the others.

49

PAPATŪĀNUKU | THE LAND

This painting by Angus Kerr depicts the battle of the mountains Tongariro, Taranaki, Tauhara and Pūtauaki, who all vied for the love of the beautiful maiden mountain Pīhanga. Eventually Tongariro won, and married Pīhanga.

Kupe separates the islands

Kupe is one of the most important of the early Polynesian ancestors who journeyed from the ancestral homeland, Hawaiki. Although their traditions are very different, Kupe, like Māui, was also responsible for shaping New Zealand. When Kupe arrived in New Zealand he found only one island. The Ngāti Kahungunu elder Īhāia Hūtana referred to Kupe separating the islands in a letter to the Māori-language newspaper, *Te Toa Takitini*:

> E kīia ana he moutere kotahi ēnei e rua, nā Kupe i tapahi ka tere te moana i waenganui, ka kīia ko 'te moana a Kupe'.
>
> *It is said that these two islands were at one time together as one. Kupe was responsible for cutting them so that the sea flowed between. This is why [Cook Strait] was called 'the sea of Kupe'.*[6]

PAPATŪĀNUKU | THE LAND

Ngāuruhoe from the slopes of Mt Tongariro, with Ruapehu in the background. In one tradition, Ngāuruhoe was one of the wives of Mt Tongariro. In another tradition the two were seen as the same mountain.

Battle of the mountains

The mountains in the central North Island once fought a great battle for the hand of Pīhanga, a mountain to the south of Tūrangi. Tribes have different versions of the story; the following is drawn from Ngāti Tūwharetoa tradition.

The story goes that in the days when the earth was young there were four mountain warriors: Tongariro, Taranaki (Mt Egmont), Tauhara and Pūtauaki (Mt Edgecumbe). There was also the beautiful maiden mountain, Pīhanga. The warrior mountains fought for her affections, and after a long battle Tongariro emerged the winner.

The defeated mountains decided that they should leave Tongariro's domain. They were to travel as far as they could before dawn, when the rising sun would fix them to the spot. Pūtauaki headed east and by daybreak reached his present position at Kawerau. Tauhara travelled slowly, all the time looking back longingly at Pīhanga; he only reached the other end of the lake. Taranaki went west and still looks back, hoping for the day when he might return to avenge his defeat. Meanwhile, Pīhanga became the wife of Tongariro, and they had a child named Pukeronaki.

The following account, given by Pei Te Hurinui Jones of the Ngāti Maniapoto tribe, illustrates how the same story can vary between tribal traditions:

Tongariro was betrothed by Rangi-e-tū iho nei (Rangi who stands above, the sky) to his own wife, Pīhanga, a mountain near Taupō. Their descendants are the snow, the winds and the rain. According to Ngāti Awa, Tongariro had two wives, Pīhanga and Ngāuruhoe. Both are mountains. Taranaki wanted these women for himself and others too pursued the women as well. And so a battle took place which resulted in the mountains being separated out. Taranaki went out to the west where it now stands. Whakaari, Paepae-o-aotea and Moutohorā went northwards off Whakatāne. Pūtauaki went northwards too and now stands south of Whakatāne.[7]

CELEBRATING KUPE'S ACHIEVEMENT

The separation of the North and South islands and the formation of others are remembered in a peruperu (dance accompanied with song).

The chief Te Rauparaha of Ngāti Toarangatira, who settled in Horowhenua at the beginning of the 19th century, recited the story to prove his tribe's links to the area. This version was written down by Mohi Tūrei of Ngāti Porou, who attributes it to the Ngāti Kahungunu ancestor Te Whatu-i-apiti.

Ka tito au, ka tito au.
Ka tito ki a Kupe!
Te tangata nana i hoehoe te
    moana.
Tu ke a Kapiti!
Tu ke Mana!
Tau ke Arapawa!
Ko nga tohu tenei a taku
    tipuna a Kupe
I whakatoreke tii-ka-puaha.
Ka toreke i au te whenua e!

I compose, I compose.
I compose for Kupe!
The man who traversed the
    oceans.
Kapiti stands apart!
Mana stands apart!
As does Arapawa!
These are symbols of my
    ancestor, of Kupe.
He traversed the land,
and so do I![8]

51

The thermal wonders

The Volcanic Plateau in the central North Island is full of mystery: mud pools, hot pools, geysers and volcanoes give vent to unfathomable powers lying deep in the earth. It did not escape Māori that there seemed to be a pattern or design in the way that 'fire' from underground could be seen at Whakaari in the Bay of Plenty all the way to Tongariro, just south of Tūrangi township.

In particular, the people of Ngāti Tūwharetoa, whose tribal lands are in the central North Island, have long maintained stories about this phenomenon. They say that the high priest Ngātoroirangi and his sisters Te Hoata and Te Pupū were responsible for bringing fire to New Zealand from the ancestral homeland, Hawaiki. Having arrived in New Zealand on the *Te Arawa* canoe, Ngātoroirangi travelled inland and discovered the lake that became known as Taupōnui-a-Tia (Taupō). He continued to Onetapu, south of present-day Tūrangi, where he encountered extremely cold weather. He called out to his sisters, who came to him from Hawaiki in the form of fire under the earth, appearing above the ground at intervals and creating the geysers, hot pools and volcanoes.

The arrival of fire from Hawaiki is commemorated in this song by the renowned composer Rihi Puhiwahine of Ngāti Tūwharetoa for her lover

> The Te Arawa people often tell the story of Tūtānekai, who lived on Mokoia Island in Lake Rotorua, and the beautiful Hinemoa, who lived on the lake's eastern shore. The two fell in love, but their families disapproved. One night, guided by the sound of Tūtānekai's flute, Hinemoa swam out to join him. After her epic swim she recuperated in a hot pool, Waikimihia, which is now a tourist attraction.

PAPATŪĀNUKU | THE LAND

Te Hoata and Te Pupū, the sisters of the high priest Ngatoroirangi first came to Whakaari (right), then made their way inland. When they arrived at Taupō, they travelled southwards along the western edge of the lake before meeting their brother on Mt Tongariro. They returned northwards via the eastern side of Lake Taupō leaving their fire at many places, including Ōrākei Kōrako (left) and Waimangu (below).

Mahutu Te Toko, of Ngāti Maniapoto:
    Kāti au ka hoki ki taku whenua tupu
    Ki te wai koropupū i heri mai nei
    I Hawaiki rā anō e Ngātoro-i-rangi
    E ōna tuāhine, Te Hoata, Te Pupū
    E hū rā Tongariro, ka mahana i taku kiri.
    I return to my homeland
    To the bubbling waters that were brought
    From Hawaiki by Ngātoro i rangi
    And his sisters, Te Hoata and Te Pupū
    Tongariro erupts and my body is warmed.[9]

Some of the places the sisters left their fire are Whakaari, Tarawera, Whakarewarewa, Tikitere, Waimangu, Ōrākei Kōrako, Tokaanu and Tongariro.

Hot springs

Hot springs have been valued from the beginnings of settlement in New Zealand. Particular pools were said by Māori to have spiritual kaitiaki (guardians), and were central to important rituals. The warm waters of

This is the Waikite geyser at Whakarewarewa before a tourist industry developed around the thermal attractions of the Rotorua area. Its hot pools were an important resource for the people of Te Arawa.

53

Lake Pūkaki, with Aoraki Mt Cook at centre, one of the glacial lakes carved by Rākaihautū as he travelled along the Southern Alps.

Hot pools at Whakarewarewa (right) have traditionally been used for cooking food, which was lowered into the water in flax bags. As the teapots indicate, the temperature was also hot enough to make tea.

When Ngātoroirangi had just arrived in New Zealand from Hawaiki, he was overcome by extreme cold at a place called Onetapu. He called out to his sisters Te Hoata and Te Pupū, who sped to him from Hawaiki in the form of fire. When they emerged above ground they created the geysers, hot pools and volcanoes renowned in that part of the country.

waiariki (large bathing pools) and ngāwhā (overflowing pools) were used for washing, relaxation and for treating diseases including skin complaints and rheumatism. Boiling pools were used for cooking and food was preserved using the available heat in the ground. Vividly coloured clays such as kōkōwai (red ochre) were used as paints and dyes.

Life in geothermal areas was not without its hazards and puia (geysers) were probably treated with caution. Henry S. Bates, visiting Ōrākei Kōrako in 1860, recorded in his diary that a Māori child had fallen into the Te Mimi-a-Homaiterangi geyser.

The lakes of the Southern Alps

The Southern Alps are the backbone of Te Wai Pounamu (the South Island). Majestic and formidable, they have inspired many tribal stories.

One of the most important narratives of the South Island tribes concerns Rākaihautū, who carved out the mountain lakes with his kō (digging stick). He arrived in the South Island aboard his canoe, *Uruao*, which came ashore near Nelson. After travelling inland to Motueka, he began a long journey south, traversing the entire mountain chain. Along the way he dug out numerous lakes, including: Rotoiti, Rotoroa, Takapō (Tekapo), Pūkaki, Ōhau, Wānaka, Wakatipu and Manawapōuri (Manapōuri).

PAPATŪĀNUKU | THE LAND

The Manawatū River was created by a huge tōtara tree which moved from its position in the Puketoi Range in Hawke's Bay under the influence of a supernatural being called Ōkatia, and gouged out the river bed.

Rākaihautū then made his way westwards and fashioned these lakes and lagoons: Waihora (Waihola), Muriwai (Coopers Lagoon), Waihora (Lake Ellesmere) and Wairewa (Lake Forsyth).

Te Āpiti

Te Āpiti (the Manawatū Gorge) provides a means of crossing the Tararua and Ruahine ranges. The river that runs along it is known as Te Aurere-a-te-tonga (flowing current of the south), and its waterfall is Te Aunui-a-tonga (great south current). A sacred rock called Te Ahu-o-Tūranga stands in the middle of the gorge. This account of how the gorge and the Manawatū River bed were formed comes from the Rangitāne tribe:

> Away in the dim past a huge totara tree growing on the slopes of the Puketoi Range in Hawke's Bay became possessed of a supernatural being called Okatia. Under the influence of the spirit the tree began to move, gouging out a deep channel towards the northwest. In time the moving tree encountered the mountain barrier of Tararua and Ruahine, but this obstacle counted for nothing as the totara turned to the west and simply forced its way right through the mountains, thus creating the gorge. The tree then meandered across the plains until it entered the sea. This provided a convenient bed for the Manawatu River.[10]

TANIWHA TALES

In many stories taniwha create lakes and harbours. According to the Ngāi Tūhoe tribe, Lake Waikaremoana, in the south-east of their territory, was formed by the thrashing of Haumapuhia, who was turned into a taniwha by her father Māhū. As she struggled to make her way to the sea, Haumapuhia formed the various branches of the lake.

PAPATŪĀNUKU | THE LAND

This ancient canoe, found in Taupō, is believed by some to have been made purely as a boundary marker, and placed at Opepe.

Ngā waewae tapu *Māori exploration*
Rāwiri Taonui

Māori traditions tell of many great journeys of exploration around New Zealand. The earliest arrivals from Polynesia sailed around the coast by canoe. Later, people headed inland on foot, discovering and naming rivers, mountains and other features.

Māori oral traditions record many great feats of exploration. These traditions often combine symbolic and historical aspects – including tapatapa whenua (naming landscapes after deeds and events) and taunaha whenua (naming landscapes to establish tribal connection to places).

Some traditions attribute several ancestors' journeys to just one person. Others may transpose current land boundaries into the past. These accounts validate a tribe's claim to land by giving mana to ancestors and longevity to land ownership. Different tribes may have their own explanations for place names, justifying their claim over an area.

PAPATŪĀNUKU | THE LAND

For instance, there are two explanations for the naming of Te Aroha peak in the Kaimai Range – in one tradition, it was named Te Aroha-o-Kahu by the Tainui ancestor Kahupekapeka, who climbed the mountain after the death of her husband. In another tradition, the peak was named by Te Arawa ancestor Kahumatamomoe.

Tribes that migrated from one area to another usually took their traditions with them. Traditions about certain canoes, for instance, are found in several areas – but this may be because the story moved with a tribe, and not because the canoe explored the whole country.

Some exploration traditions explain natural phenomena. For example, geothermal activity in the North Island is explained as fire sent from Hawaiki by Ngātoroirangi's sisters as he climbed Mt Tongariro (see pages 52–54). In other traditions, explorers created natural features, or stocked them with resources. For instance, Pāoa, the captain of the *Horouta* canoe, made rivers by urinating, and the explorer Tamatea put freshwater crayfish into the Moawhango River. Such accounts use symbolism to reinforce a tribe's claim to an area through an ancestor.

Some explorers were said to travel by supernatural means – for example, the sisters Reitū and Reipae flew from their homeland, the Waikato, to Northland on a bird. These accounts occur where the explorers passed over areas of no interest to their descendants, or where they have limited importance. In some traditions, landscapes merge with people. For instance, Matiu (Somes Island) and Mākaro (Ward Island) in Wellington Harbour were said to be the daughters of the legendary explorer Kupe.

Canoe explorations

Several of the voyaging canoes from Polynesia extensively explored the New Zealand coastline.

Tainui

The *Tainui* and *Te Arawa* travelled together from Whangaparāoa in the eastern Bay of Plenty to the Whangaparāoa Peninsula, just north of Auckland. The *Tainui* crossed the Tāmaki portage in Auckland and explored the west coast between Manukau and Mōkau harbours, while *Te Arawa* returned to the Bay of Plenty and landed at Maketū.

Rakataura, the tohunga of the *Tainui* canoe, appears in several traditions. In one, the *Tainui* left him behind at Māhia Peninsula. Rakataura dived under the ground and came up again at Kāwhia, on the opposite coast, before the canoe arrived.

In another account, he left the canoe in Auckland after his request to marry Kahurere, daughter of the *Tainui*'s captain, Hoturoa, was refused. Rakataura went down the west coast of the North Island, lighting fires at the entrances of the Waikato River, Whāingaroa (Raglan), Aotea and Kāwhia harbours to stop the canoe from entering.

Eventually, Hoturoa and Rakataura made peace. The *Tainui* landed at Kāwhia Harbour, and Kahurere and Rakataura married. They travelled throughout the Waikato, climbing the mountains Pirongia, Kakepuku, Hākarimata, Pureora, Puke-o-Kahu (where Kahurere died), and Te Aroha in the Kaimai Range – where Rakataura also married Hinemarino.

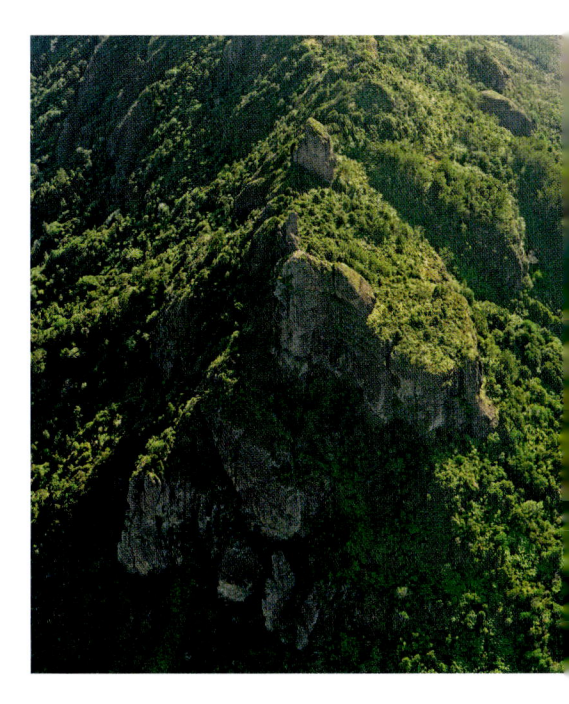

In one tradition, Te Arawa explorer Kahumatamomoe climbed the highest point on the Kaimai Range, naming it Te Muri-aroha-o-Kahu, te aroha-tai, te aroha-uta (the love of Kahu for those on the coasts and those on the land). This has been shortened to Te Aroha.

This tekoteko (carved figure on the gable of a house) depicts Hoturoa, captain of the *Tainui* canoe (top) and Rakataura, the canoe's priest (directly below Hoturoa). The pair quarrelled, and Rakataura left to explore parts of the North Island.

PAPATŪĀNUKU | THE LAND

HOROUTA

The *Horouta* canoe, captained by Kiwa and Pāoa, landed at Ahuahu (Great Mercury Island) and Ōhiwa Harbour, where it needed repairs to its haumi (bow-piece). Pāoa walked inland and climbed Maunga Haumi to find a suitable tree. Unable to carry it back, he urinated the Waipāoa, Waioeka and Mōtū rivers into being and floated the timber down to the coast.

After the canoe was repaired, Kiwa sailed it around the East Cape to Tūranganui (Gisborne), which he named Te Tūranganui-a-Kiwa (the great standing place of Kiwa). Cliffs east of Gisborne (Young Nick's Head, right), were named Te Kurī-a-Pāoa (the dog of Pāoa). Pāoa went on to Gisborne through the Waioeka valley, which he called Te Whai-a-Pāoa (the going of Pāoa).

Another crew member, a woman named Hinekau-i-rangi, made an even longer overland journey. She led a large party to Tōrere, across the Mōtū River, through the Raukūmara Range, down the Tapuwaeroa Stream to the Waiapu River, and then south to Tūranganui.

Te Arawa

Ngātoroirangi and Tia arrived in New Zealand on the *Te Arawa* canoe, which landed at Maketū in the Bay of Plenty. They went inland, towards the centre of the North Island. Tia took a westerly route along the Kaituna River and Mamaku Plains, reaching Ātiamuri (Tia who arrived after earlier people) and Te Aratiatia (the stairway of Tia) on the Waikato River. Further south, he saw some cliffs that resembled his cloak, and named them Te Taupō-nui-a-Tia (the rain cloak of Tia). The name later came to refer to the lake. Tia explored both sides of the lake before settling at Tītīraupenga in the Pureora Forest.

Ngātoroirangi headed east from Maketū. He then followed the Tarawera River, which he named Te Awa-a-te-atua (the river of the atua), inland to Ruawāhia, the northern peak of Mt Tarawera. From there he crossed the Kāingaroa Plains and Waikato River before climbing the summit of Tauhara mountain and surveying Lake Taupō southward to Mt Tongariro.

Ngātoroirangi climbed Tongariro. Freezing, he called to his sisters in Hawaiki for help, 'Kua riro ahau i te hau tonga' (I am seized by the cold from the south) – hence the name Tongariro. Assisted by the fire gods, the sisters sent fire to save their brother (see also page 52).

Kahumatamomoe was the son of Tamatekapua, captain of the *Te Arawa* canoe. He arrived on the canoe at Maketū, with his nephew Īhenga. Heading inland to Rotorua, they named Te Rotoiti-kite-a-Īhenga (Lake Rotoiti) and Te Rotoruanui-a-Kahumatamomoe (Lake Rotorua) before heading north. On their journey, they named Manukau Harbour Te Mānuka, after Kahumatamomoe planted a stake to claim a tribal connection to that place. Arriving at Poutū on the lower northern Wairoa River, the home of Īhenga's brother Taramainuku, Kahumatamomoe named the adjacent harbour Te Kaiparapara-a-Kahumatamomoe after the king fern (kaipara) that Taramainuku fed them.

Kurahaupō

The *Kurahaupō* canoe is known in Northland, Taranaki and the coasts of the lower North Island. Some have suggested that there were three different canoes with the same name. Others think that the same canoe visited all three areas. It may be that the *Kurahaupō* landed in one place, and its descendants took the story of its arrival to different regions.

Whātonga was the captain of the *Kurahaupō* canoe, which landed at Māhia Peninsula. He explored the Wairarapa coast and the upper South Island by sea, returning via the west coast of the North Island. He disembarked and went up the Manawatū River, crossing the Tararua Range to the Tāmakinui-a-Rua area (Dannevirke to Pūkaha Mt Bruce), reaching a great forest which he named Te Taperenui-o-Whātonga.

Whātonga married Hotuwaipara. Their son was Tara-ika or Tara-nohu (named when his mother cut her finger on the barbs of a fish). Tara was the ancestor of the tribe Ngāi Tara, which occupied the lands around Wellington and the northern South Island.

Tautoki was Whātonga's son by his second wife, Reretua. Tautoki's son Rangitāne was the ancestor of the Rangitāne tribes.

Tara and Tautoki made a sweeping journey around the lower North Island, from Māhia Peninsula to Rangiwhakaoma (Castlepoint), Ōkoriwa (Palliser Bay) and Parangārehu (Fitzroy Bay). They explored Wellington Harbour and the Hutt Valley, before heading up the west coast to

The Tarawera River, named by Ngātoroirangi of the *Te Arawa* canoe Te Awa-a-te-atua (the river of the atua).

Māhia Peninsula was the landing place of the *Kurahaupō* canoe.

PAPATŪĀNUKU | THE LAND

Porirua Harbour and the Rangitīkei River. They followed the river and the Hautapu tributary to Waiōuru and Moawhango before proceeding to Tongariro and Lake Taupō, and across the Tītī-o-kura saddle on the Maunga Haruru Range, then back to Nukutaurua at Māhia.

Mataatua

The *Mataatua* explored between Whakatāne in the Bay of Plenty and Tākou Bay in Northland. Northland tribes say that the captain was Puhi and the canoe landed in the north first. Whakatāne tribes believe that Toroa was the captain, and the boat made landfall in their region first. In a less well-known tradition, Mirupōkai was the captain and the *Mataatua* circumnavigated the North and South islands. Tāneatua was a tohunga on the *Mataatua* canoe, and the half-brother of Toroa, the captain. He explored the Urewera forest after the *Mataatua* landed at Whakatāne in the Bay of Plenty. Tāneatua began each of his journeys at the hill called Ōtarahioi or Te Kurī-a-Tāneatua (after one of his pet dogs), still a distinctive mound in the settlement of Tāneatua.

On Tāneatua's first journey, he explored the Ōwhakatoro stream to its source, which he named Te Wai-pōtiki-a-Tāneatua. He then travelled up the longer Whakatāne River, naming it Hinemataroa after his wife. He named many other places along this river, including Ngā Māhanga-a-

Maungapōhatu, climbed by Tāneatua, tohunga of the *Mataatua* canoe.

60

PAPATŪĀNUKU | THE LAND

This view shows Taranaki Point and the entrance to Aotea Harbour. The *Aotea* waka landed in a bay inside the harbour, and its captain, Turi, began exploring inland.

AOTEA

The *Aotea* explored Kaipara Harbour (below) and the Auckland isthmus before landing in a small bay named Hawaiki-iti, inside Aotea Harbour. From there, Turi, the captain, led an overland expedition along the coast around Mt Taranaki. Going over the hill from Aotea, Turi named a larger harbour Kāwhia, Te awhinga o Turi (the embracing of Turi). He called the next harbour Marokopa (lame) because he sprained his ankle climbing a steep hill. Turi also named several rivers, including Moekau (place where he rested), Urenui (big penis), Waitara (wading) and Mangatī (stream lined with cabbage trees). He called the last river Te Pāteanui-a-Turi (Turi's large cloak).

Tāneatua (the twins), at the junction of the Kānihi and Ōhora streams. He placed the feathered plumes of the *Mataatua* canoe at Pūrakau, where the settlers built a village on the banks of the Tāneatua Stream. He went inland as far as the summit of Whakataka in the Huiarau Range, before visiting and climbing Maungapōhatu and returning to Ōtarahioi.

On Tāneatua's next trip he went up what is now the Waimana River, which he named Tauranga when he stood at its starting point. He branched eastward along the Te Waiiti River and reached a large plain, which he burned to clear the land for growing aruhe (fern root). He named the area Te Wera-a-Tāneatua (the burning of Tāneatua). Tāneatua placed many guardians and tipua (supernatural creatures) in the rivers, streams and waterfalls he discovered.

Ngātokimatawhaorua is housed at the Treaty Grounds, Waitangi. It is named after the original *Ngātokimatawhaorua*, which was re-adzed from Kupe's canoe, the *Matawhaorua*.

This statue of Kupe, on the Wellington waterfront, shows the legendary explorer with his wife, Hine Te Apārangi, and his tohunga, Pekahourangi. The country's Māori name, Aotearoa, came when his wife saw a long white cloud and realised that land was nearby.

Great explorers

Kupe

In tribal tradition, Kupe was an important early explorer. The northern tribes have many stories about Kupe. Ngāti Kurī believe Kupe first saw New Zealand when he mistook Houhora mountain for a whale. Ngāti Kahu say that Te Aukānapanapa (the flashing current) guided Kupe to land below Whakarārā mountain in Matauri Bay. Te Aupōuri and Te Rarawa hold that Kupe landed in the Hokianga Harbour.

The Ngāpuhi tribe say that light reflecting from Te Ramaroa mountain guided Kupe into the Hokianga Harbour, where his people settled at Kohukohu, Te Pouahi, Whānui, Koutu, Pākanae and Whirinaki. All the northern tribes say that Kupe returned to the Polynesian homeland of Hawaiki from the Hokianga – hence the name Te Hokianga-a-Kupe (the place of Kupe's return).

Hauraki traditions say that Kupe visited the Coromandel Peninsula, and the place names Taputapu-ātea and Te Whitianganui-o-Kupe commemorate his time there. Ngāti Ruanui believe that Kupe arrived at the Pātea River mouth, while Te Āti Haunui-a-Pāpārangi say that he landed at the mouth of the Whanganui River, at a place called Te Kaihau-o-Kupe (where Kupe ate wind). According to the Te Āti Awa tribe, Kupe explored the entire west coast of the North Island, from Auckland to Cook Strait. Tribal traditions in the lower North Island say that he arrived

PAPATŪĀNUKU | THE LAND

The great explorer Kupe named a number of features in Wellington Harbour – including Matiu (Somes Island) and Mākaro (Ward Island), after his daughters. Kupe is on the right side of this panel, with Matiu and Mākaro at the bottom. On the left is the demigod Māui, and below him, the two taniwha (supernatural creatures) of Wellington Harbour, Ngake and Whātaitai.

off the northern Wairarapa coast and travelled southward through the Wellington region and to the top of the South Island. He named rocks near Cape Palliser Mātakitaki (gazing out), because he could see Tapuae-o-Uenuku (the highest mountain in the Kaikōura ranges).

Kupe eventually moved to Wellington Harbour, naming Matiu (Somes) and Mākaro (Ward) islands after his daughters. Steeple Rock, near the harbour's entrance, was named Te Ure-o-Kupe (the penis of Kupe).

Tōhē

Tōhē, a chief of the Ngāti Kahu people, lived at Maunga Piko in Kapowairua Bay. When he was very old he announced his intention to travel south and see his only daughter, Rāninikura, who had married a man from the Kaipara near Dargaville. His people, concerned about his health, asked him not to go. Tōhē replied that although one could shelter from the wind, one could not shelter from the longing to see a daughter one last time.

He made his way south, naming over 100 places along the western coast, but died at Whāngaiariki near Maunganui Bluff before reaching his daughter's home. Tōhē's place names stand as a memorial to this journey. The most well-known are Te Oneroa-a-Tōhē (the long beach of Tōhē), also called Ninety Mile Beach, and Kapowairua (catch my spirit), named in memory of his last words to his people.

RĀHIRI

There are several traditions about the explorer Rāhiri. In a journey that took several years, he first went from the far north to Auckland (naming Mt Eden Maungawhau after the whau trees that grew there). Further south, he crossed the summit of the Kaimai Range, naming it Te Aroha (loving remembrance) in memory of his relations in the far north and Bay of Plenty. Rāhiri continued around the coast to Tauranga, Whakatāne and the East Coast, visiting Wharekāhika (Hicks Bay), Horoera, Waiapu, Tūpāroa, Tawhitiroa, Tokomaru and Tūranganui (Gisborne) before heading south through Te Wairoa and Ahuriri (Napier) to Te Whanganui-a-Tara (Wellington). From there he went north, up the west coast through Taranaki and Kāwhia.

From this extensive trip, Rāhiri is known as an ancestor of Ngāpuhi in Northland, Ngāti Rāhiri-tumutumuwhenua in Hauraki, and Ngāti Ruanui and Ngāti Rāhiri in Taranaki (where he is called Rāhiri-pakaraka).

63

PAPATŪĀNUKU | THE LAND

The ancestor Matanginui followed a flock of birds through the Wairarapa and Taihape. The people of the Rangitīkei River area are descended from him.

HINEĀMARU

Hineāmaru, the ancestor of the Ngāti Hine tribe, is famous for her trip from Waimamaku, near the Hokianga, to Waiōmio in the Bay of Islands. With her people, she travelled inland to Waimā, Te Hāwera (present-day Mataraua), Awarua, Tautoro and Pouerua before going on to Ngāwhā Springs, Mōtatau and Waiōmio, where the group settled. Hineāmaru later married Koperu, and the descendants of their disabled son, Whē, spread through the hills toward Whatitiri and Whāngārei. Because of this, the tribe is also called Ngāti Hine-pukerau (Ngāti Hine of a hundred hills).

Haunui

Haunui was an ancestor of tribes descended from both the *Aotea* and *Kurahaupō* canoes. Haunui's journey began in pursuit of his wife, Wairaka, who had eloped with another man. He named several rivers on the lower west coast: the Whanganui (wide river mouth) for its size; the Whangaehu (cloudy river) after the ash in its waters from Mt Ruapehu; the Rangitīkei (striding) because it could be waded when the water was low; the Manawatū (startled breath) for its fast, deep waters; Ōhau after himself; and Waikanae because it was a good mullet (kanae) fishery.

Haunui caught up with Wairaka, her lover and their entourage at Pukerua Bay, where he turned them into a group of rocks off shore. He then climbed the Tararua Range, which he named Te Pae-a-Whaitiri (threshold of thunder). From the top he saw a shining lake, which he named Wairarapa (glistening water). He then returned north on a comet.

Matanginui

Matanginui, an ancestor of the people in the Rangitīkei River area, explored much of the land between Wairarapa and Taihape following a flock of birds – one of the more mystical traditions in Māori oral lore. Matanginui followed the birds northwards from the Ruamāhanga River in Wairarapa, along the eastern flank of the Tararua Range to Pahīatua. He crossed what is now called the Pahīatua track to Aokautere (near Massey University), then went to Tāhuna-a-rua (near Palmerston North). From there he headed to Te Aorangi (Feilding) and the Pūrākau and Te Rākauhou forests on the sides of Mt Stewart.

Matanginui followed the flock northwards along the eastern side of the Rangitīkei River. He spent a night in the open at Te Whakamoetakapū (by the present-day railway bridge at Kākāriki), and implanted a stake at Tokorangi, a hill just south of where the Waituna Stream intersects the Rangitīkei River. Heading through a deep gorge, he heard the birds on the high ridge to the west, which he called Parorotangi. Blowing his pūtōrino (horn) in response he named the ridge to the west (between Hunterville and the Rangitīkei) Pūtōrino.

By the time he reached Rangitoea peak (southeast of Taihape), Matanginui was exhausted and ready to give up the chase. However the birds were also tired and could not fly any further, so Matanginui and his children caught and killed them. The family settled in the area, intermarrying with the Ngāti Apa and Ngāti Hauiti tribes.

Many years later Matanginui made a return journey to his people in the Wairarapa, crossing the Ruahine Range at Hikurangi peak and heading through the Rangi and Waipawa saddles. Reaching the Waipawa Plains to the east he named the Whakaara Range (now called the Whakarara Range) before heading south towards home.

Tamatea

Tamatea is one of the greatest explorers in New Zealand's history. He was known as Tamatea-pōkaiwhenua (land explorer), and Tamatea-pōkaimoana (sea explorer). Northland traditions say that Tamatea explored the Kaipara and Hokianga harbours before settling at Awanui and Kaitāia on Rangaunu Harbour. According to Tauranga traditions,

PAPATŪĀNUKU | THE LAND

After completing his exploration of the South Island, the Waitaha ancestor, Rākaihautū, settled on Horomaka (Banks Peninsula). His stick, Tuhiraki, forms a rocky peak, known to Europeans as Mt Bossu, above Akaroa Harbour. Tuhiraki rises on the opposite side of the harbour from the town of Akaroa.

Tamatea was one of New Zealand's greatest explorers, and has been described as the Māori Marco Polo. He circumnavigated the North and South islands and also explored inland. He was sometimes called Tamatea-pōkaiwhenua (land explorer) or Tamatea-pōkaimoana (sea explorer). This poupou (post, right) stands in the wharenui at Te Herenga Waka marae in Wellington.

Tamatea explored their region. On Maunga Tawa he built a pā, planted flax and left his son Ranginui, who became the ancestor of Ngāti Ranginui.

Tamatea rounded East Cape and headed south to Hawke Bay, landing at Tūranganui (Gisborne), Māhia, Wairoa, Ahuriri (Napier), Heretaunga (near Hastings) and Pōrangahau. He went up the Mangakopikopiko River and over the Tītī-o-kura saddle via Pohokura to Lake Taupō. The Ōtamatea river and swamp, on the eastern side of the main pre-European route through the Ahimanawa and Huiarau ranges, are named after him.

The traditions of Ngāti Whitikaupeka, Ngāti Hauiti and Ngāti Apa tell how Tamatea went up the Ngaruroro River and across the upper Rangitīkei River into the Waiōuru and Taihape districts, where he stocked the Moawhango River with freshwater kōura (crayfish). Tamatea is also the name of a place in Ahuriri (Napier).

Early South Island accounts say that Tamatea sailed down the east coast. His canoe was wrecked at the southernmost end of the South Island, and became the Tākitimu mountain range. Tamatea walked northward to Kaiapohia, near Christchurch (now Kaiapoi), where he called on the North Island mountain, Tongariro, to help him. The mountain sent fire, which burned out the channel of the Whanganui River and Cook Strait before arriving at Kaiapohia. Tamatea took the fire and, heading northward on foot, left fire at several places along the coast before walking across Cook Strait and up the Whanganui River.

RĀKAIHAUTŪ AND ROKOHOUIA

In traditions of the Waitaha tribe, their founding ancestor, Rākaihautū, landed the *Uruao* canoe at Whakatū (Nelson). He is credited with carving out the string of lakes in the centre of the South Island with a giant kō. Rākaihautū eventually settled on Banks Peninsula, where his digging stick forms Tuhiraki, a prominent peak above Akaroa Harbour. Several South Island names derive from the explorations of Rākaihautū and his son Rokohouia. Cliffs near Kaikōura, where Rokohouia gathered seagulls' eggs, are named Kā Whatakai-a-Rokohouia (the food stores of Rokohouia). The two explorers took hao, a type of eel, from the river where they met up, which is still called Waihao. The southern lakes are known as Kā Puna-karikari-a-Rākaihautū (the springs of water dug by Rākaihautū).

65

PAPATŪĀNUKU | THE LAND

Lewis Tamihana Gardiner's artwork (below), 'Te ara kōhatu' (the stone trail), relates to a story about the location of stone resources. The taniwha Poutini kidnapped the wife of Tamaāhua from Tūhua (Mayor Island), and was pursued to a number of places – all of them stone quarries. In the end, Poutini turned the woman into pounamu at the Arahura River.

Tūhua, Mayor Island

The Arahura River on the West Coast of the South Island was a major source of pounamu, much prized by Māori for making tools, weapons and jewellery. According to one tradition, the Pounamu were once a people who escaped from their enemies in Hawaiki. But when their canoe, the *Tairea*, was wrecked, they were turned into greenstone boulders.

Ngāhue and stone trading

Ngāhue is an important ancestor of the Te Arawa tribe. Te Arawa say he landed at Tūhua (Mayor Island in the Bay of Plenty). Ngāhue explored inland in the South Island, and found pounamu (greenstone) in the Arahura River. This was made into the adzes that fashioned the *Te Arawa* and *Tainui* canoes. Pounamu was sometimes called Te Ika-o-Ngāhue (Ngāhue's fish) because of his exploits in retrieving it. Tūhua was a major source of obsidian for tools, and Ngāhue may have been involved in networks trading South Island greenstone and North Island obsidian and basalt.

Poutini and Tamaāhua

The legend of Poutini and Tamaāhua is an oral map of the places where valuable stone resources could be found. Poutini was a taniwha and guardian for Ngāhue in the coastal seas. One day while sheltering at Tūhua in the Bay of Plenty, he saw a beautiful woman, Waitaiki, bathing. Smitten, he grabbed her and headed for the mainland, pursued by her husband Tamaāhua.

Tamaāhua chased Poutini through a number of places in the North Island and on the West Coast of the South Island – each the site of an important stone resource. They include:
- Tahanga in the Coromandel (basalt for adzes)
- Whangamatā near Taupō (obsidian)
- Rangitoto (D'Urville Island) in the Marlborough Sounds (argillite for adzes)
- Whangamoa, above Nelson, and Farewell Spit (argillite)
- Pāhua, on the West Coast of the South Island (flint)
- Takiwai at Milford Sound (bowenite)
- the Arahura River (pounamu for adzes).

Finally, trapped in the Arahura River, Poutini cast Waitaiki into the river to form pounamu. He fled to the coast, where he cruises back and forth as a guardian of the precious stone. Tamaāhua and Tūhua are the names of hills above the Arahura River. The tradition matches archaeological evidence for stone trade networks centuries ago. Poutini and Tamaāhua represent two great centres of stone trade: North Island obsidian and basalt, and South Island pounamu. The struggle between the taniwha and the man may symbolise the tension between the two trading centres and those who used the stone.

PAPATŪĀNUKU | THE LAND

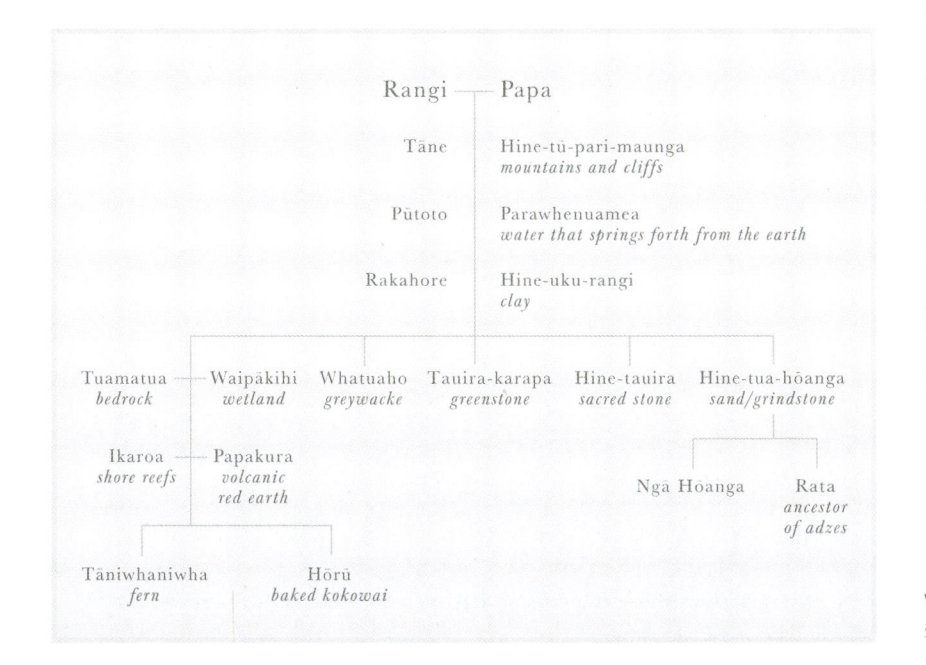

Varieties of pounamu

ARA POUNAMU (GREENSTONE TRAILS)

Before Europeans arrived in New Zealand, Māori had extensively explored the South Island. They developed the 'greenstone trails' across the Southern Alps, tracks for moving raw materials from west to east for trade with North Island tribes. Routes included the present-day Heaphy and Wangapeka tracks, the Kawatiri (Buller) River, the Māwhera and Īnangahua rivers, the Maruia River (Lewis Pass), Noti Taramakau (Harper Pass), Ōtira–Waimakariri (Arthur's Pass), and the Amuri, Hope, Harman, Whitcombe and Tioripātea (Haast) passes. They also include the many Whakatipu trails in and around Queenstown – among them the famous Milford and Routeburn tracks.

There are stories about the discovery of two of the more difficult passes. Noti Raureka (Browning Pass) was said to have been discovered by a woman named Raureka from the Ngāti Wairangi tribe. Tū-te-kawa, a notorious figure, discovered Ō-Tū-te-kawa (Mathias Pass).

```
                    Rangi ── Papa
                    
              Tāne       Hine-tū-pari-maunga
                         mountains and cliffs
              
              Pūtoto     Parawhenuamea
                         water that springs forth from the earth
              
              Rakahore   Hine-uku-rangi
                         clay
```

Tuamatua — Waipākihi — Whatuaho — Tauira-karapa — Hine-tauira — Hine-tua-hōanga
bedrock   wetland   greywacke   greenstone   sacred stone   sand/grindstone

Ikaroa — Papakura   Ngā Hōanga — Rata
shore reefs volcanic   ancestor
             red earth   of adzes

Tāniwhaniwha — Hōrū
fern   baked kokowai

Whakapapa of rocks and stones (left).

PAPATŪĀNUKU | THE LAND

This argillite adze was found at the top of the South Island.

Tūwiri (drills) had two cords. The tip was a hard, sharp stone. Sand and water were used as an abrasive during drilling.

Kaiapoi pā, at the eastern end of routes across the Southern Alps, became the centre of working and trading in the prized stone pounamu. This magnificent greenstone hei tiki was found at Kaiapoi pā.

KŌHATU *MĀORI USE OF STONE*

TOOLS

The most important tools were adzes (toki) and chisels (whao). Initially, the majority of adzes were made from basalt or other hard rock, but later adze styles were more restricted. In the North Island, the main type was a relatively simple form without a defined butt, generally made from greywacke or basalt, but in some cases from nephrite, argillite and gabbro (a coarse-grained plutonic rock). Similar adzes in the South Island were more commonly made from nephrite. Drill points were used to make holes in both wood and stone, and were made from various materials, particularly chert, but also obsidian and some of the same rock types used for adzes.

ORNAMENTS AND PENDANTS

The early settlers from East Polynesia brought pendants, necklaces, and other ornaments, and for several hundred years Māori continued to make and wear items in similar styles. As fashions changed, new styles of pendants, particularly those made from pounamu, became popular.

Typical early Māori stone ornaments were reels and pendants. Reels were usually made of serpentine, a relatively soft metamorphic rock obtained mainly from the Nelson region. It ranges in colour from dark brown to green, and is easily carved. Serpentine reels, which were probably strung to form necklaces, have been found (often singly) in early sites in both islands, sometimes with human burials. Pendants shaped like whale teeth, and decorated discs were also made from serpentine. One remarkable whale-tooth pendant from Southland is over 20 centimetres long and weighs almost 2 kilograms, but most were much smaller and possibly worn as part of a necklace. Disc pendants, worn on the chest, are extremely rare and have been found only in the South Island. These were decorated with notches around the rim, and one spectacular example has two fish shapes carved on the front.

Pounamu ornaments appear to be a later development, perhaps after 1500 AD. The main items were hei tiki (neck pendants) and ear pendants, both of which were widely worn in the early years after the arrival of Europeans in New Zealand. Small pounamu adzes and chisels were sometimes made into pendants by drilling a hole at one end for a cord.

WEAPONS

During the 17th and 18th centuries, patu (short hand clubs) were typical Māori stone weapons. Patu ōnewa were commonly made from greywacke, various volcanic rock types – including pumice – and from nephrite (mere pounamu). These appear to have been used mainly in the north, and are well represented among artefact collections from Ōruarangi pā on the Hauraki Plains. In the South Island, patu may have been used for killing seals and moa.

FISHING

Fishing was an important activity in Māori life, as shown by the numerous fish hooks of bone and

68

PAPATŪĀNUKU | THE LAND

shell found in some archaeological sites. Stone trolling lures (also called minnow lures), with bone or shell points attached, were used to catch fish such as kahawai and barracouta. They were commonly made from argillite, schist or greywacke, but also from other materials, including limestone and serpentine. Stone sinkers were made by forming a shallow groove around a pebble or cobble and winding a line around it. Large stones were occasionally used as anchors, and pumice as floats for fishing nets.

GARDENING

Māori used stone extensively for gardening. They added sand and gravel to garden soils, to make them friable, retain moisture, and improve their heat retention – critical for subtropical plants growing in New Zealand's temperate climate.

Cobbles and rough stones were used to make low, elongated rows 1 to 2 metres wide and up to tens of metres long. These were usually in groups, called stone row systems, and were laid out more or less parallel, often in association with circular stone mounds 1–2 metres in diameter.

Some stone rows appear to mark garden plot boundaries. Other stones were dug from nearby underground deposits or brought from streams or river beds and put into purpose-built shallow trenches. The excavated soil was then replaced over the stones. The stones improved heat retention and warmed the soil above them, and the rows themselves were probably gardened.

OTHER USES

One valuable plant was flax, which was prepared for use as a fibre by beating it with stone pounders (patu muka). These pounders were often made from greywacke or volcanic rock. Rounded stones were widely used in cooking, particularly in earth ovens (hāngī or umu). Hāngī stones were carefully selected because certain rocks explode violently when heated in a fire. Good stones would sometimes be presented as a gift to other tribes. Volcanic rocks were the most suitable, while greywacke was also used.

Stones were also used to boil water. They were heated in a fire, then put into the vessel containing water. Water-smoothed cobbles (autoru) were used for crushing kōkōwai, a naturally occurring red or yellow iron oxide. The powder was used in body painting and on carvings, and stored in pumice pots. Red kōkōwai or ochre is still used on carvings.

For entertainment, children and adults used spinning or whipping tops, generally made from pumice but also greywacke, volcanic rock, and wood. They were spun with a flax whip. Some nose flutes (nguru), particularly those found at Ōruarangi on the Hauraki Plains, were also made from stone, including sandstone, pumice, and hard volcanic ash.

Phil Moore and Bruce McFadgen

These stone rows are at Okoropunga in the Wairarapa. The rows are in groups known as stone row systems and are generally parallel. In some cases stone rows are thought to mark boundaries, in others, such as Okoropunga, they were probably gardened, as the soil in the rows tends to be warmer and better for cultivating subtropical plants.

The patu muka, right, often made from greywacke or volcanic rock, was used to pound the inner fibres of flax.

This mere pounamu (hand weapon), named Hine-nui-o-te-pāua, was gifted by the Ngāti Pāoa tribe to Governor George Grey to indicate their desire for peace with the Europeans. The mere was believed to have great status and to be extremely sacred. Mere pounamu were often used to seal peace agreements between tribes.

PART III

Tangaroa
the sea

West Coast, near Greymouth

TANGAROA | THE SEA

One of the small offshore islands in the Bay of Plenty.

This taumata atua (god stick) was found at Ōngare Point, north of Tauranga. It has been suggested that the carved figure may represent Tangaroa.

Tangaroa *the sea*
Te Ahukaramū Charles Royal

In Māori culture the sea is often considered to be the source and foundation of all life. Islands are fish drawn up from the water, and people evolved from amphibious beginnings. But Tangaroa, god of the sea, can also be destructive. Traditions tell of vengeance wrought by the sea upon those who fall out of favour.

Māori and their Polynesian forebears have been island peoples for many generations, so it is not surprising that water, particularly the sea, figures prominently in their world view. In some traditions the oceans' depths are considered to be the origin and source of all life. The islands are believed to be fish, pulled up from beneath the sea, and humans are thought to have evolved from aquatic beginnings.

The sea dominated traditional Polynesian and Māori life for many practical reasons. It was an essential source of food and other resources. A number of Polynesian islands were sometimes inundated by high tides or storms, causing those who lived there to fear and revere its waters. After Polynesians settled in New Zealand, life was centred less around the sea, but it nevertheless retained its mystery and power.

Traditional Māori knowledge includes genealogies of fish and other creatures that live under the sea. Numerous legends and stories are dramas of underwater life.

Māori noted different types of waters. Seas could be calm and refreshing, boisterous and masculine, or extremely dangerous. Water was considered to be an energy possessing myriad characteristics, shapes and natures. It upheld life, yet was also able to bring terrible destruction. This energy with all its forms, moods and expressions is called Tangaroa. The common translation, 'god of the sea', does not adequately convey its meaning.

This epa (house post, left) was discovered in Waitara, Taranaki, in 1919. The figure at the top is a marakihau, sometimes described as a sea taniwha. However, some view it as an ancestor with the bulbous head, three fingers, and serpentine body that reflects the Māori view that humans had amphibious origins.

In some traditions the waters off the East Coast of the North Island are named Te Tai Tamawahine – 'peaceful, female waters'. The picturesque Tokomaru Bay, shown above, illustrates this concept.

```
Ranginui ─── Papatūānuku
         │
Tangaroa ─── Heketangawainui
         │
       Punga
         │
      Ikatere
         │
  ┌──────┼──────┬──────────┬──────────┐
Pātiki  Kōkiri  Whaitere  Wheketoro  Tāmure
Flounder Leatherjacket Stingray Octopus Snapper
```

Traditional Māori knowledge includes whakapapa of fish and other underwater species. This chart shows Ranginui and Papatūānuku as parents of Tangaroa, god of the sea. Tangaroa married Heketangawainui and they had Punga, the ancestor of the fish and octopuses.

Creation

In the most well-known version of the Māori creation story, Tangaroa is the son of Papatūānuku, the earth mother, and Ranginui, the sky father. He is one of the 70 children who, when earth and sky were separated, went to live in the world that was created.

In other versions, however, Tangaroa is the husband of Papatūānuku and a competitor of Ranginui. The following account was dictated to Sir Donald McLean by Hūkiki Te Ahukaramū of the Ngāti Raukawa tribe, in 1856:

Ka moe [a] Rangi i a Papatūānuku, te wahine o Tangaroa, i pūremutia e Rangi … Ka puta ki waho ko … Tānenui-a-rangi … Ka whakaaro rātou kia puta iho te rā i te kēkē o Rangi. Ka mea [a] Tānenui-a-rangi 'Tēnei te rā kei runga e whiti ana.' Ka mea [ia], 'Me toko tō tātou matua kia waiho ko te wahine ko Papa hei matua mō tātou.' Ka mea rātou, 'Tokona, wehea rāua, kia tau kē te wahine kia tau kē te tāne, kia tupu ai tātou ki te Ao.' Kātahi ka tokona te rangi. E tū iho ana a Rangi; e takoto nei a Papa.

TANGAROA | THE SEA

The sky [Rangi] cohabited with the earth [Papa] who was the wife of the sea [Tangaroa]. She was seduced by the sky. They had a child whom they called Tānenui-a-rangi, 'Tāne, great of the heavens.' The family thereupon decided that the sun should be allowed to shine through the armpit of the sky. 'Tāne-great of the heavens' said, 'The sun shines above.' He then said, 'Let us raise our father above and leave the female, Papa, as our parent.' They joined in and said, 'Raise him up, separate the two. Let the female be set apart, let the male be set apart so that we may prosper in the world.' The sky was then raised above. Hence, the sky stands above and the earth lies below.[1]

It is likely that this version of the creation story – where water lies between the earth and sky – reflects an islander's view of the world, where much of the earth appears to be under the sea. Following the separation of the adulterous lovers by their child, the earth returns to her place beneath the water and what is left above is the whenua – a word meaning both land and placenta, which comes from the womb of the earth and floats on the sea. The Māori term for island is moutere – 'floating land'.

Tangaroa, enraged at some of his children deserting him, and, being sheltered by god of the forests, Tane, has ever since waged war on his brother Tane, who, in return, has waged war against him.

Hence, Tane supplies the offspring of his brother Tumatauenga with canoes, spears and fish-hooks made from his trees, and with nets woven from his fibrous plants, that they may destroy the offspring of Tangaroa; whilst Tangaroa swallows up the offspring of Tane, overwhelming canoes with the surges of his sea, swallowing up the lands, trees, and houses that are swept off by floods, and ever wastes away, with his lapping waves, the shores that confine him, that the giants of the forests may be washed down and swept out into his boundless ocean, that he may then swallow up the insects, the young birds and the various animals which inhabit them.[2]

From George Grey's
Polynesian mythology

Te Rerenga Wairua, Far North

TANGAROA | THE SEA

WATER AS THE SOURCE OF LIFE

In Māori culture, many tribes directly or indirectly consider water as the source or foundation of all life. This is reflected in traditions which speak of te taha wairua, often translated as 'the spiritual plane (of existence)'. The term te taha wairua is widely used to refer to the 'real world', which lies both behind and within the world of normal experience. Much of life, according to the traditional world view, is concerned with coming to see, experience and understand the interplay of this 'real world' with our more limited everyday life. Te taha wairua can literally be translated as 'the dimension of two waters', a conception that likens spirituality to water. However, it might be argued that te taha wairua does not mean 'the spiritual plane' at all. Instead, references to te taha wairua might be saying that there is a fundamental dimension to all life and it takes the form of water.

In one tradition Te Manuhauturuki, the son of Ruatepupuke, went fishing with a kahawai lure, like the one above. Tangaroa became angry that the lure had been named after him but the proper karakia had not been said, and he turned Manuhauturuki into a tekoteko (carved gable figure).

This tekoteko on the ancestral house of Te Herenga Waka marae is of Kupe, who is said to have discovered New Zealand.

Ruatepupuke and the origin of carving

The story of the discovery of whakairo (wood carving) from under the sea is famous in Māori tradition. It tells of the imprisonment of Te Manuhauturuki, the son of Ruatepupuke. Te Manu was captured by Tangaroa, taken to his house deep in the ocean, and mounted on the gable. Ruatepupuke undertook the journey to find his son.

The following translation is from a version of the story recounted by Mohi Ruatapu and Hēnare Pōtae of the Ngāti Porou tribe:

This is the story of Ruatepupuke, who first made wood-carving known. The cause of his discovery was the going of his child, Te Manuhauturuki, to sail a boat. The child was captured by Tangaroa, taken to his home, and set up on the gable of his house as an image. When the child was missed, his father set forth to look for him ... he went there, and so found the body of his child set up on the roof-gable of the house.

When Rua entered the house the carved posts were talking amongst themselves; he heard the posts talking, but those outside remained

76

silent. He closed up all the interstices of the house … and when the sun had set, Tangaroa and his family arrived and sought repose within their house. There they amused themselves with posture-dancing, hand-clapping contests, cat's cradle and other games, as is usual when many folk meet together … When day came the interior of the house was still in darkness …

By this time Ruatepupuke had come and taken a position in the porch of the house with his weapon at the ready … He set the house on fire, and the folk inside ran out; the first was Kanae (mullet) … then came Maroro (flying fish) … then came Kōkiri (trigger fish) … But most of Tangaroa's children were destroyed … The carved posts of the outside of the house were taken away; some of those did not talk, and so it is that carved images of the present time do not have the power of speech.[3]

Categories of water

In traditional Māori knowledge, wai (water) is classified in a number of ways. Some of these categories include:
- waikino – dangerous water, sometimes inclement seas or swollen rivers
- waitapu – sacred water, waters used for ceremonial purposes
- waimāori – pure water, water rich in mauri, used for cleansing and for ceremonial purposes
- waitai – sea water, saline water
- waimanawa-whenua – water from under the land
- waikarakia – water for ritual purposes
- waiwhakaika, waikotikoti – water to assist in the cutting of hair.

The pounding waves along the western coast are sometimes called Te Tai Tamatāne – 'rough, masculine waters'. These waves are rolling onto a west coast beach north of Wellington.

'Papaki tū ana ngā tai ki Te Rēinga' is a phrase often used in chants. It describes the meeting of the two seas at Cape Rēinga, at the tip of the North Island, where the waves clap together. It is an important place in Māori culture – many believe it is where the spirits of the newly deceased depart.

Te whānau puha *whales*

Bradford Haami

In Māori traditions, whales guided the canoes on their great journeys to New Zealand. They carried people to safety, and were called on for protection. Whales were a source of food, and the jawbone was carved into weapons, combs, walking sticks and jewellery.

Whales in Māori tradition

Māori have a long association with whales. While whales provided food and utensils, they also feature in tribal traditions and were sometimes guardians on the ancestors' canoe journeys to Aotearoa. Oral histories recall interactions between people and whales in tribal stories, carvings, specialised language and place names. There is also a wealth of tribal knowledge about whales.

Names for the different species of whales vary from tribe to tribe. One of the old terms for whales was 'ika moana' – fish of the sea. They were part of the family known as 'te whānau puha' – the family of animals that expel air. While 'tohorā' (or tohoraha) is considered an all-embracing term for whales, it also refers to the southern right whale.

TANGAROA | THE SEA

Parāoa female and calf

Other names are:
- hakurā or iheihe – scamperdown whale (also known as Grey's beaked whale)
- miha pakake – a whale calf
- paikea – southern humpback whale, or a whale with a white belly and deep grooves along its length
- pakake – minke whale
- parāoa – sperm whale
- ūpokohue – blackfish or pilot whale.

Poetic names for whales or families of whales are Tūtarakauika, te Kauika Tangaroa, Wehengakāuki, Ruamano, Taniwha and Tū-te-raki-hau-noa.

Whale origins

There are many tribal versions of the origin of whales. Some say Tangaroa is the ancestor of sea creatures, while others name Te Pūwhakahara, Takaaho and Tinirau as progenitors of whales. Another tradition cites Te Hāpuku as the main ancestor of whales, dolphins and seals as well as tree ferns, which are often known as 'ngā ika o te ngahere' – the fish of the forest.

The story of the whale and the kauri places trees and whales in their environments. The Tohorā asked kauri to return with him to the sea, but kauri preferred the land. Tohorā then suggested they exchange skins, which they did. This is why the bark of the kauri is so thin, and as full of resin as the whale is of oil.

THE PAKAKE MOTIF

Many carved houses and pātaka feature the pakake (whale) motif on their maihi (bargeboards). Some believe this design depicts the story of the death of Tinirau's pet whale Tutunui at the hands of Kae. Some versions of the story say Kae built a house to commemorate his wretched act, showing the hauling of Tutunui ashore on one maihi and the cutting up and preparation for cooking the whale on the other. The bones of Tutunui were suspended on the framework of the interior of the house. Tinirau was also said to have built a house to honour the sad event.

Tohorā (southern right whale)

TINIRAU AND KAE

The story of Tinirau and Kae is very old, and numerous versions exist in New Zealand and the Pacific Islands. The story begins with the difficult birth of Tūhuruhuru, the son of Tinirau and his wife Hineteiwaiwa. Following the birth, Tinirau needed to find a priest to conduct the baptism. He travelled to Te Tihi-o-Manono, where he secured the services of Kae. They returned to Tinirau's island where the ceremony was performed. Afterwards, Tinirau summoned his pet whale, Tutunui, and cut off a piece of flesh, which he gave to Kae as payment. Tinirau also offered Kae a waka to travel home in, but Kae asked if he could ride on the whale's back instead. Tinirau reluctantly agreed, giving explicit instructions that when they neared the shore and the whale shook himself, Kae must disembark.

Despite these instructions, Kae drove Tutunui towards the shore and beached him. The whale was cut up and cooked in the village ovens, and the aroma of the flesh was brought by the winds to Tinirau's home. Learning of the creature's fate, Hineteiwaiwa convened a group of women, including Raukatauri, goddess of flute music, to travel to Kae's home and capture him. Unsure what Kae looked like, the women were advised to make the villagers laugh – they would be able to identify Kae by his niho tāpiki, a tooth that has grown over the top of another.

When the women arrived at Kae's village, people were gathered in the whare tapere for the evening's entertainments. Kae assumed his customary place nearest the door. The women danced and told stories, but they could not get Kae to laugh. It was not until their dances became more erotic that they finally succeeded in spotting the tooth and confirming Kae's identity. The women removed him from the house and placed him on a waka, taking him while he slept to Tinirau's island and into a house identical to his own. When Kae finally awoke, he wondered why Tinirau was sitting in his house. Tinirau killed Kae and avenged Tutunui's slaughter.

Charles Royal

In Māori tradition, Paikea was known as Kahutiaterangi and was the son of Uenuku. As depicted in this carving (above), Uenuku placed a comb in Kahutiaterangi's hair to indicate he was of high birth. However, when another son, Ruatapu, asked why he had not also received a comb, he was told it was because he was illegitimate. In revenge, Ruatapu tried to drown Kahutiaterangi and others at sea by sinking their canoe. Kahutiaterangi survived by calling on a sea god, who sent a whale to carry him to shore. On reaching land he changed his name to Paikea.

TANGAROA | THE SEA

This carving on the threshold of a meeting house depicts Paikea, who was saved by whales – they were tipua or his tīpuna (ancestors).

Whales and Māori voyaging

Many traditions mention that whales accompanied or guided the canoes on their journeys to Aotearoa. Waitaha followed his sister Hāhuru to New Zealand from Hawaiki, guided by the whale Tūtarakauika. They eventually landed at Ō-tara-muturangi, near Matatā.

The song 'He oriori mō Tuteremoana' describes a canoe, believed to be the *Tākitimu*, safely following in the wake of a pod of whales during a storm. Some of the whales are specifically named in this song. The tohunga on board the *Tākitimu* was Ruawharo. He possessed the mauri (life force) of whales, which he laid to rest at Māhia Peninsula to attract whales to the region. Pane-iraira was a taniwha, thought to be a whale, who calmed the waves for the journey of the *Tainui* canoe.

Tohunga responsible for navigation exercised their powers during storms, appealing to sea creatures to escort the canoes and shield them from the fury of a storm. Often the tohunga would pull a hair from his head and throw it to the whale or taniwha as recognition of assistance. This tradition may have been prompted by the reported habit of toothed whales and dolphins presenting gifts of seaweed to each other.

A whale of a Trojan Horse

The origin of the name for the Ngāti Kurī tribe of Muriwhenua is linked to the construction of a whale made of dog skins. This became a Trojan Horse, concealing 100 warriors as it appeared to lie beached on the coast, in front of an unsuspecting enemy village. The people left the safety of their pā to gather the valuable whale meat and were met with a surprise.

This same ploy was used by the Ngāti Kahungunu warlord Taraia, who dressed his warriors in black cloaks and ordered them to lie on the beach in front of Heipipi pā to lure the enemy out. The people thought a pod of pilot whales had stranded, and streamed out of the pā, to their demise.

WHALE RIDERS

Whale riding, illustrated in the legend of Tinirau and Kae (opposite), is a common theme in Māori oral storytelling. It was made popular worldwide by the film *Whale rider*, based on the Ngāti Porou tribe's tradition of Paikea.

According to the story, the ancestor Paikea was enticed on a fishing trip with others. During this, his jealous brother Ruatapu sank the canoe in an effort to drown them. Paikea called on the guardians of the sea to help him. A taniwha in the form of a whale was sent to take him to safety. He eventually landed at Aotearoa (New Zealand). A similar tradition, thought to be from the Waikato, is that of Waihuka, who was also carried back to land on a whale, after being abandoned by his brother who left him to drown at sea. Other famous whale riders are:
• Te Tahi-o-te-rangi, an ancestor of the Mataatua tribes, who rode a whale named Tūtarakauika from Whakaari (White Island) to the mouth of the Whakatāne River
• Tūnui, the Hawke's Bay tohunga, who was seen riding his pet whale, Ruamano, out of the Keteketerau outlet on his way to Cape Kidnappers.

Moutohorā, an island off the coast at Whakatāne.

Whales and Māori society

The whale has often been commemorated in place names. These include:
- Moutohorā (whale island), an island off the coast at Whakatāne
- Te Ara-a-Kewa (the path of the right whale), the name for Foveaux Strait
- Te Ara-a-Paikea (the path of Paikea), a whale-shaped hill on the Māhia Peninsula
- Whangaparāoa (bay of sperm whales) in Auckland and the East Cape
- Te Waiū-o-Te-Tohorā (the milk of the whale) is the name of a spring of white water associated with hills around Welcome Bay and Pāpāmoa in the Tauranga area. The hills represent a family of whales (mother, father and baby) that lost their way. After drinking from a magical spring at Karikari, they were all transformed into the ranges in this region.

Whale resources

It is thought that Māori did not actively hunt whales, but they were known to force whales to beach themselves. Whales provided meat, which was eaten fresh, hung to dry or cooked in a hāngī. Milk was taken from a suckling mother, oil was used for polish and scent, and teeth were made into ornaments and jewellery such as the prized rei puta (whale-tooth neck ornament). Whalebone, in particular the jawbones from the parāoa, was

Traditionally, whales were perceived as aristocratic. 'Te kāhui parāoa', a gathering of sperm whales, indicates a group of chiefs. A sight such as these pilot whales (ūpokohue) beached at Ōpoutere, South Auckland, gave rise to the saying, 'He paenga pakake' (a group of beached whales) – describing a number of chiefs who had fallen on the battlefield.

These whales were brought ashore to be processed at Houhora, Northland, in 1910. Once a whale was landed, the next step was to flense it – strip the skin and blubber from the carcass.

TANGAROA | THE SEA

The tail of a parāoa (sperm whale, left) off the coast of Kaikōura, in the South Island.

MODERN MĀORI AND WHALES

More recently, Māori have moved into ecotourism ventures. Members of Ngāti Kurī, a hapū of the Ngāi Tahu tribe, created Kaikōura Whale Watch. Tourists observe the migratory parāoa, Hector's dolphins and other attractions along the Kaikōura coastline (on the north-east coast of the South Island). Māori have also asserted their rights, under Article Two of the Treaty of Waitangi (New Zealand's founding document), to harvest resources such as bone from stranded whales that die. Some tribes are actively involved in this as a way of recovering their cultural traditions relating to beached whales. The people of Wharekauri (the Chatham Islands), Te Tai Poutini (the South Island's West Coast), Ngāti Haumia (at Paekākāriki), Ngāti Wai (in Northland) and other tribes all take part.

fashioned into weapons like patu, taiaha, tewhatewha and hoeroa, and other objects like heru (combs), tokotoko (walking sticks), and hei tiki.

Disputes over resources were common. At Whangaparāoa on the East Coast, Pou-mātangatanga of the Tauira tribe sought to claim a stranded parāoa. This was challenged by Taikehu from the *Tainui* canoe who had already fashioned a patu from the jawbone. This led Pou to relinquish his claim and shift to Maraenui. Kauaetangohia (extracted jawbone) is the name of an ancestor, a hapū, and a marae that commemorate this incident. In another dispute, when a pod of whales was stranded near Te Awanga in Hawke's Bay, the chief Tamaariki arrived home to find that his son had not been given a share of the meat. He was offended and left the district.

From whaling to tourism

With the advent of whaling in Aotearoa in the later 18th century, many Māori became involved in the industry. By 1804, they were said to be participating in whaling, and by the 1840s whaleboats were being widely used by them. Māori men played a major role at shore stations, some reaching the position of headsman in command of a whaleboat. Around most of the country, as many as 40% of the whalers may have been Māori, and in Otago the figure was higher.

Visiting European whalers had profound impacts on Māori society. Many were highly dependent on Māori for food and repairs, and a number married local women. Many Māori can trace descent from marriages between Māori women and Pākehā whalers. Well-known whalers such as Dicky Barrett, George Fyfe, Paddy Gilroy, Thomas Halbert, Happy Jack Greening, William Haberfield, John Hughes, Manuel Lima, Jacky Love, William Morris, James Spencer, Phillip Tapsell and Edward Weller all fathered children with Māori women.

Māori continued whaling in the late 19th century, long after most of the whaling stations had closed. Increasingly, they pursued it as a seasonal, part-time activity, hunting humpbacks and the occasional sperm whale. This remained an important practice until the mid-1920s for the Te Whānau-ā-Apanui tribe, and for families around Cook Strait and further south.

Māori traditionally treasured stranded whales for their jawbones, which were used for carving. When three sperm whales beached and died at Paekākāriki in 1996 (right), local Māori removed the jawbones.

TANGAROA | THE SEA

Taniwha
Basil Keane

Supernatural creatures – some terrifying, others protective – are legendary in Māori tradition. Known as taniwha, they lurk in watery dens, or in caves, and were often depicted as dragons or serpents, with fiery eyes and lashing tails. Crucial to the stories of deadly taniwha were the heroic slayers, who triumphed with their cunning and courage.

What are taniwha?

Taniwha are supernatural creatures whose forms and characteristics vary according to different tribal traditions. Though supernatural, in the Māori world view they were seen as part of the natural environment. Taniwha have been described as fabulous monsters that live in deep water. Others refer to them as dragons – many taniwha looked like reptiles, had wings and ate people. They could also take the shape of animals such as sharks, whales, octopuses or even logs. Some taniwha could change their shape, moving between different forms.

Taniwha were either male or female. They usually lived in or near the water – lakes, rivers or the sea. They hid in lairs known as rua taniwha, which could be deep pools, caves or dangerous waterways – areas that people avoided. In some traditions, taniwha were terrifying creatures that captured people and ate them. Occasionally, it was said that they would kidnap women to live with them as wives. These monsters would inevitably be killed and the women returned to their families.

Others were kaitiaki, or protectors, of iwi and hapū. These ones were respected, and people who passed by their dens would say the appropriate karakia (charm) and leave an offering, often a green twig.

Taniwha and chiefs

Taniwha were also a symbol for great chiefs. There is a proverb from Waikato:

Waikato taniwha rau, he piko he taniwha.
Waikato of a hundred taniwha, every bend a taniwha.

For some this refers to the many taniwha of the Waikato River, while for others it is about the many important chiefs of the area.

This figure of speech is used in laments for chiefs who have passed on, such as this one for Te Haupā, chief of the Ngāti Pāoa tribe:

Unuhia noatia te taniwha i te rua.
Withdrawn now is the dragon from his lair.[4]

Taniwha of the sea

Many taniwha were associated with the sea. A large number were said to have come with the voyaging canoes that brought the Polynesian ancestors of the Māori people to Aotearoa.

Issued in 1960, this stamp features a taniwha design based on the cave drawing known as the Ōpihi taniwha. This was drawn on a limestone cave shelter overlooking the Ōpihi River in South Canterbury.

This carving is of Ureia, a taniwha of the Hauraki region who lived in Tikapa (the Firth of Thames). Ureia was a symbol of fertility and prestige.

TANGAROA | THE SEA

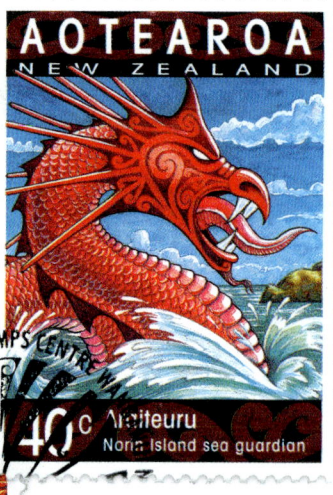

Āraiteuru is the famed taniwha represented on this stamp. She is said to have arrived in New Zealand with the early voyaging canoes, and her 11 sons are credited with creating the various branches of the Hokianga Harbour.

The taniwha Tuhirangi accompanied the legendary explorer Kupe on his voyage of discovery to New Zealand. It was reputed that Kupe placed Tuhirangi in Te Moana-o-Raukawa (Cook Strait) as a guardian.

Kupe was the great navigator who is reputed to have discovered New Zealand while travelling in the *Matawhaorua* canoe. He placed one of his guardian taniwha, Tuhirangi, in Cook Strait where the taniwha guided and protected canoes.

In the late 1800s and early 1900s a white dolphin known as Pelorus Jack guided ships across a dangerous stretch of water around French Pass, in the Marlborough Sounds. Some Māori believed that this dolphin was Tuhirangi, a taniwha that had escorted the explorer Kupe from the traditional homeland, Hawaiki. In 1900, a correspondent for the Māori-language newspaper *Te Pipiwharauroa* described this dolphin playfully escorting his steamer near the French Pass. He described it as an 'ika tipua' (supernatural fish) and suggested it could be a taniwha.

In the Far North in the summer of 1955–56, a friendly female dolphin delighted thousands of children and adults by playing with them in the sea at Opononi. Nicknamed Opo, she was believed by many Māori in the area to be a taniwha.

It was believed that a taniwha that acted as a protector for Ngāti Tamaterā of Hauraki would take the form of a dolphin and play about in the river to warn its people of an impending invasion.

IS THAT REALLY A TANIWHA?

In 1907 *Te Pipiwharauroa* newspaper received a letter about a taniwha sighting at Waimārama. The taniwha, which emerged from the sea, had a head like a dog and fur on its body. It was killed by a local. The editor responded, '[K]o te ingoa o te taniwha na he kekeno he oioi ranei, he taniwha tapu, kua turengia e te Kawanatanga'[5] (that taniwha is either a sea lion or seal. It is a sacred taniwha protected by law). He noted further taniwha should be left alone to avoid prosecution.

Āraiteuru and her sons

Āraiteuru was a female taniwha, believed to have escorted the *Māmari* canoe to New Zealand from Hawaiki. In other traditions Āraiteuru and another taniwha named Ruamano guided the *Tākitimu* canoe.

When she arrived, Āraiteuru gave birth to 11 sons. All went exploring, and on the way they dug trenches – creating the branches of the Hokianga Harbour. One son, Waihou, burrowed inland and lashed his tail about to form Lake Ōmāpere. Another, Ōhopa, was angered by the large number of rocks he encountered, and came to hate all living things. He terrorised the people near the Panguru mountains.

Āraiteuru was a guardian of the Hokianga Harbour, and had her lair in a cave there. She lived at the south head of the harbour, and her companion, known by some as Niua, lived in the north head.

Whātaitai and Ngake

Whātaitai and Ngake were also sea taniwha who created Wellington Harbour. In tribal tradition the harbour was once a lake in which these taniwha lived. But Ngake was restless and smashed his way through to

TANGAROA | THE SEA

Kawautahi is a small lake 15 kilometres up Rētāruke River, a tributary of the Whanganui. It was avoided by Māori because a ferocious taniwha was said to live in it. In 1892 a surveyor employed three Māori from Taumarunui – Wārahi, Pita Te Aitua and Piki – to assist him in his work at the lake. Despite their concerns, they agreed because of the good wages on offer. However, while there they were allegedly attacked by the taniwha, and although slightly wounded, they all survived. They later told their story to T. W. Downes, who based this image loosely on their description.

nearby Cook Strait. Whātaitai tried to get out a different way and became stranded on dry ground. It is said that his spirit took the form of a bird named Te Keo, which flew to the top of Wellington's Mt Victoria and mourned (tangi), hence the name of the mountain, Tangi te keo.

Whales

In some traditions, taniwha took the shape of whales. One story tells of four such taniwha, Hine-kōtea, Hine-mākehu, Hine-kōrito and Hine-huruhuru, who escorted the voyaging canoe *Tākitimu* from Hawaiki, the Polynesian homeland. Another, Pane-iraira, was a taniwha who swam with the *Tainui* canoe from Hawaiki. The famed east coast ancestor, Kahutiaterangi, later known as Paikea, was rescued from drowning by a taniwha in the form of a whale.

In another story, Te Tahi-o-te-rangi, a well-known tohunga (priest) from Whakatāne, was abandoned by his people on Whakaari (White Island). He chanted a spell and called up the great whale-shaped taniwha Tūtarakauika, who took him back to the mainland.

This photograph of the Whanganui River, taken in 1955, has an anonymous inscription on the back: 'On many (?) occasions a large flow of water gushes up from the head of the Wanganui River below the bluff at Buckthaughts Redoubt just past the village of Upokongaro. This phenomenon is accompanied by a loud bubbling noise and small pieces of waterlogged wood and debris are brought to the surface...' Such events were often taken as signs that taniwha were present.

This watercolour of Te Rēinga falls near Wairoa was painted in 1845. One tradition tells of Hine-kōrako, a female taniwha who married a local man. After being insulted by his people, she went to live under Te Rēinga falls. One day, when the Wairoa River was in flood, a canoe carrying local people was being swept towards the falls. In desperation a kaumātua (elder) called out to her, and she rescued those on board.

Freshwater taniwha

Taniwha were also believed to inhabit lakes, rivers and other freshwater areas. Te Tau-a-Porirua was a taniwha from Heretaunga (Hastings), said to live on the Ruataniwha plains. A chief named Tara was responsible for capturing this taniwha, which had killed many people. Tara made a giant hīnaki (eel pot), put in 200 dogs as bait and set the pot in the Roto-a-Tara lake. Lured by the dogs, the taniwha entered the trap. Tara then dragged the creature ashore and killed it. When it was cut open, more than 200 victims were found inside. They were buried, and the taniwha was eaten by Tara and his people.

Hine-kōrako was a female taniwha who married a human named Tāne-kino. They had a child named Taurenga. Some of Tāne-kino's relatives insulted Hine-kōrako, so she left and went to live under Te Rēinga waterfall in Wairoa. But she remembered her ties to the community when the Wairoa River was in flood, threatening the lives of some. An old man called out to her as a canoe was being swept towards the falls. She managed to slow the canoe and then push it upstream so those on board were saved.

In the 1870s, Mohi Tūrei, an elder of Ngāti Porou, sent a letter to the Māori language newspaper *Te Waka Maori o Niu Tirani*. He described the case of a girl who was said to have been killed by a taniwha.

On 20 December 1876, four young girls had gone to bathe in a waterhole at Waipapa. This spot was renowned as the lair of a taniwha

TANGAROA | THE SEA

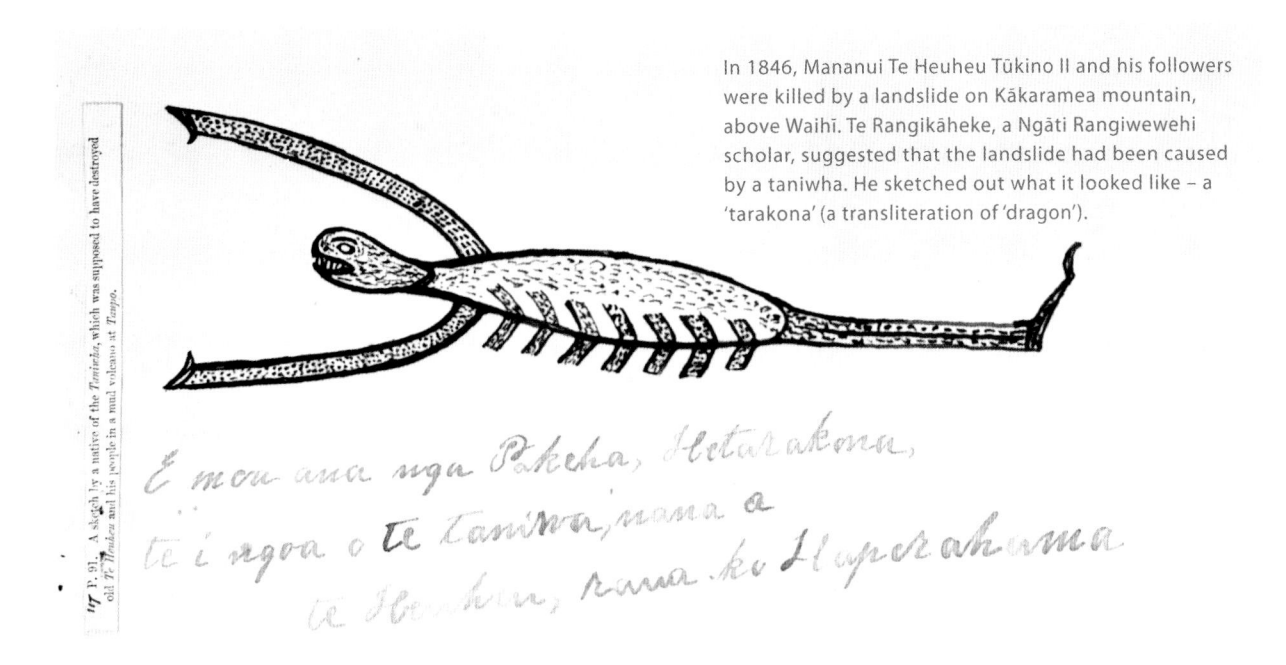

In 1846, Mananui Te Heuheu Tūkino II and his followers were killed by a landslide on Kākaramea mountain, above Waihī. Te Rangikāheke, a Ngāti Rangiwewehi scholar, suggested that the landslide had been caused by a taniwha. He sketched out what it looked like – a 'tarakona' (a transliteration of 'dragon').

named Tāminamina. While three of the girls began to bathe, the fourth, Mereana, swam to the other side of the waterhole, climbed out onto the rocks, and began sucking nectar from the red flowers of the sacred rātā tree. Suddenly, she slipped back into the water. Her friend Rāhera tried to grab her, but failed. The two other girls screamed, because they saw the water whirling near where she had fallen, and knew it to be the taniwha named Tāminamina who had got their friend. Rāhera dived to find her, but could not. Rāhera swam to shallow waters and then saw the water was rising into waves. Days later Mereana was found, back on the rock where she had slipped. But when a group came to get her body, she had once again disappeared. An elder believed she had been taken by the taniwha as punishment for sucking the flowers of the sacred rātā tree.

Ngārara – giant reptiles
Ngārara Huarau

It was believed that many taniwha took the form of giant reptiles. They were known as ngārara, and less commonly as kumi. One that is known by tribes throughout New Zealand is Ngārara Huarau.

In one tradition, Ngārara Huarau wreaked havoc first at Waimārama in Hawke's Bay, before visiting his sister, Pari-ka-whiti, in the Wairarapa. When he left his cave in Waimārama, his scales remained and became tuatara. He began to eat passing travellers until eventually one escaped and returned home, alerting his people. The chief of the village came up with a strategy to capture and kill the taniwha.

Along the path used by Ngārara Huarau a number of trees were cut almost to the point of falling. A spell was cast on a dog, which was then sent to the taniwha's cave. It barked, provoking the taniwha to give chase. Pursuing the dog, Ngārara Huarau reached the cut trees and struck them, making them fall. He tried to wriggle out, but all the trees fell and crushed him.

TAKERE-PIRIPIRI

Takere-piripiri looked like a giant tuatara with a spiky tail. He acted as guardian at Ōtautahanga pā, a stronghold of the Ngāti Raukawa tribe. The people prospered under his protection, and would place a basket of the best food below the walls of his cave. One day a gift of eels was mostly eaten by the people who brought it. In his anger Takere-piripiri ate those who had taken his food. He then went to the Maungakawa Range, where he began to eat the travellers passing by. Eventually, warriors from the Ngāti Hauā tribe trapped him in a giant, cage-like eel pot, and speared him to death.

TANGAROA | THE SEA

Sharks' teeth form a serrated blade on the māripi (shark-tooth knife). In tradition, Ao-kehu, a taniwha slayer, climbed into a hollowed log, to be swallowed by the taniwha in the Whanganui River known as Tūtaeporoporo. He used two māripi to cut his way out, killing the taniwha in the process.

Sharks

Some taniwha took the form of sharks. The northern bay of Mangōnui (great shark) is named after a guardian taniwha in the form of a giant shark that accompanied the canoe *Riukaramea* into the harbour. There are several stories of these taniwha in Māori tradition.

Pānia and Moremore

'Pānia of the Reef' is one of the great romantic stories in Māori tradition. Pānia was a sea maiden who swam ashore at sunset and returned to the sea before dawn. She would hide in a clump of flax beside a freshwater spring at the foot of Hukarere cliff in Napier. One day Karitoki, a chief in the area, was thirsty and came to the spring for a drink. He caught sight of Pānia, and took her home to be his wife. But every morning Pānia would return to the sea.

After some time Pānia had a son, Moremore, who was without hair. The chief worried that he might lose his son and wife to the sea people. He consulted a tohunga, who told him that if he placed cooked food on the mother and child while they slept, they would never return to the sea.

He did this, but the ritual did not work and Pānia was turned into a rock, forever in the ocean. Moremore became a taniwha in the form of a shark. He lived in a cave in the sea, and his descendants used to frequent the Ahuriri harbour. He was a kaitiaki, patrolling the coastal waters and inner harbours while his people fished and gathered seafood.

Tūtaeporoporo

Tūtaeporoporo, the renowned taniwha of the Whanganui River, also began life as a shark. A chief named Tuariki caught a shark and kept him as pet in a nearby river. The shark soon grew until he was as large as a whale. Then he began to change, with hard, spiky skin, bat-like wings, a lizard-like tail, webbed feet and claws like a hawk's. His head became like that of a featherless bird, but he retained shark's teeth. Later the chief Tuariki was killed by warriors from Whanganui. Tūtaeporoporo set out to avenge his master's death, making his way to the mouth of the Whanganui River. He made his home in a cave under a high cliff. After a while some canoes came down the river. The taniwha swam out and, though the people tried to escape, he swallowed them and their canoes whole.

Logs float down the Whanganui River where the chief Tuariki used to keep his pet shark, Tūtaeporoporo. When Tuariki was killed, Tūtaeporoporo, who had grown as big as a whale, set out to avenge his death. He enjoyed eating people so much he began preying on anyone who travelled the river.

TANGAROA | THE SEA

LET THE MONSTER SLEEP

Here is a translation of a karakia (charm) to slay a taniwha.
> The monster there!
> Vast as a rock he lies!
> How angrily his eyeballs glare!
> How flash his fiery eyes!
> Come Sleep, come Sleep;
> Let the slumberous spells be laid
> In depths below, in depths below;
> Let Sleep be as of night,
> Like the Great Night,
> The Long Night,
> The Sleep-bringing Night,
> Sleep on – sleep on![6]

Tāmure wrestles with Kaiwhare, a man-eating taniwha who lived in an underwater cave at Piha. Tāmure lived at Hauraki and was reputed to have a mere pounamu (greenstone weapon) with the power to defeat any taniwha. He came to Piha at the request of the local people and fought the creature. He hit it with the mere, and though he did not kill it, its wounds prevented it from eating people. From then on it lived on crayfish and octopus.

Kā kau ā Tāmure i te moana.

Ka *hopukia ē ia taua taniwha rā, ka patupatua ē ia.*

This was the first time he had tasted human flesh, and he liked it. He devoured everyone who travelled down the river, and so the people began to look for ways to slay him. An old chief named Tama advised them to find Ao-kehu, renowned as a taniwha slayer. They did, and Ao-kehu returned with them to Whanganui, taking 70 people and two māripi (shark-tooth weapons). He got his people to take a log and hollow it out so that a man would fit inside. A lid was then made. Ao-kehu got in, the lid was fitted, and any holes in the log were filled with clay to make it watertight. The taniwha Tūtaeporoporo smelt Ao-kehu, and came down and swallowed the log. Then Ao-kehu used his māripi to cut the ties around his container and slash his way out of the taniwha's stomach.

Tūtaeporoporo was soon defeated. When his body floated to the river bank, the people came and cut a hole in it. Inside they found people, canoes, weapons, tools and pounamu pendants. They buried the people, and left the body of the taniwha for the birds and fish.

Rākau tipua *enchanted logs*

Enchanted logs were known as rākau tipua. Other things such as fish, dogs, stones, trees and mountains might also be described as tipua. For example a kōhatu tipua was an enchanted rock. But rākau tipua in particular were usually thought to be taniwha. Whaiwhaiā was an enchanted log which was mainly seen drifting in rivers in the Waikato area. However, it was believed to have travelled to other areas, including the South Island. Because of the numerous places it was seen, a saying arose: 'Ngā paenga he rau o Whaiwhaiā' (the many stranding places of Whaiwhaiā).

At Waikaremoana there was a log, known as Tūtaua, which would sing. When the ethnographer Elsdon Best heard it, he compared the sound to the whistling of the wind. Others would say, 'Kō Tūtaua e waiata haere ana' (it is Tūtaua singing as it goes).

A taniwha named Humuhumu acted as a guardian of the *Māhuhu* canoe on its voyage to New Zealand. Later he acted as a guardian for his people, Ngāti Whātua in Kaipara. He was seen as a tōtara log drifting in a lagoon near the harbour. Like other rākau tipua he was recognised as a taniwha because he moved against the currents. He was said to have finally disappeared because his people had taken shellfish from his lagoon.

Another enchanted log was Mataura, who would mourn the death of a chiefly person by appearing as a huge tree on the water.

Taniwha slayers

Although many taniwha were kaitiaki, or protectors of iwi and hapū, others were killers, sparking the need for heroic slayers. They often used ingenious methods to capture the dangerous creatures.

Pitaka

Hotupuku, a taniwha on the Kāingaroa Plains, was lured out by some fast runners acting as decoys. He raced into a large noose woven from cabbage tree leaves. Led by Pitaka, these slayers used a different method for a taniwha named Pekehaua in Rotorua. They wove a large basket from supplejack and bush lawyer, and decorated it with pigeon feathers. Some of the men climbed into the basket and were lowered into the depths of a

TANGAROA | THE SEA

Te kōhatu o Hatupatu (above) is beside State Highway 1 at Ātiamuri. Hatupatu was being chased by Kurangaituku, a tipua who was part woman, part bird. He said a karakia to allow the rock to open and let him hide inside.

The pool (right) at Ngāwhā springs (photographed in 1913) was one of the places where the taniwha Takauere was said to appear in the form of a log.

spring, where they said karakia to weaken the taniwha. Pitaka placed a noose around the taniwha, tugged on the rope, and the rope was pulled up, killing the creature.

Tāmure
Kaiwhare was a taniwha who lived near Manukau Harbour in an underwater cave and blowhole, named the Gap, south of Piha. After being lured out, he was maimed by a man named Tāmure with a special mere that had the power to destroy taniwha.

Pōtoru
Te Kaiwhakaruaki was a fearsome taniwha who lived near Collingwood, in Golden Bay. A seal hunter tried to slay him by punching him in the snout. The first blow hurt the taniwha, but on the second blow the hunter's hand went into the taniwha's gaping mouth, along with the rest of him. Pōtoru, a chief from Arahura, had a more successful strategy. His party divided into three, the first to lure the taniwha into a trap, and the other two groups to flank him – one would attack and as he swung to them they would retreat and the other group would attack. This plan succeeded and the beast was slain.

In many cases, like the dragon slayers of old, these heroes also rescued maidens from the clutches of the taniwha, and were rewarded with their love.

TANIWHA TODAY

In the early 2000s two construction projects caused debate because they were planned for areas where taniwha were believed to live. In 2002, the Ngāti Naho hapū in Waikato objected to construction of a highway in a particular area because it would destroy the lair of one of their taniwha, known as Karutahi. Eventually, Transit New Zealand agreed to partially reroute the highway.

The building of a prison in Ngāwhā, Northland, was also opposed because of belief in a taniwha. Takauere, a taniwha in the form of a log, was said to have been created by a Ngāpuhi ancestress, Kareariki. While he was mainly located at Lake Ōmāpere, he was also believed to manifest himself at Ngāwhā Springs and other geothermal areas. Local hapū were concerned that the prison would impede his travel. Ultimately, against these objections, the prison was built.

In both cases, raising taniwha as an objection led to controversy. Even among Māori there was disagreement as to whether the concerns about taniwha were genuine or not.

While debate continues, taniwha continue to play an important role in the cultural identity of many tribal groups.

Ngārara *reptiles*
Bradford Haami

To Māori, reptiles were the descendants of Punga – the ugly god whose progeny were repulsive. Lizards and tuatara were feared as bringers of bad luck, and stories tell of hideous giant reptiles that captured women and married them. However, reptiles were also seen as kaitiaki (guardians).

What are ngārara?

Ngārara is the Māori name for reptiles – including tuatara, lizards and the giant reptiles of Māori tradition.

The tuatara is named for its appearance – tara means spiny, and tua means back. Māori call lizards (skinks and geckos) mokomoko. The kawekaweau, now extinct, was the world's largest gecko. It was described as 'about two feet [60 centimetres] long, and as thick as a man's wrist; colour brown, striped longitudinally with dull red'.[7] Māori also believed in giant reptiles, although no scientific evidence of them has been found. Simply called ngārara, they were a type of taniwha and looked like lizards or tuatara.

Reptiles are believed to be descended from Punga, a son of Tangaroa. 'Te aitanga a Punga' (the progeny of Punga) traditionally refers to a wide range of sea and land creatures. As well as lizards and tuatara, it includes sharks, sea and freshwater fish, eels, lizards, stingrays, octopus, insects and various birds. As Punga's descendants these creatures are seen as repulsive, ugly or offensive.

TANGAROA | THE SEA

The tuatara (left) is a unique reptile found only in New Zealand. Inland taniwha were often described as looking like giant tuatara, and were known as ngārara.

The mokomoko, or skink, was another of Punga's offspring.

This carving of a ngārara is on a post of Tamatekapua meeting house at Whakarewarewa. Traditionally, ngārara are rarely represented in Māori carving. However, when they are depicted, it is usually as kaitiaki or guardians.

NGĀRARA SIGHTINGS

In the late 19th century there were a number of sightings of large ngārara. In 1875, a large reptile, said to have six legs, was caught near Hokianga. However, its Māori captors were so horrified that they hacked it into unidentifiable pieces. In 1898 a Māori bushman said he had seen a giant lizard, 1.5 metres long. It disappeared, but its footprints were photographed by W. D. Lysnar, the owner of the farm where it was seen.

There are various tribal traditions about the identity of Punga. In most, he is the son of Tangaroa. In other traditions, he was the eldest son of Whaitiri, the goddess of thunder, and her husband Kaitangata. Punga was named after the anchor stone of his father's canoe.

'Te aitanga a Punga' or 'te whānau a Punga' (Punga's offspring) were terms for ugly people or dark-skinned, ill-favoured people.

The saying 'Me aha hoki, ngā uri o Punga aruaru kai' (what does it matter, these are descendants of Punga who chased food), describes an objectionable person who is likely to be shunned at a feast. It refers to Punga's behaviour in his guise as a shark – when he approaches food, the other fish move away quickly.

Punga's son Tū-te-wanawana, along with Tūpari, produced the following offspring: the large gecko kawekaweau, tuatara, the mokopāpā or the Pacific gecko and the mokomoko or skink.

95

BEASTS ON BOARD

An ancestral canoe of the Ngāti Porou tribe, the *Māngārara*, was said to have brought a cargo of reptiles, insects and a bird to New Zealand. The chief Wheketoro set them free on Whangaokeno Island (East Island) by East Cape. Wheketoro made the island sacred, and made a home for the tuatara in the fern. He took the other creatures to the mainland, but his canoe was wrecked at Pariwhero, and turned to stone. The reptiles ran and hid under overhanging banks, where they are still said to live today.

In another tradition, a tuatara called Ngārara argued with his younger brother Mangō (shark) over whether to live in the sea or on land. Ngārara chose the land, while Mangō remained in the sea. Just as Ngārara moved onto the shore, Mangō swam up and asked him to return to the sea. Ngārara cursed his brother: 'Stay in the sea to be served on a dish of cooked food for man to eat.' Mangō replied, 'Go ashore and be smoked out of your hole with burning fern leaves.' Ngārara replied, 'Indeed, I will go on ashore, away unto the dry land, where I shall be looked upon as the personification of Tū [the war god], with my spines and ridgy crest, causing fear and affright, so that all will get out of my way, hurrah!'

The brothers' curses came to pass. Māori often ate dried shark as a relish with kūmara (sweet potato) or potato, and caught reptiles by lighting a fire at the entrance of their hole.

Ngārara traditions

Some tribes have other traditions that explain the origins of reptiles. In one tradition, reptiles originated from Peketua (the son of the earth mother, Papatūānuku, and the sky father, Ranginui). He made an egg from clay, and took it to Tāne, god of the forest, who said, 'Me whakaira tangata' (give it life). This egg then produced the first tuatara.

In some stories lizards originate from the death of a ngārara – a hideous giant reptile. The reptilian monster Te Ngārara Huarau was a terrifying giant reptile that burned to death. Its scales escaped and turned into lizards. Another ngārara, Te Whakaruaki, forcibly took a woman as his bride. Her family trapped and burnt him inside a house. As he was dying, his tail broke off and escaped, becoming the father of the mokopāpā (Pacific gecko). It is said that since then, lizards have shed their tails when they are in danger.

From sea to land

Punga, son of Tangaroa, had two offspring: Ikatere (fast fish) and Tū-te-wehiwehi, also called Tū-te-wanawana (reptiles). After the separation of Ranginui and Papatūānuku, Tangaroa was forced to flee into the sea. His offspring argued over staying in the sea or going onto the land.

Ikatere and his descendants, some species of fish, decided to stay in the sea. Tū-te-wehiwehi chose the land. The saying 'tāua ki uta, tāua ki te wai' (we of the land, we of the sea) refers to the choices they made for their descendants. Ikatere told Tū-te-wehiwehi, 'Fly inland, the fate of your race will be a frightful one. You will be caught by men. When you are cooked they will burn your scales over a wisp of lightened fern.'

Tū-te-wehiwehi shouted back, 'Go to the sea. Do you know what will happen to you? When they put the baskets of cooked vegetables in front of the people, you will be placed on top as a relish.'

These lizards were illustrated in an article by naturalist Walter Buller. In Māori tradition lizards were descended from Tū-te-wehiwehi, who came from the sea but chose to live on land.

TANGAROA | THE SEA

REPTILES AS GUARDIANS

Lizards and tuatara were often seen as kaitiaki and released near burial caves to watch over the dead. They were also used as kaitiaki for mauri – a talisman, usually a stone, which was thought to protect the health and vitality of a forest or tree. Lizards – often the moko kākāriki or moko tāpiri – were released near mauri, and were believed to stay there forever. Lizards were also sometimes buried under a post supporting the ridge pole in a whare wānanga (house of learning) or other important buildings.

This is the Northland moko kākāriki (green gecko). Its chattering sound was traditionally believed to be laughter, and was feared.

This waka kōiwi (burial chest) was found in a burial cave at Waimamaku, near Hokianga. The lizard acts as a kaitiaki, or guardian. Lizards – real or carved – were believed to act as kaitiaki, as they were often feared.

Guardians or enemies?

Māori feared lizards (skinks and geckos), and to a lesser extent tuatara. Lizards were seen as representatives of Whiro, the god of darkness, evil and death. The East Coast ancestor Kahungunu kept a kawekaweau in a special bowl, and brought it out to scare approaching enemies. When moko kākāriki, green geckos, lifted their heads and chattered in a sound believed to be laughter, it was seen as a bad omen.

A Waikato woman who eloped with a Rotorua warrior later asked her elders' blessing. They challenged the warrior by making him swallow a lizard. He rose to the challenge, and became known as Ngārara nui (great reptile). A carving showing him swallowing a lizard is sometimes placed on the front of a house as a guardian.

Another of Tū-te-wanawana's offspring was Tū-tangata-kino, who took the form of a reptile and produced insects, spiders and lizards. Tū-tangata-kino was thought to be a spiritual reptile that crawled into people's mouths while they were asleep and gnawed their stomachs, causing illness.

Taranaki and Whanganui people believe that Tū-tangata-kino guarded the house of Miru, ruler of the underworld, with Moko-hiku-waru, another reptile.

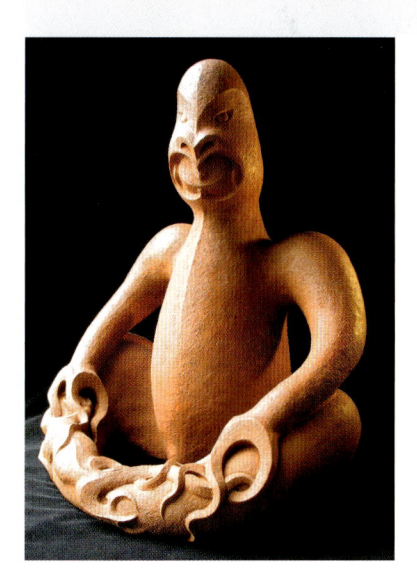

This clay sculpture, 'Whakapakoko III', by Manos Nathan, is a contemporary take on traditional burial chests (whakapakoko), which contained bones and were placed in burial caves. Between the hands of the figure is a lizard, both a guardian and a symbol of misfortune.

97

PART IV

Te Waonui-a-Tāne
the forest

Kaitoke Regional Park, near Wellington

Te Waonui-a-Tāne *forest mythology*

Te Ahukaramū Charles Royal

New Zealand's forests provided Māori with rich inspiration for sayings and expressions, as well as the means of life. Tāne, the god of the forest, separated earth and sky and let light into the world. These actions became the basis for important rituals and oratory on the marae.

When the ancestors of Māori arrived in New Zealand, they found it was very different from their Polynesian homeland. They had been primarily seafaring people, but on these larger, colder islands, they also needed to know about the bush.

Understanding the forest was vital to life. As Māori explored and learnt about the forests, Tāne, the god of the forest, found an important place in tribal consciousness and traditions. People developed a reverence for and knowledge of Te Waonui-a-Tāne – the great forest of Tāne.

Tāne is a figure of great importance in tribal traditions. Tāne separated earth and sky and brought this world into being; he fashioned the first human; he adorned the heavens, and brought the baskets of knowledge, wisdom and understanding down from the sky to human beings.

Tāne is sometimes given different names to reflect his different roles. He is called Tāne-mahuta as god of the forest, Tāne-te-wānanga as the bringer of knowledge, and Tānenui-a-rangi as bringer of higher consciousness.

TE WAONUI A TĀNE | THE FOREST

The kauri tree Tāne Mahuta stands in the Waipoua Forest in Northland. It is 51.5 metres tall, has a trunk diameter of 4.5 metres and is estimated to be 1500 years old. Trees like this are believed to symbolise Tāne, propping up the sky from the earth.

Tāne is a model for masculinity and action in the world. His various names suggest freshness, youth, someone who can overcome others' actions, and who is true, loyal and authentic. He is seen as upright and able to bear the weight of an enterprise; he has his roots in the earth and his head in the heavens.

Trees in the forest are seen as Tāne-mahuta, rising to separate earth and sky. Tāne, the tree, holds the sky aloft, bringing light into the world. The widespread felling of forests in New Zealand in the 19th and 20th centuries was calamitous to the traditional world view of tribes that lived in the forest – it was like the sky rejoining the earth, and the world returning to darkness.

The felling of forests also went against traditional models of behaviour. The word 'tika' means erect, upright and correct – as a tree is upright and erect. It informs the concepts of tikanga – correct behaviour or action – and whakatika, which means to arise. Correct behaviours arise from within a person, as a tree rises from the ground.

Symbolism of trees and plants

In the traditional Māori world view, plants and animals were rich in meaning. The diverse heights, girths and other features of trees suggested the variety of human dimensions. Children were named after trees, plants and birds, and people's characters were likened to features of the forest.

TŌTARA

The tōtara is symbolic of a great chief. The following expression describes the death of a chief:

Kua hinga te tōtara i
Te Waonui-a-Tāne.
A tōtara has fallen in the great forest of Tāne.

A great chief is also referred to as a tōtara haemata – a strong-growing tōtara. Another saying compares people to the tōtara and the pukatea:

Ka haere te tōtara haemata,
ka takoto te pukatea wai nui.
The tōtara floats, while the pukatea lies in deep water.

This proverb suggests that young people are like the soft-wooded tōtara – they move around easily and can attend meetings in different areas. Older people are more settled – they are like the pukatea, a tree with heavy wood that grows in swamps.

The ti-kouka, or cabbage tree, often grows alone, symbolising stoic independence.

TE WAONUI-A-TĀNE | THE FOREST

The harakeke (flax) plant represents the whānau in Māori thought. The rito (shoot) is the child. It is protectively surrounded by the awhi rito (parents). The outside leaves represent the tūpuna (grandparents and ancestors).

The raukawa (below) evokes romantic love.

Many whakataukī (sayings) use trees and plants as symbols and metaphors. Some reflect the human qualities associated with certain plants. The tī-kouka, or cabbage tree, which often grows alone, symbolises stoic independence. It was sometimes called tī-tahi – the lone cabbage tree. Another proverb notes that when a person dies, they return to Te Pō (the darkness) forever, unlike the tī kōuka, which grows back even if it is cut down.

Ehara i te tī e wana ake.
Man is not like the tī, which renews itself.

The raukawa evokes romantic love – it was used to make perfume for the East Coast ancestor Māhinaarangi's meetings with her lover Tūrongo. They named their child (the ancestor of the Ngāti Raukawa tribe) after the plant.

Harakeke (flax) symbolises the family and the cycle of life. Similarly, the flax bush represents the family – the new leaf at its centre is the child, and larger leaves on the outside are older relatives.

The maire is a hardwood, and represents strength. A saying about the maire asks where to find the most important part of a speech:

Kei whea te maire o ngā kōrero?
Where is the maire of the speechmaking?

A mother often sang this song while nursing a child.

Taku hei piripiri
Taku hei mokimoki
Taku hei tāwhiri
Taku kati taramea.
My little neck satchel of sweet-scented moss
My little neck satchel of fragrant fern
My little neck satchel of aromatic gum
My sweet-smelling neck locket of speargrass.

All these plants were admired for their scents. Their leaves, or gum in the case of the tāwhiri, were worn in satchels around the neck.

Symbolising strength, a bold and committed person is compared to the maire:
E, ko te matakahi maire.
Like a wedge of maire.

103

TE WAONUI-A-TĀNE | THE FOREST

The tawa (right) could symbolise cowardice (the soft berry), or courage (the hard kernel).

PERILOUS PRICKLES

Māori were cautious of two thorny plants in the bush. Ongaonga or tree nettle has 6-millimetre-long stinging hairs that can kill small animals such as rats and cats. Dogs, horses and cattle can also die, and in 1961 a tramper died after pushing through a thicket of it. Tātaramoa or bush lawyer has hooked thorns that snag clothing and rip or prick the skin. Its fruit can be eaten, and the vine yields water when cut.

The ongaonga's hairs give a painful sting. A difficult or 'prickly' person was likened to this plant.

A difficult person is identified with the stinging ongaonga:
   He tangata ongaonga.
   A prickly person.
Cowardice is likened to the soft berry of the tawa:
   He tawa para, he whati kau tāna.
   The pulp of the tawa berry is easily crushed.
Whereas a courageous person is compared to the tawa's hard kernel:
   Ka mahi te tawa uho ki te riri.
   Well done, tawa kernel fighting away.
Another proverb refers to the tough climbing frond of mangemange:
   Kia pēnei te mārōrō o tō kākahu me te mangemange.
   Let your clothes be as strong as the mangemange, which never wears out.
   Even māheuheu (weeds) played a symbolic role. They represented abandoned places, and were sometimes deliberately cultivated to hide sacred sites, giving the impression that they had been abandoned.

TE WAONUI-A-TĀNE | THE FOREST

This rāpaki (wrap), made from flax, is a beautiful example of strong but attractive clothing. One proverb urged people to make their clothes as strong as mangemange which never wore out.

Symbolism in oratory

Trees and plants came to represent poetic and symbolic ideas, expressed in classical oratory and storytelling. In the 19th century, Europeans (and perhaps uneducated Māori) sometimes struggled to understand orations despite speaking the Māori language, because they did not know the symbolism behind the words.

A tongi (saying) from Tāwhiao, the second Māori king, used native plants as symbols:

Māku anō e hanga tōku whare
Ko tōna tāhuhu, he hīnau.
Ōna pou he māhoe, he patatē
Me whakatupu ki te hua o te rengarenga,
me whakapakari ki te hua o te kawariki.
I will build my house
Its ridge pole will be made of hīnau.
Its posts will be made of māhoe (whiteywood) and patatē (seven-finger)
Those who inhabit that house shall be raised on rengarenga (rock lily),
and nurtured on kawariki.

His tongi has been interpreted to mean that the native plants used to build the house and feed its inhabitants represent Māori self-sufficiency.

Pou and tumu

A pou, or post, is made from a tree and re-erected in another place to make a statement. For example, a pou rāhui is a boundary post that marks a restricted area.

A person was also sometimes described as a pou. This meant that they too had been carved – tattooed with a moko – and were then commissioned to do certain tasks. They often had to take a position, stake a claim and uphold the weight of an enterprise – doing metaphorically what a post does literally.

A tumu is another kind of post – a tree stump that remains in the place where it grew, rather than a tree that is felled, carved and erected in another place. Canoes were tied up to stumps, which were firmly rooted in the ground. High chiefs were compared to stumps, because they remained in the lands where they were born and were not easily overcome by the events of the day:

Ko te tumu herenga waka.
Like a tree stump to which the many canoes are tied.

This woven tukutuku panel is from Te Herenga Waka marae, Victoria University. The panel has the same name as the marae – meaning 'the hitching post of canoes'. In the centre is the tumu (stump) to which the waka (canoes) are tied. This represents the ethos of the marae – a place where people from all areas can 'hitch' their waka. The tumu is usually a tree stump, and represents the tribe's solid foundation.

Te ngahere *forest lore*
Rāwiri Taonui

In Māori tradition, people and forests are vitally connected – both were created by the god Tāne. A magical realm guarded by lizards, birds and other creatures, the forest also provided Māori with the necessities of life. They depended on its trees and shrubs for food, medicines, building materials and clothing.

Māori revered the forest for its beauty, spiritual presence, and bountiful supply of food, medicines, and weaving and building materials. The forest is called by many names – ngahere, ngāherehere, nehenehe, ngahengahe, wao, waonui and waoku. In Taranaki, motu or motu rākau refer to a stand of trees or patch of bush.

Māori believed that the life principle or mauri of a forest could be concentrated into objects such as stones and thereby protected and fostered. Stones were chosen for their unusual shape or appearance, and buried in significant places such as at the foot of well-known, bird-frequented trees. Lizards such as the moko kākāriki (common green gecko) and moko tāpiri (Pacific gecko) were often released to guard the mauri. Māori believed these guardians were immortal.

However, forces could conspire to deplete the mauri itself, and tohunga (priests) from other tribes could recite incantations to negate

TE WAONUI-A-TANE | THE FOREST

Barrett Bush Scenic Reserve, Waikato

This Pacific gecko is on Hauturu (Little Barrier Island). Lizards were released near mauri stones to act as guardians.

This mauri stone (right) was found on Moutohorā (Whale Island) in the Bay of Plenty. Māori believed that the mauri of a forest, tree or waterway could be concentrated in a stone or other object for protection.

or steal it. Tohunga were called on to protect or revitalise the mauri.

Respect for Tāne's forest was shown by performing certain tikanga (customs). Their importance is reflected in the story of Rātā who saw the hakuturi (forest guardians in the form of birds, insects and other life) replant a tree he had felled. When he confronted them, they told him he had failed to perform the appropriate rites. He then did so, and the hakuturi released the tree.

The early Polynesian settlers hunted the moa to extinction and burned large tracts of forest. Over a period of about 500 years, indigenous forest cover was reduced from about 80% to 50%. In the 200 years since European settlement, it has dwindled to 24.8%.

But Māori knowledge of forest plants, foods, medicines, building materials and other resources shows a deep understanding of the natural world.

TE WAONUI-A-TĀNE | THE FOREST

Tōtara

Kauri

MAKING FIRE

The demigod Māui, wanting to discover the secret of fire, visited the goddess Mahuika. She gave him one of her fingernails, which contained the fire. To trick her, Māui deliberately put out the flame and returned for another fingernail. He repeated this until Mahuika, realising she had been duped, cast the last nail down and set the underworld alight. Fire became implanted in kaikōmako, rimu and tōtara. Since then, fire has been made by rubbing sticks from these trees in grooves of māhoe or patatē wood.

The great trees

Tōtara

Tōtara had pride of place among the tall trees. Found throughout New Zealand and growing up to 40 metres high, their strong, straight trunks were ideal for building waka taua (war canoes). The bark was used to make roofs, splints for broken limbs, and food and water containers called pātua or papa tōtara.

Kauri

Kauri reaches 30 to 60 metres tall, has a massive girth, and can live as long as 2000 years. Tāne Mahuta in Waipoua Forest, Northland, is the largest living specimen. Kauri grows naturally in the north of the North Island, its southern limit crossing the country from Raglan harbour, through Hamilton to just south of Tauranga. The timber was ideal for canoe hulls.

Kauri gum was called kāpia. Older gum was used as an accelerant for fires and a fuel for torches. Gum from kauri, tarata and kōhūhū was chewed. The stalk of the pūhā plant was cut to release juice. This hardened and was rolled into a ball, to be chewed like gum.

Beech

Beech trees were known as tawhai or tawai. They grew mainly on the Volcanic Plateau in the central North Island and along the mountain chains of the North and South islands, and could reach 20 to 30 metres in height. Three varieties were recognised: tawhai (silver beech), tawhairauriki (black beech and mountain beech) and tawhairaunui (red beech and hard beech). Kiore (Pacific rats) lived in beech forest and became abundant when beech seeds were plentiful. A name for kiore in Whanganui was kiore tawai (beech rat). Kiore were a favourite food of Māori (see pages 174-177).

Kahikatea

New Zealand's tallest tree, at up to 60 metres, kahikatea was the dominant tree of swampy lowlands around the country. Its wood was not durable, but it was often used for canoes as it was plentiful near waterways. It bears edible berries, known as koroī.

TE WAONUI-A-TĀNE | THE FOREST

TREE FERNS

There are several varieties of **whekī** and **whekī-ponga** ferns, growing 5 to 20 metres high. **Whekī** (rough tree fern) has peg-like extensions marking where old fronds have fallen off, and is found throughout New Zealand.
Whekī-ponga (brown tree fern) is distinguishable by its large skirt of old brown fronds, and grows south of Auckland. Both provided building materials — the trunks were used for walls, and the fronds for roofs.
Ponga (silver fern) grows in the North Island and the east and north of the South Island. Its fronds have a distinctive silver underside. Māori laid them silver-side up as track markers — in the dark they were lit up by burning torches. The leaves of rangiora were used in the same way.
Mamaku tree ferns grow in damp gullies throughout New Zealand. Reaching 20 metres in height, they have oval-shaped frond scars on the trunk. The white pith of the trunk and the koru (new shoots) are edible, although slimy when first cut. Māori stripped the trunk's outer layers so the slime could dry or drain away. The plant was then cut down and cooked whole. Alternatively, koru were hung to dry. Baking was the preferred way to cook mamaku, to separate the stringy fibres from the flesh. Although the taste is bland, the nutritional value is high.
Kātote (soft tree fern) grows throughout New Zealand and is half the size of mamaku. It was a favourite food of South Island tribes.

Mamaku koru are called pikopiko. Slimy when fresh, they were sometimes hung to dry before being eaten.

Rimu

Rimu is found throughout New Zealand and can reach 50 metres in height. The tree and its wood have a number of uses. The red cap that holds the seed is edible. The inner bark and leaves were pulped and applied to burns and other wounds. The resinous heartwood was split into slivers and tied in bundles for torches.

Matai and miro

Matai and miro grow to 25 metres high, matai in lowland forests around New Zealand and miro in both low and high altitude forest. Miro produce fruit all year round, and were a favourite of kūkupa or kererū (New Zealand pigeons) and kākā in autumn and winter. Snares were set to catch the birds.

Mānuka and kānuka

Although strictly shrubs and small trees, mānuka and kānuka were very important to Māori all over Aotearoa. Incredibly versatile plants, their bark provided a waterproof layer for roofs, and poles were used as battens and rafters, and for spears or paddle shafts. The leaves were used to scent hair oil, and flexible saplings and new branches were made into snares and traps.

> Kua takoto te mānuka.
>
> *The challenge has been laid down.*

Mamaku can grow to a height of 20 metres in damp gullies in the forest.

TE WAONUI-A-TĀNE | THE FOREST

Puawānanga (below) was said to be the child of the stars Puanga (Rigel in Orion) and Rehua (Antares in Scorpio). In some traditions, the appearance of Puanga signalled winter and Rehua summer – puawānanga trees flowered in the months between them.

When the pōhutukawa (above and right) blooms, summer has arrived. For some, this also signals that the yellow roe of the kina (sea urchin) is fat.

Flowering plants

Puawānanga
Oral traditions say that white-flowered puawānanga (clematis) is the child of Puanga (Rigel, the top star in Orion) and Rehua (Antares in Scorpio). Puanga's rising in June marks the beginning of winter, and the rising of Rehua in December signals summer – puawānanga blooms in the months between them. Garlands were made from the flowers.

Kōwhai
When the bright yellow flowers of kōwhai bloom, in late winter and early spring, it is time to plant kūmara. Pigment for yellow dye was extracted from the flowers, and the flexible branches were good for making houses and bird snares.

Pōhutukawa and northern rātā
Pōhutukawa reaches 20 metres high, and grew wild north of Kāwhia, Lake Taupō and Ōpōtiki. Its distinctive red flowers signalled the arrival of summer. The boiled juice of the inner bark could cure diarrhoea, and the nectar was good for sore throats. This was a coastal tree, and the curving nature of the lower branches meant that they were ideal for carving out one-piece fish hooks.

The main inland relation of the pōhutukawa, the northern rātā, is found north of Kaikōura and grows up to 25 metres tall. It usually begins life as a vine that grows around host trees, and finally engulfs them completely. The bark was used to help heal wounds and burns, and cure diseases.

Some species of rātā never become trees, but grow into a mass of vines. These were cut and drained of drinking water.

This rātā vine has grown around a rimu tree.

TE WAONUI-A-TĀNE | THE FOREST

The cabbage tree was an important fibre plant for early Māori. They used the leaves to weave food-carrying baskets or kete, such as the one shown here.

This kiekie is growing on Breaksea Island, Fiordland. Māori wove kiekie leaves, and ate the fruit and bracts around the flower.

Plants for weaving

Harakeke and wharariki (mountain flax) were the main plants used for weaving (see page 112). Their tough, sword-shaped leaves were woven into kete (baskets), sails, tukutuku panels and fishing nets. But there were other plants that could be used to provide the raw materials needed to create clothing, shelter, storage and cooking vessels. Many of these plants also provided food and medicine.

Nīkau, New Zealand's only native palm tree, is found as far south as Banks Peninsula and Greymouth in the South Island. It grows up to 10 metres tall. The trunks were used for house posts or walls, the fronds for roofs, and the leaves for weaving. The base of the frond, which holds rainwater, was used as a bowl. The young leaves in the heart of the bowl can be eaten raw or cooked, although removing them can kill the tree. They have a mild laxative effect, and pregnant women ate them to relax their lower body. Nīkau's large, immature flower pods and green seeds make good eating before they open, in late summer to early autumn. Also edible are the tender centre shoots of young plants on the forest floor.

Tī kōuka (cabbage tree) grows up to 12 metres tall. The leaves were used for weaving. Drinking the juice of the boiled leaves cured diarrhoea. The roots, tender new shoots and core of the trunk are rich in fructose and good to eat. New shoots were eaten raw or cooked. The usual method was to chop off the top, strip the bark and leave the tree to stand for a couple of days. The trunk was then felled and steamed for 24–48 hours, then the flesh separated from the fibre. Preparing the roots involved a similar process.

Generally speaking, the smaller the tree the better the taste – tī rauriki (dwarf cabbage trees) were particularly good. Several other species, including the multi-headed tī tōī (mountain cabbage tree), are also edible.

Neinei (grass tree) is found only in the upper North Island. Looking like a slender cabbage tree, its foliage was used for weaving. The scrambling climber or ground plant kiekie was another important weaving plant. The white bracts around the flower and the protruding fruit were eaten.

These nīkau palms are growing alongside the Heaphy Track in the South Island. The trunks were used for house posts or walls, the fronds for roofs, and the leaves for weaving. The bowl at the base of the fronds held rainwater.

HARAKEKE FLAX

After Māori arrived in New Zealand, from around 1250, they discovered the useful properties of flax. The nectar from its flowers made a sweet drink. The roots could be crushed to make poultices for skin infections, and to produce a juice with disinfectant and laxative properties. The gum from the base of the leaves eased pain and healed wounds, especially burns. The leaves themselves could be used as bandages and to secure broken bones.

At first, Māori women used flax in the same way they had used the pandanus plant in Polynesia – weaving baskets, containers and mats from the leaves. They then learned to obtain the strong fibre (muka) from the leaves by scraping the green flesh away with a sharp shell. The muka was pounded until soft, then washed and sometimes dyed. Twisted, plaited and woven, it was used to create a wide range of items, such as fishing nets and traps, footwear, cords and ropes.

Flax became so crucial for Māori that when 19th-century missionary William Colenso told chiefs that it did not grow in England, they would reply 'How is it possible to live there without it?' and 'I would not dwell in such a land as that'.[1]

The first Māori arrivals had found that their tapa cloth garments, made from the aute plant (paper mulberry), were too thin. In any case the aute did not thrive in New Zealand. Muka could be woven (often with feathers and dog skin) into warm clothing – vital in New Zealand's cooler climate.

Various types (cultivars) of flax were seen as having specific uses by different iwi. For instance, the cultivar 'Māeneene' was used by the Ngāi Tūhoe people of Urewera to weave fine patterned mats. Ngāti Porou sought the 'Tākirikau' cultivar for making piupiu (kilts). The 'Kōhunga' cultivar produced muka that Ngāti Maniapoto used for their finest cloaks. Whanganui tribes chose the 'Ate' cultivar for making eel nets and kete.

Special flax plants were tended in a plantation (pā harakeke) and there were traditions about when and how they could be harvested. The plant was seen as a family. The central shoot or rito was the baby and the leaves on either side of it the awhi rito or mātua (its parents). Only the leaves on the outside – the tūpuna, or grandparents – were cut, to avoid weakening the plant.

Flax was not just useful – it was a way of passing on culture. Through the patterns in woven articles, stories were told and beliefs affirmed. Although European clothing replaced flax garments, weaving as an art has survived.

Nancy Swarbrick

A piupiu is a skirt-like garment made of flax strands that hang from a belt. When the wearer moves, the strands sway to and fro.

There are two species of New Zealand flax. *Phormium tenax* (left), also known as harakeke or swamp flax, has stiff leaves, red flowers, and upright seed pods. It grows mainly on lowland swamps throughout New Zealand. *Phormium cookianum* (right), also known as wharariki or mountain flax, has softer leaves and yellow flowers. The seed pods droop and twist, becoming thin and papery with age. This species is found on mountain slopes and coastal cliffs.

TE WAONUI-A-TĀNE | THE FOREST

Karaka berries at various stages of ripeness (left) were an important food source, but required careful preparation to make them safe to eat.

Fruiting trees

Fruiting trees were a vital source of food for Māori, though some fruits required a lot of preparation to make them more palatable or, in the case of karaka, even safe to eat. The poroporo produces its yellow fruit year-round, but unripe fruit is poisonous – it is edible only when the skin has split.

The hīnau grows in forests throughout most of New Zealand and its fruit was an important food for Māori, who pounded or soaked it to remove the flesh from the stones, dried it, then baked it into large cakes. The bark was used to make pātua (food containers) and black tattooing pigment. Cakes were also made from the pungapunga (pollen) of raupō (bulrush), another plant found throughout the country. The rhizome of this plant provided a starchy food.

The kernels of tawa and taraire, which mature in late summer to early autumn, were a staple of forest tribes north of Lake Taupō. The kernels were boiled, steamed or roasted in embers. When dried they kept for several months. Tawa was also used to make taoroa (long bird spears) and as fuel to light fires.

Growing from 5 to 15 metres tall and found in coastal and lowland forest around New Zealand, karaka was probably the most important source of kernels. These had to be carefully prepared because in their raw state they are poisonous. They were boiled or steamed for up to 12 hours, then immersed in running stream water for one or two weeks. The kernels could then be stored for several months. Re-cooking softened them for eating. The raw flesh of the bright orange fruit is also edible after the kernel is separated, and has a strong apricot flavour. Māori planted groves of karaka trees near the bays and harbours they seasonally visited.

Tutu was another plant that needed special preparation to neutralise its deadly toxicity. Every part of the plant is poisonous except for the petals (which look like long strings of small, dark fruit). To extract the juice, Māori crushed and strained the petals through toetoe and other fibrous plants. It was used to sweeten and flavour other foods such as aruhe (fern root) and dishes made from mamaku and karaka.

Māori made cakes from the pollen of raupō, and its rhizome provided a starchy food.

All parts of the tutu plant are poisonous except for the petals. Māori crushed and strained the purple petals through toetoe grass, using the juice to sweeten aruhe (fern root).

TE WAONUI-A-TĀNE | THE FOREST

A flax bag (below) called a kopa or tāwiri was used to squeeze tītoki berries (right). The berries were placed inside the bag and pounded, then the bag was squeezed. The oil dripped into a receptacle underneath.

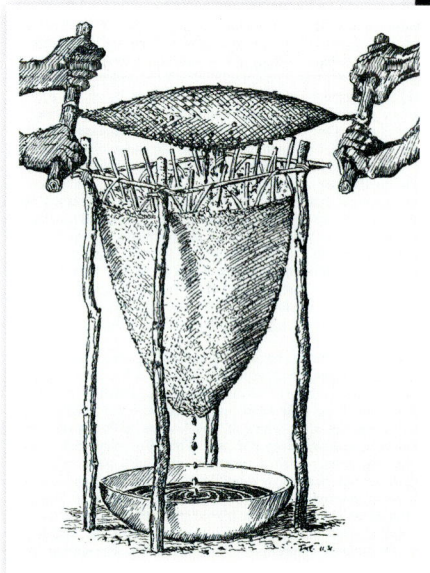

Fragrant taramea or wild Spaniard was highly valued. South Island Māori held the leaves over a fire to release the oil, which was collected in a small container.

Tītoki and parapara

Tītoki grows up to 20 metres tall and is found on the coast and lowlands of the North Island and northern South Island. Its red berries were used in scented sachets, or crushed, washed, then pressed to make hair oil. The oil was stored in tahā hinu (small gourd vessels) and perfumed with leaves of heketara, raukawa, mānuka or the moss kōpuru. Pia and ware (gums) extracted from tarata and taramea were also added.

The parapara is found in the northern parts of the North Island. The Ngāti Porou tribe extracted oil from the seeds by steaming, pounding and pressing them.

Ground ferns

Aruhe is the root of rārahu or rauaruhe (bracken fern), a tough ground fern with reddish-brown stems, which grows up to 2 metres tall. Fern root was the most important wild vegetable for Māori and several traditions explain its origin:

- Aruhe was a grandchild of Rarotimu and Rarotake, and grew on the back of Ranginui. When Tāne separated his father Ranginui from his mother Papatūānuku, Aruhe tumbled down to the ground.
- When Tāne separated the earth and sky, he was attacked by his brother Tāwhirimātea (god of the winds). In fright, another brother, Haumia (god of wild or uncultivated foods), fled into the folds of their mother. Fern-root fronds are said to be Haumia's hair sticking up out of the earth.
- The explorer Kupe brought the first fern root from Hawaiki on the canoe *Tapuwaeputuputu* (the canoe's remains are said to be at Waimā in the Hokianga).
- Aruhe is said to have come from the fairy-like beings tūrehu or patupaiarehe. In former times, working parties offered the first three roots they collected to these ancient creatures.

TE WAONUI-A-TĀNE | THE FOREST

EAT YOUR GREENS

The best-known Māori 'green' is pūhā. However, a number of others were also eaten, including pōhue, raupeti (black nightshade) and the young leaves of puahou (five-finger).

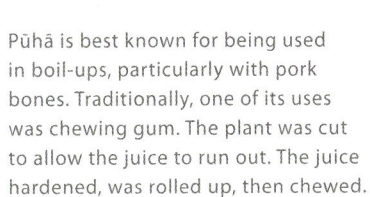

Pūhā is best known for being used in boil-ups, particularly with pork bones. Traditionally, one of its uses was chewing gum. The plant was cut to allow the juice to run out. The juice hardened, was rolled up, then chewed.

Māori harvested aruhe (fern root) from bracken fern throughout the year.

Harvest and preparation

Bracken fern flourishes in open woodlands where felled or burnt forest is regenerating. Māori harvested the roots and shoots throughout the year, although late spring to early summer was the optimum time. The best plants were about three years old and had rhizomes 2–3 centimetres in diameter. These were dried, steeped in water, roasted, boiled or steamed, and then pounded to separate the edible flesh from the fibres. The resulting paste was formed into large blocks or cakes, and sweetened with tutu juice or wai kōrari (harakeke nectar).

Māori ate other ground ferns, including the young fronds or shoots of kōwaowao (hound's tongue fern), rereti, mouku (hen and chickens fern) and huruhuru whenua (shining spleenwort). They ate the koru or fiddleheads of kiokio and pikopiko (common shield fern).

MOVEABLE FEAST

Large flocks of kūkupa travelled from forest to forest in the North Island to eat the fruit as it ripened. In spring and early summer they ate miro, pūriri and taraire in Northland. By March (early autumn) they had moved south to Pirongia and Te Aroha in the Kaimai Ranges; in May and June they were at Rangitoto and Ranginui near Te Kūiti; and in July and August (late winter) they feasted at Tītīraupenga, Pureora and Ketemaringi.

TE WAONUI-A-TĀNE | THE FOREST

This portrait by George French Angas, done in the 1840s, shows a chief of Motupoi pā, by Lake Rotoaira in the central North Island. His weapon is adorned with feathers, and his wife appears to be wearing a pōhoi toroa (albatross-feather earring).

This waka huia contains a single huia feather. While the main purpose of waka huia was to hold these prized feathers, they were also used for other taonga (treasures). The intricate carving shows how important the boxes were.

Ngā manu *birds*

Kelly Keane

Birds had a vital place in traditional Māori life, providing food, and feathers for adornment and cloaks. Their habits were closely observed, and were a rich source of metaphor and poetry. Birds' behaviour was used to predict the weather, and sometimes the future.

In traditional Māori thought, many birds were seen as chiefly and the feathers of certain birds were used as adornment for high-born people – particularly plumes worn in the hair. Chiefs wore the kahu huruhuru (feather cloak), made from the feathers of the most beautiful birds. The huia, extinct since the early 20th century, had black tail feathers with white tips, which high-ranking people wore in their hair. The group of 12 feathers from a huia's tail, usually still joined at the base, was called a mareko, and was worn by high chiefs going into battle. Huia feathers were kept in a carved wooden chest called a waka huia.

The male huia had a straight beak, while the female's was curved. One story explains its origin. A chief found a female huia in a trap, and plucked two tail feathers as plumes. He enchanted the bird so she would return when he needed more plumes. One time she arrived with feathers ruffled from sitting on her nest. Annoyed, the chief gave her a long, curved beak so she could reach her tail feathers and lift them out of the way.

TE WAONUI-A-TĀNE | THE FOREST

North Island brown kiwi

Kākāpō

Kākā

The kākā, a cheeky parrot, has red feathers under its wings. Māori associated the colour red with high rank, and only high-status people wore cloaks made with kākā feathers. Kākā were kept as pets, and were often used as decoys when fowling. The kākā has a loud, harsh call, so Māori describe talkative people as he kākā waha nui ('big-mouthed kākā') or he pane kākā ('kākā heads'). Another parrot, the flightless and nocturnal kākāpō, was used for food, and its beautiful yellow-green and brown feathers were used to make cloaks for high-born people. Kākāpō also made good pets.

A very important bird both for its feathers and as a valued food source was the kererū, New Zealand pigeon. The kererū's colourful feathers were used to make cloaks and their tail feathers adorned tahā huahua and pātua – containers for holding preserved birds.

In one tradition, the kererū's feathers were originally white. The demigod Māui wanted to find out where his mother, Taranga, went during the day. He hid her skirt to delay her, but she left anyway. Māui changed into a white kererū to follow her, still holding the skirt, which became the bird's beautiful multi-coloured plumage.

The kiwi was known as 'te manu huna a Tāne', the hidden bird of Tāne, because it came out mostly at night and was seldom seen. Kiwi meat was considered fit for chiefs. Their feathers were woven into rare, beautiful cloaks called kahu kiwi, which were considered taonga (treasures). The cloaks were used on special ceremonial occasions, such as the tangi (funeral).

This 1848 lithograph by John Gould shows a pair of huia – a male (top) and female. The huia's tail feathers were highly prized and worn by people of rank.

117

TE WAONUI-A-TĀNE | THE FOREST

Tākapu

Kōtuku

Tara

The regal-looking kōtuku (white heron) appears in a well known whakataukī, 'He kōtuku rerenga tahi' (a white heron of a single flight). This can refer to a distinguished visitor who visits only rarely. Long plumes from the kōtuku's broad wings, called piki kōtuku, were prized as head ornaments by people of high rank.

Sea birds

Tākapu (gannets) were valued for their white down and plumes. The plumes were used as hair adornments, and the soft belly feathers were made into pōhoi – feather balls worn in the ear by men and women of rank. Māori associate tara (terns) with high status because of the birds' beauty and grace. A group of chiefs might be honoured or praised as 'he tāhuna ā-tara' – a sand bank of terns. The prized white feathers of the toroa (albatross) were worn on important occasions by leading men. Toroa feathers used as plumes are known as raukura or kaiwharawhara. Soft feathers from the belly were made into pōhoi toroa – feather-ball earrings.

Birds associated with death

Some birds were linked with death and grieving. In Māori tradition, spirits leave this world at Te Rēinga in the far north. Similarly, kūaka (godwits) gather near Te Rēinga to migrate. Departing spirits are compared to kūaka in the saying 'me he kāhui kūaka' (like a flock of godwits).

To some tribes, the mātātā (fernbird) is tapu. When a chief died and was buried, men would catch a mātātā from a swamp. The bird was used in a ceremony to help lead the dead man's spirit to the legendary Polynesian homeland of Hawaiki.

The male matuku (bittern) has a loud booming cry to ward off other males in the breeding season. It was thought the matuku boomed from loneliness and sorrow, and that hearing its call could help people express grief. A lament sung by a grieving person describes the singer as a matuku:

Kei te matuku, e hū ana i te repo, i!
A bittern booming in the marsh!

The call of the moho pererū (banded rail) sometimes sounds like laughter. In one story, Māui tried to overcome death by passing through

ISLAND FEATHERS

The tail feathers of the huia, the dorsal plumes of the kōtuku, and a full headdress of albatross feathers were all known as 'te rau o Tītapu' (the feathers of Tītapu). Tītapu was said to be an island in Cook Strait that was visited by albatrosses, but has since sunk beneath the sea.

118

Tūī imitate the songs of other birds, and can also imitate people. The birds were sometimes tamed and taught to speak. They were taught mihi (greetings) which they would recite when visitors arrived, as well as prayers and proverbs. They were often trained to sound like the loud and deep voice of a chief. A tūī that spoke like this was called a manu rangatira – a chiefly bird. Sometimes a tūī was named after a tribe's famous ancestor, and kept by the chief.

Some people consider the tīwaiwaka (far left) to be a harbinger of death when seen inside a house. In one story, the bird was responsible for the death of the demigod Māui when he tried to overcome Hine-nui-te-pō, the goddess of death. It was thought that hearing the booming call of the matuku (left) could help people express grief.

the body of the sleeping goddess of death, Hine-nui-te-pō. His attempt to enter her was halted by the moho pererū, which laughed and woke the goddess. This is recalled in an old lament:

Ehara i te taru te mate.
Kua mate mai i mua, i a Māui –
Nā te pātātai i kata, ka motu ki roto rā …
Death is no light matter.
There was death in the past, with Māui –
When the pātātai (moho pererū) laughed, Māui was cut off within …

The fantail has 20 or 30 different Māori names. As well as tīwaiwaka, it is commonly called pīwakawaka, tīwakawaka or tīrairaka. In one tradition, it was the fantail that caused Māui's death, so it is a harbinger of death when seen inside a house. A fidgety person is described as a fantail's tail, because of the bird's restless movements.

Tohu – signs and predictions

The behaviour of some birds was believed to foretell the future. Their call, or arrival, was thought to bring good or bad luck.

Māori believed that the kāreke (marsh crake) could foretell the future. If someone heard the kāreke cry to their left, bad luck lay ahead; if they heard the cry on the right, it brought good luck.

Gulls evoke sun, sea and surf for both Māori and Europeans. It was thought to be a bad omen to see karoro (black-backed gulls) inland.

The kūaka (godwit) migrates north in autumn from Te Rēinga – the same place that spirits of the dead are believed to depart this world. When many people die at the same time, they are compared to a flock of kūaka leaving Te Rēinga.

TE WAONUI-A-TĀNE | THE FOREST

Kōmiromiro

Ruru

Tarāpunga

LOVE MEDICINE

The kōmiromiro (tomtit) was sometimes used as a go-between for estranged husbands and wives. The abandoned partner would consult a priest for an ātahu (love charm). It was believed that the bird would fly to the missing wife or husband and land on their head. Unable to resist the spell, they would return home. The kārearea (falcon) was also used to bring back a straying partner by dropping a feather on their head. Kōmiromiro could also be bearers of good news. An observant person was said to have 'he kanohi kōmiromiro', the eye of a tomtit, referring to the careful way the bird looked for small insects. Like kōmiromiro, pōpokotea (whiteheads) were thought to have a positive influence on people's wellbeing. In the Whanganui district they were believed to be the spirits of the dead. In other regions, they showed that spirits would soon arrive.

A person habitually living by the sea was called a 'karoro that drinks the tide'. Gulls were sometimes kept as pets – they kept garden pests under control. Tarāpunga (red-billed and black-billed gulls) are firmly entrenched in Māori lore. They were made tapu after their loud cries alerted the Te Arawa tribes to Ngāpuhi invaders paddling to Mokoia Island, and prevented a surprise attack.

Now extinct, the piopio (New Zealand thrush) was also known as tiutiu kata (laughing tiutiu) because its call sounded like ominous laughter. Hearing or seeing the bird was considered bad luck, and it was called a manu aituā – a bird of ill omen.

The ruru (morepork), New Zealand's native owl, has large, staring eyes and a mournful cry, echoed by its name. Ruru provide a rich source of symbolism for Māori. Their haunting cry and watchful nature are linked with tapu, guardianship, forewarning, grief and awareness.

The turiwhatu (dotterel) appears in a number of songs. Poets predicting a cataclysmic disaster claim that no-one will survive but the little turiwhatu. The whēkau (laughing owl), now extinct, had a call that was thought to warn of bad fortune. Its name means entrails, because it ate the entrails of the kiore, the native rat, and small birds.

TE WAONUI-A-TĀNE | THE FOREST

The call of the migratory pīpīwharauroa was a welcome signal that spring had arrived.

Tōrea

Predicting the weather

Māori observed birds carefully, and their actions were often believed to predict the weather. Māori saw hurupounamu, the now-extinct bush wren, as tapu, and believed that if one was killed, snow would fall.

The cry of the kārearea (New Zealand falcon) was believed to foretell the weather, as in the saying:

Ka tangi te kārewarewa ki waenga o te rangi pai, ka ua āpōpō.
Ka tangi ki waenga o te rangi ua, ka paki āpōpō.
When a kārearea screams in fine weather, next day there'll be rain.
When it screams in the rain, next day will be fine.

The calls of the migratory pīpīwharauroa (shining cuckoo) and koekoeā (long-tailed cuckoo) heralded the arrival of spring. These birds laid a single egg in another bird's nest. The intruder's egg hatched first, and the chick pushed the other eggs out of the nest so it was the only mouth for the parent birds to feed. A lazy, irresponsible parent was said to be like the pīpīwharauroa or the koekoeā ('ka rite koe ki te koekoeā').

The position of the riroriro's (grey warbler's) nest was believed to indicate the prevailing wind, as the nest's entrance faced away from the wind, and the riroriro's song signalled the time to plant crops. The bird is also mentioned in a saying about a lazy person who doesn't help plant the seeds, but turns up later to eat the harvest:

I whea koe i te tangihanga o te riroriro, ka mahi kai māu?
Where were you when the riroriro was singing, that you didn't work to get yourself food?

When the tōrea (pied oystercatcher) cried 'keria, keria' (dig, dig), it was seen as a sign of an approaching storm – in other words, dig for shellfish before the storm comes. After a storm, the bird is said to call 'tōkia, tōkia', meaning that calm has settled and all is well.

The call of the kārearea (New Zealand falcon) was said to foretell the weather. If the bird screamed on a fine day, there would be rain the day after – if it screamed in wet weather, the next day would be clear.

121

TE WAONUI-A-TĀNE | THE FOREST

Kōkako (right) are known for their beautiful birdsong; male and female birds sing duets. The blue wattles are said to be ears full of water which the kōkako brought for the demigod Māui.

This kawau pāteketeke (spotted shag) was photographed at Little Akaloa, Banks Peninsula. Kawau extend their necks as they prepare to fly.

Sayings, metaphors and stories

As with the trees and plants of the forest, birds were also used in whakataukī and metaphors. Often people's behaviour was compared with that of birds – favourably or unfavourably. Birds make many appearances in stories – notably those about Māui.

The kāhu (harrier) was believed to be noble like a chief, while the kārearea (New Zealand falcon) was seen as bold, assertive and treacherous. A saying suggests that people should take care to identify their allies and their enemies:

Homai te kāeaea kia toro-māhangatia
Ko te kāhu te whakaora – waiho kia rere ana!
The kārearea (falcon) must be snared
And the kāhu saved – let it fly on!

The term kawau mārō means a column of men who advance to face their enemy and perform a haka (war dance). It comes from the saying 'Ka mārō te kakī o te kawau' (the neck of the shag is stiffened), referring to the way a kawau stretches its neck before flying.

Kōkako are well known for their beautiful song. In one story, Māui asked the different birds for water. The kōkako agreed, and filled its ears with water. Māui rewarded the bird by stretching its legs so it could move with swift hops. The 'water' can be seen in the kōkako's blue wattles.

The koreke (New Zealand quail) was extinct by about 1875. When disturbed in their tussock habitat, quail fly up quickly with a whirring of feathers. Māori likened this to a sudden encounter with an enemy. The koreke's frightened response is described in the saying:

Whiti koreke, ka kitea koe!
Haere whakaparirau i a koe, haere whakamanu.
The koreke springs up – you're found!
Go get yourself wings, go turn into a bird.

Great singers and orators were praised by being compared to the korimako (bellbird), a beautiful singer.

He rite ki te kōpara e kō nei i te ata.
Just like a korimako singing at dawn.

Māori admired the kōtare (kingfisher) for being like a watchful sentry. The bird perches motionless, then attacks its prey in a sudden blur. The word kōtare sometimes referred to the elevated platform in a pā used to watch for enemies.

The moa, a large flightless bird, became extinct centuries ago. Knowledge of moa was passed down through stories, songs and whakataukī. One saying, lamenting the death of many people, is 'Kua ngaro i te ngaro o te moa' (we are lost, lost like the moa).

The way the pārera (grey duck) feeds is compared to a greedy person's behaviour, in the saying 'He pārera apu kai' (the duck is a gross feeder).

Hauraki legend compared Pāoa, an important chief, to the poaka (pied stilt) because his dignified bearing and long strides were like the bird's.

Ka kohure a Pāoa, me te turuturu-pourewa te āhua e haere atu ana.
Pāoa was taller than any of them, walking along like a poaka.

Pūkeko were known for their bold scheming and determination – they raided gardens for kūmara (sweet potato) and taro. A stubborn, annoying person was compared to the bird, and was said to have pūkeko ears (taringa pākura).

One tradition explains the origin of the pūkeko's red bill. When Tāwhaki, a handsome high chief, lay dead and bleeding, his blood marked the pūkeko's bill.

Weka are inquisitive birds, a trait which makes them easy to catch. A saying about weka questions whether a person will make the same mistake twice:

Makere te weka i te māhanga e hoki anō?
Will a weka that has escaped the snare return?

TE WAONUI-A-TĀNE | THE FOREST

Pītoitoi *Kākāriki*

WHAT'S IN A NAME?

The male kiwi's cry was said to be 'koire' or 'hoire', and the female's was 'poāi'. The shrill whistle of the male calling its mate sounded like 'kiwi' – so this may be the origin of its name. Others believe that the kiwi's name is adapted from kivi, the bristle-thighed curlew, which early Māori settlers may have remembered from their Polynesian homeland. The call of the pītoitoi (robin) sounded like pi-toi-toi-toi. It was also known as karuwai (water eye) because of its watery eyes. The bird's call was thought to bring good or bad news, depending on the time and place.

Birds' names

Māori often named birds after their call, their plumage or their behaviour. In one of the many stories about the demigod Māui, the hihi (stitchbird) refused to fetch water for him after he had captured the sun and slowed it down. Māui threw the bird into the fire, burning its feathers. Hihi means rays of the sun, and the bird's name refers to the male's yellow breast plumage – a reminder of sun and fire.

The giant hōkioi (Haast's eagle) is extinct, and known only through oral tradition. The hōkioi was seldom seen, and its cry was considered a bad omen. The bird's name sounds like its call: 'Hōkioi, hōkioi, hu!' In the south, it was known as Te Pouākai.

Kākā means parrot, and riki means little. The saying 'He kākāriki kai ata' (a kākāriki eating in the morning) refers to a person who acts like the kākāriki, eating greedily in the morning before working.

The name of the kea sounds like its call – 'keee aaa'. Although the meat of this mountain parrot was tough and lean, it was included in the Māori diet. The Waitaha tribe believed that kea, along with the kāhu and ruru, were kaitiaki (guardians) of their people.

The name of the kuruwhengu (shoveler) means 'snuffle'. It refers to their method of feeding as they up-end in shallow water. The pāpango's (scaup's) name refers to its dark plumage – as does another of its names, matapōuri (dark face).

The pīhoihoi (pipit) was believed to be noisy; hoihoi means 'Be quiet'. Another of its names, whioi, means whistler.

The takahē was believed to be extinct until it was rediscovered in 1948. It was known as a solitary bird – hence its other name, moho (hermit). The takahē's night cry was described by Māori as sounding like two pieces of pounamu struck together.

TE WAONUI-A-TĀNE | THE FOREST

This artwork by John Bevan Ford depicts the bird known as Te Hōkioi, or Te Pouākai in the south – the extinct Haast's eagle. The bird weighed up to 13 kilograms, with a wing span up to 3 metres.

The whio (below left), gets its name from the distinctive whistling call of the male. Whio means whistle in Maori. The name of the hoiho (below right), also comes from its call.

Tētē whero (brown teal) comes from 'tētē', the Māori rendition of the ducks' quacking, and whero (red) referring to their reddish-brown plumage.

The name tīeke (saddleback) sounds like the birds' call when disturbed. Another name, tīeke rere, comes from their cry when alarmed.

The rifleman is called tītiti pounamu. Tītiti refers to the bird's high-pitched call, while pounamu probably describes the male's bright green feathers. Because tītiti pounamu often lived in beech forest, they were also known as momo-tawai (the beech-tree species).

Whio (blue duck) live in turbulent white-water rivers and remote high-country waterways. They are named for the male's call – whio means whistle in Māori.

The name of the hoiho (yellow-eyed penguin) comes from its call. The pokotiwha (Fiordland crested penguin) is named for its yellow crest and eyebrow stripes (poko means head, tiwha means gleaming). The name of the kororā (blue penguin) is probably a rendition of one of its calls.

The kea (mountain parrot) got its name from its screeching call, 'keee aa'. The Waitaha people of the South Island believed it to be a kaitiaki (guardian).

TE WAONUI-A-TĀNE | THE FOREST

This is the wētā punga (Cook Strait giant wētā). All wētā were considered repulsive, and the wētā punga especially so – it was named after the 'ugly god' Punga.

Te aitanga pepeke *the insect world*
Bradford Haami

Why do sandflies bite us so fiercely? They are taking revenge on Tū, the god of humankind, for killing Namuiria, the first sandfly. Midges, moths, cicadas, mosquitoes and other insects feature in many traditional Māori stories, especially the battles fought by Tāne, guardian of the forest and its tiny creatures.

What is te aitanga pepeke?

'Te aitanga pepeke' refers to a wide range of insects and other creatures in the Māori world that share certain features: they have four or more legs, sit in a crouching position, and some can leap or jump. Mosquitoes, butterflies and moths, spiders and sandflies belong to this group.
The words used for this group of creatures refer to their characteristics:
- The root word 'peke' means to spring, leap or jump.
- Pepeke means to move quickly, and is used for the whole group of insects.
- Pēpeke (the first 'e' is long) means to draw up the legs or arms, or to crouch.

Whiro, Tāne and the army of insects

The insect world features in the Māori creation stories, particularly those about the rival brothers Tāne and Whiro (god of the underworld).
  In the narratives of the Wairarapa region, Whiro competed with Tāne to obtain the three baskets of sacred knowledge from the heavens. He sent

This pare (lintel, below) hangs over the entrance to the New Zealand arthropod collection (Te aitanga a pepeke o Aotearoa), at the Mt Albert Research Centre in Auckland. Featuring a unique mix of contemporary and traditional aspects, it was carved by Denis Conway, a student of the late Henare Toka, from 100-year-old recycled kauri wood. The traditional style of the Ngāti Whātua people is combined with contemporary features, including realistic creatures such as a spider and dragonfly – unusual in Māori carving.

The odd-looking giraffe weevil (above) may have been the 'pepeke-matarūwai' (insect with a silly face) in the tradition about Tāne fetching the baskets of knowledge.

a war party of insects – namu poto (small sandflies), naonao (midges), rō (stick insects), peketua (centipedes), pepe-te-nuinui (butterflies), and pekepeke-haratua (hopping things of the May season), as well as birds and bats. His aim was for them to pursue Tāne, strike his head and kill him, but they could not get close enough – Tāne called on the winds, who spun the army in circles.

Having gained the baskets of knowledge, Tāne descended to the heaven known as Rangi-te-wanawana, only to be met by Whiro and a war party of beetles, including pekepeke-matarūwai (beetle with a silly face), pekepeke-haurutua (beetle with dew on it), pekepeke-harakuku (scraping beetle) and pekepeke-matanui (beetle with large face).

Tāne also defeated this army, and took Whiro's army of birds and insects down to earth as prisoners. Among them were waeroa (mosquitoes), namu poto, naonao, rō, wētā, pepe (moths and butterflies), rango (blowflies) and kāwhitiwhiti (grasshoppers). There they dwelt among the trees under the care of Tāne, whose domain was the forests.

In this artwork by Robert Jahnke, the god Tāne is attacked by insects as he retrieves the three baskets of knowledge from the heavens. The insects were sent by his brother Whiro, who wanted the baskets for himself. Tāne repelled their attacks by calling on the wind to blow them away.

TE WAONUI-A-TĀNE | THE FOREST

SUMMER BUGS

Māori know the bright star Antares as Rehua. It was linked with summer, when it became visible. 'Ngā manu a Rehua' (Rehua's birds) is a term for the winged insects that appear in summer, such as kēkerewai, a small green beetle found on mānuka trees, and tūtaeruru, a night-flying beetle.

The huhu beetle's larva was engulfed by the ocean when Tangaroa, the god of the sea, waged war on Tāne, god of the forests.

In the Māori world view, pūngāwerewere (spiders) were also insects. This is a Nelson cave spider on the wall of a cave near Karamea on the West Coast.

Tāne and Tangaroa

Tāne also battled with his brother Tangaroa, god of the sea. Tangaroa's ocean-dwelling children included the families of lizards and fish. When Tāwhirimātea, the wind god, attacked the sea with storms, the fish decided to stay there, but the lizards moved into the forests. In retaliation Tangaroa waged war by wearing away the land with large oceans that swept away the forests, drowning birds and insects. Inside the broken tree trunks were two of Tāne's descendants – tātaka, the larva of the huhu beetle, and pepe (a butterfly). Tangaroa engulfed them, casting them to the hungry mouths of the fish. Tāne struck back – he allowed the trees to be made into canoes, hooks and spears, so that humans could snare and catch fish, the sons of Tangaroa.

Insects and canoes

Insects play a role in two traditional stories of voyaging canoes. The first is about respecting nature, and the second explains how insects came to New Zealand.

Rātā and the multitude

'Te Tini o Hakuturi' means 'the multitude of bow-legged ones', which included insects, birds and fairy spirits. They had the task of avenging any desecration of the forest's sacredness.

An old tradition tells of a man named Rātā, who did not say the required incantations before he felled a large tree in the forest, cutting off its branches to make a canoe from the trunk. The insects and birds were

TE WAONUI-A-TĀNE | THE FOREST

...hukura is a general name for butterfly, while pūrerehua ...n mean butterfly or moth. Of the Māori names that ...ve been collected for insects, the greatest number refer ... butterflies and moths (including larvae and pupae).

This beautifully carved taurapa (sternpost) is part of the renowned waka *Te Toki a Tapiri*. In one tradition, spiders were said to have carved the stern and prow of the first waka. That is why the web-like spiral form (known as mata kupenga) features so prominently on the stern and prow of many canoes.

angry, and after Rātā had retired for the day, they raised the tree up again, calling on all the branches and broken pieces to bind together. Twice Rātā felled the tree, and twice the multitude of Hakuturi raised it up.

Finally Rātā hid, and saw the forest creatures raising the tree. He accused them of interfering in his work. The creatures asked him, 'What authority do you have to fell the forest god to the ground? You had no right to do so.' Rātā was so overcome with shame and remorse that Te Tini o Hakuturi told him they would build him a canoe, if he returned to his village. The ornamental stern and prow of the vessel were carved by the spiders (pūngāwerewere).

This story is one of many throughout Polynesia that explain proper conduct. It emphasises the importance of paying respect to your kinsfolk and the forest trees, and the importance of placating the spirit world before taking something from nature.

How insects arrived in New Zealand

A Ngāti Porou tribal account describes how the *Māngārara* canoe, led by Wheketoro and other chiefs, brought insects and reptiles to New Zealand from Polynesia. On board were the insect family of weri (centipedes), whē (caterpillars) and other crawling species, and the reptile family, including teretere (geckos) and tuatara. The *Māngārara* left Hawaiki, the traditional homeland of Māori, and came to Whanga-o-keno Island on the East Cape. Before travelling on to the mainland, Wheketoro left most of his insect and reptile passengers on the island, to save them from 'the plundering propensity of man'.[2]

BITERS ON BOARD

In one tradition, an ancestor named Manaia brought the namu (sandfly) and waeroa (mosquito), whose bites cause intense itching, to New Zealand on his canoe. He did this as an act of revenge against some of the tribes who had not invited him to join in their hākari (feasts). He released them in the Bay of Islands, in the north, and from there they are said to have spread far and wide.

129

After the eggs of the pūriri moth hatch, the larvae gnaw into the trunks of trees such as the pūriri and tītoki. They live on the sap, eventually causing the tree's death – hence the saying 'he iti mokoroa e hinga pūriri' (the little mokoroa grub fells a pūriri tree). This reminds people that small things can have a big impact.

The giant pūriri moth (below) has huge, bright green wings that may span 15 centimetres.

PEPETUNA

According to a Ngāti Kahungunu tradition, an ancestor named Hinepeke (jumping woman) married Tūteahuru, a grandson of Tāne. They produced a vast number of insects and lizards that dwell within the earth, on the land or stones, and in the water.

One descendant was the pepetuna, commonly known as the pūriri moth or ghost moth, a parasite of pūriri trees. Because it flies at dusk and into the night, commonly regarded as the realm of spirits, the pepetuna was known as a spiritual messenger, or a ghost of an ancestor returning to visit his or her descendants.

Pepetuna means 'eel moth': the caterpillars were used as bait for eels. The term could also refer to the fact they are eaten by migrating eels that head for the sea on rainy nights, between September and January, when the moths lay their eggs as they fly through the forest. They then die, falling to the forest floor.

Moths

The origins of many insects are explained in tribal narratives and whakapapa. The Ngāti Awa tribe have a whakapapa for the kūmara and the caterpillars that live on it. For example, according to the Ngāti Awa whakapapa concerning the origin of the kūmara, Whānui (the star Vega) is known as the celestial parent of the kūmara. One day, Whānui's younger brother Rongomāui stole some kūmara tubers and took them to the earth as a food source for mankind. Whānui was so angered that he sent three creatures, Anuhe, Toronū and Moko, down to earth in punishment for the theft. Ever since then, they have ravaged the leaves of the kūmara. They are all the caterpillars of the kūmara moth.

Mosquitoes and sandflies

In a whakapapa from the Tūhoe region, certain insects originate from Haumia, god of the bracken fern rarauhe and its edible root, aruhe. Haumia gave rise to te mōnehu (the fine, rusty fern spores), who produced the biting insects waeroa and namu, along with rōtāne (male mantis), pūngāwerewere and other insects.

TE WAONUI-A-TĀNE | THE FOREST

```
                    Haumia
                      |
                  Te Mōnehu
    ┌─────────────┬──┴──┬─────────────┐
   Namu         Wairoa  Aruhe          Rō
  Sandflies    Mosquitos Fern root   Stick insects
```

Haumia (above) is the god of bracken fern and its edible root, aruhe. Among other creatures, a large number of insects are said to descend from him. See the whakapapa of Haumia (left).

A rō (stick insect, above left) seeks to disguise itself on a leaf of harakeke (flax).

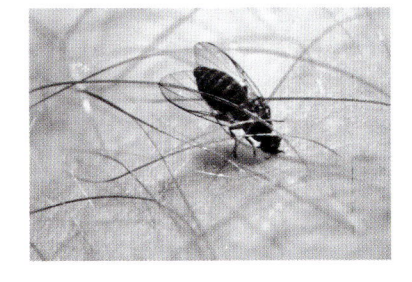

Namu (sandflies, above) and waeroa (mosquitoes) made war on the god Tūmatauenga by attacking people – sandflies chose to attack by day.

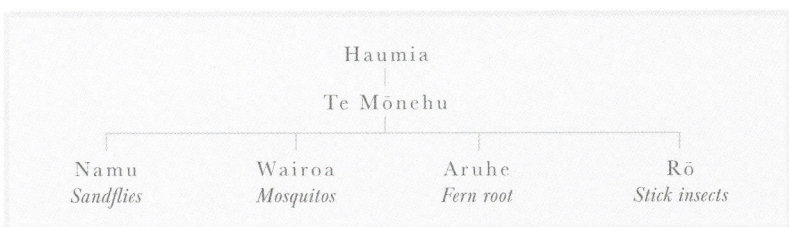

These creatures are strongly associated with their fern habitat, which sheltered them. Also, to relieve the intensely itchy bite of the mosquito and sandfly, Māori would rub moisture from the bruised fronds of the bracken fern onto the skin.

An old tradition explains the origins of the fierce bite of these insects. The god of humans, Tūmatauenga (Tū), killed Namuiria, the first sandfly, when the creature stole his spiritual essence. In retaliation, the tribes of Waeroa (mosquitoes) and Namu (sandflies) attacked the sons of Tū – humankind. Waeroa suggested striking at night, as his army might perish in the daylight. But Namu said, 'Let us fight in the light of day. I am going while it's light. Although I will die in great numbers, what does it matter, so long as his blood flows? If you attack at night, when the fires are burning, you will be smothered in smoke.'

The army of sandflies set out in daylight and were defeated by Tū, dying in their thousands. Waeroa observed their downfall and commented in a song that it was better for the mosquito to wait for the darkness of night and hum in the ears of humans, even though he might be suffocated with smoke. The sandfly repeated, 'What does it matter, brother, if I am killed, as long his blood gushes forth? None but the offspring of Mahuika [fire] shall stop me from fighting. Only then will I flee, and you will run too.' That is why the sandfly bites in the daytime, and the mosquito at night.

Patupaiarehe

Martin Wikaira

In the misty mountain tops or deep in the forests lived the patupaiarehe – fairy-like beings who were seldom seen. They could lure people away from safety with the music of their flutes, and had magical powers and special knowledge. Some believe that red-haired Māori are their descendants.

In Māori tradition patupaiarehe, also known as tūrehu and pakepakehā, were fairy-like creatures of the forests and mountain tops. Although they had some human attributes, patupaiarehe were regarded not as people but as supernatural beings (he iwi atua).

They were seldom seen, and an air of mystery and secrecy still surrounds them. In most traditions, those who encountered patupaiarehe were able to understand their language. But in one account they were unintelligible.

Patupaiarehe had light skin, and red or fair hair. Historian James Cowan was told that 'they were a lighter complexion than Maori; their hair was of a dull golden or reddish hue, *urukehu*, such as is sometimes seen in Maori of today.'[1]

Unlike Māori, they were never tattooed. Mohi Tūrei of Ngāti Porou described their skin as white, albino or the colour of red ochre. Their eye colour varied from light blue to black.

TE WAONUI-A-TĀNE | THE FOREST

Patupaiarehe, also known as tūrehu and pakepakehā, were fairy-like beings who were believed to live in the forests, hills and mountains. They often had blonde hair and played kōauau or pūtōrino (flutes). Although this patupaiarehe is blue, their skin colour was described as white or red.

Forest near Rotorua

The pūtōrino is a type of flute which, along with the kōauau, was played expertly by patupaiarehe. It is said that while playing their music they were able to lure young women into their clutches.

NAMING MOUNTAINS

The explorer Īhenga became thirsty while climbing a mountain in Rotorua, and a patupaiarehe woman gave him a drink from a calabash. So he named the mountain Ngongotahā ('drink from a calabash'). In another story the mountain Mauao, in Tauranga, was rejected by the beautiful mountain Pūwhenua. The lovelorn mountain asked his patupaiarehe friends to drag him to the sea. As they did so, the dawn rose, forcing them to flee. Stranded at the water's edge, the mountain became known as Mauao ('caught at dawn').

There is still debate about their height. The Tūhoe tribe records that they were small, but others say they were similar in size to humans. Whanganui stories claim them to be giants, more than 2 metres tall.

Patupaiarehe were generally found deep in the forests, or on mist-covered hilltops. In these isolated places they settled and built their homes, sometimes described as forts. In some stories their houses and pā were built from swirling mist. In others, they were made from kareao (supplejack vine).

In the North Island they were said to live mainly in the Waikato–Waipā basin, the Cape Colville–Te Aroha range, the hills about Rotorua, the Urewera ranges and Wairoa districts, and the Waitākere Ranges in the Auckland region.

South Island traditions had them living mainly in the hills around Lyttelton Harbour, Akaroa and the Tākitimu Range, and in the hills between the Arahura River and Lake Brunner.

Patupaiarehe were said to be expert net makers. In this artwork by Brian Flintoff, 'Patupaiarehe making nets and dreaming fish into them', the patupaiarehe are on either side of the net, catching many different types of fish.

HOW MĀORI CAME TO USE A NET FOR FISHING

One traditional account tells of a chief, Kahukura, who when travelling north found himself on a lonely beach just as night set in. He slept in the sand dunes, but was awoken by the sounds of voices and laughter. At the water's edge a group of patupaiarehe were catching great numbers of fish in a net of woven flax. Despite his fear Kahukura crept among them, hoping to take the net and find out how it was made. As it was dark, and he was short and fair like the patupaiarehe, they did not notice him as being different. He knew that if he could delay them until dawn they would flee to avoid the sun, leaving the net behind. He helped thread the gutted fish onto lines, but tied his knots so they would come undone again. This tactic worked, and the fairy people fled as the sun rose. From this Kahukura discovered the secret to making the net, and taught it to his people.

What kind of people were they?

Patupaiarehe society was kinship-based, similar to Māori society. In 1894 Hoani Nahe, an elder of the Ngāti Maru people, recalled three sub-tribes of patupaiarehe: Ngāti Kura, Ngāti Korakorako and Ngāti Tūrehu. Tahurangi, Whanawhana and Nukupori were important chiefs. They were generally a closed group who shunned intruders, and were unfriendly to those who ventured into their midst.

Patupaiarehe were hunters and gatherers, surviving on raw forest foods and sometimes fishing from the shores of the sea or a lake. Their canoes were made of kōrari (flax stalks). Cooked food was offensive or foul to them. In different traditions, albino birds and eels, red flax and red eels were considered their property, and trouble befell Māori who took any of these.

Fearing the light, they were active mainly in the twilight hours and at night, or when the mist was heavy enough to shield them. They wore flax garments (pākērangi), dyed red, but also rough mats (pora or pūreke). They were also known for playing kōauau and pūtōrino (flutes).

Ponaturi

Ponaturi are sometimes described as sea fairies. They had red hair and white skin, and fingers with long, evil claws. They spent their days under the sea, only coming onto land at night. Like the patupaiarehe they feared sunlight and fire. One tradition tells of Tāwhaki taking revenge on the ponaturi for killing his father. He tricked them into staying in his house after dawn. Then he and his brother opened the doors and windows to let light flood into the house, in order to kill their captives.

Encounters with patupaiarehe

Patupaiarehe were known to lure people, especially attractive women, to their midst. A patupaiarehe would use hypnotic magical sounds from his flute to lure a young woman to his side, and then take her back to his camp. There he would make love to her before taking her home. The spell he had cast on her meant that he could call her at any time and she would be compelled to return to him.

The urukehu (red-heads) and albinos among Māori were said to be the descendants of such unions of patupaiarehe and mortal women. Men who were captured were either mistreated and then released, or killed.

TE WAONUI-A-TĀNE | THE FOREST

This photograph is from *The old-time Maori* (1938), by Mākereti Papakura. She notes that the blonde, fair child and the father, Tonihi (right), are both Urukehu.

PĀKEHĀ

Pakepakehā is another name for patupaiarehe. It may have given rise to the term Pākehā (a New Zealander of European descent). To Māori, Europeans resembled the pakepakehā or patupaiarehe, with their fair skin and light-coloured hair.

Warding them off

There were different methods of avoiding the sometimes evil intentions of the patupaiarehe. Homes would be smeared with kōkōwai (iron oxide mixed with shark oil) when patupaiarehe were known to be close. Also the cooking ovens were put into operation. The smell coming from both the kōkōwai and cooked food was repugnant to patupaiarehe, and kept them at bay. Patupaiarehe were also afraid of the light of open fires, so as long as the campfire was still glowing at night, people considered themselves safe. Young children too were warned not to stray from the village 'in case the patupaiarehe gets you'.

Miru

A patupaiarehe named Miru is credited with giving Māori the sacred knowledge and wisdom of his mysterious world. Married to a mortal woman, Miru took his father-in-law to his world and taught him these things. In this way the rites of mākutu (magic arts), ātahu (love charms) and other priestly skills were passed on to the Māori world. Miru's people also taught the visitors whai (string games) and tititorea (stick games).

Several parts of the North Island were renowned haunts of patupaiarehe. One favoured lair was Moehau (below), a hilltop where they were reputed to inhabit a large fortified pā in the swirling mists.

These children hold different forms of whai (cat's cradle), a well-known traditional pastime. It has been said that it was patupaiarehe who passed their knowledge of whai to Māori.

135

PART V

Te mahinga kai
food gathering

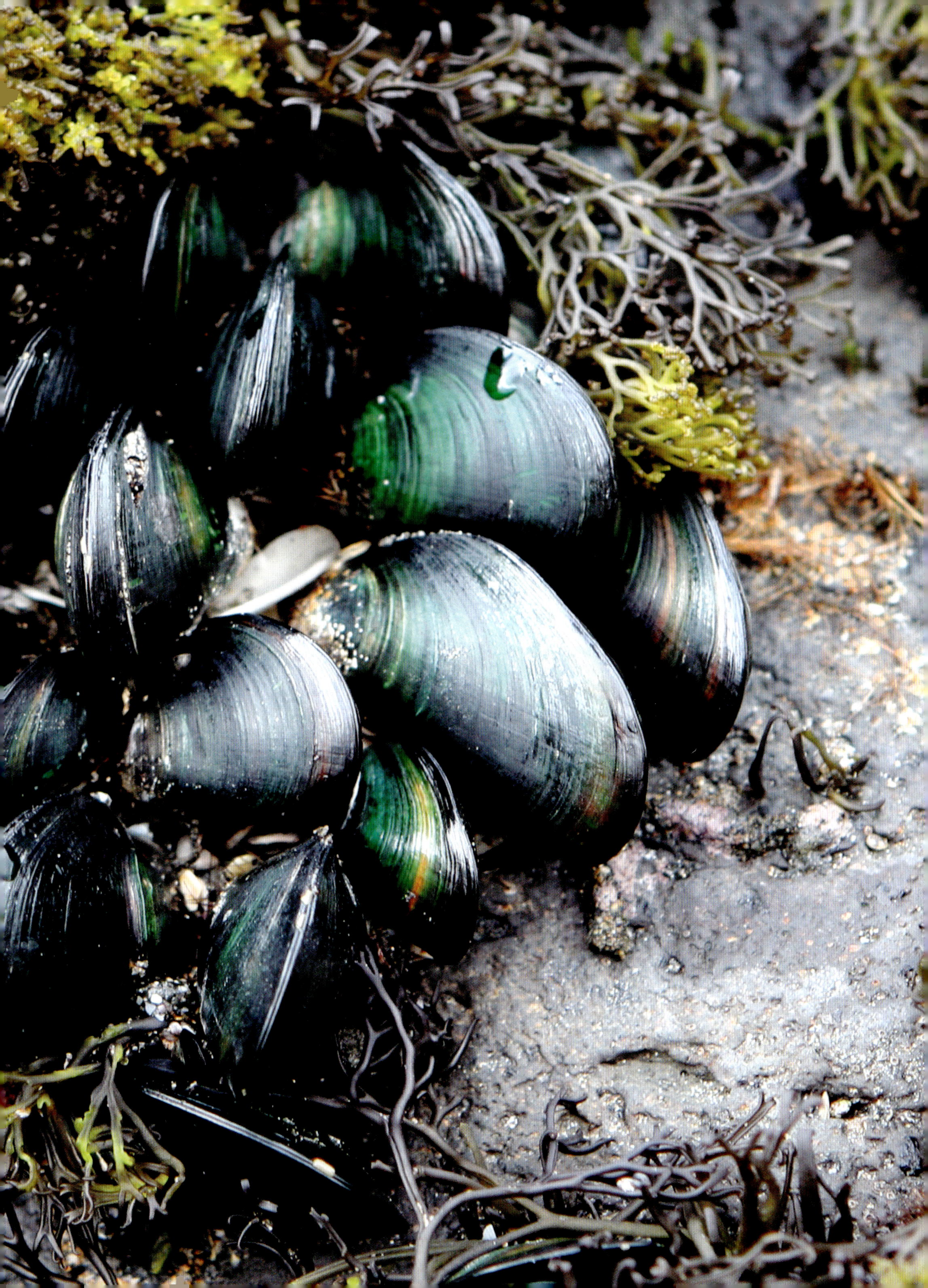

TE MAHINGA KAI | FOOD GATHERING

Te hī ika *Māori fishing*
Paul Meredith

Traditional fishing was both a practical and a spiritual activity. There were many ingenious methods and tools, from complex calendars to iridescent lures and woven traps. But fish were also seen as the descendants of Tangaroa, god of the sea. Rituals and talismans were an important way to ensure his favour and protect the bounty of the ocean, lakes and rivers.

An array of Polynesian fishing equipment was adapted for conditions in New Zealand: the kupenga (net), aho (line), matau (hook), matira (fishing rod), pātia (spear), tāruke (pot), hīnaki (trap) and pā (weir).

The construction of nets was a tapu activity – certain rituals and restrictions had to be followed. Most nets were made of green flax, and they ranged in size from individual tītoko ika (hand nets) to very large kaharoa (seine nets). The base was weighed down with māhē (stone sinkers), and gourds or light woods were sometimes used as pōito (floats).

The largest net documented was made in 1886 by Te Pōkiha Taranui (also known as Major Fox) and 400 others of Ngāti Pikiao, at Maketū in the Bay of Plenty. About 1.6 kilometres long, it was used only once to procure tens of thousands of fish for a major tribal gathering. Handling such nets required community effort.

Lines and hooks were very popular for catching hapuku and kahawai. The lines were very strong, and made of dressed flax fibre that was twisted into cord.

Māori fashioned fish hooks from ngāruru (Cook's turban), a common coastal sea snail, as its thick shell could be worked into a strong point or even an entire hook.

Photographed at Waiapu on the North Island's East Coast, Te Rangi Hīroa (Peter Buck), the Ngāti Mutunga anthropologist, measures a tāruke kōura (crayfish pot) with two kaumātua.

TE MAHINGA KAI | FOOD GATHERING

Displayed left are a number of matau (fish hooks) from various tribes. The materials include bone, wood, and pāua shell.

Māori used a number of nets and pots to catch fish and eels. On the tree is a tāruke kōura – a pot for catching crayfish. On the ground in front of it are a hīnaki (eel trap) and a tītoko ika (hand net). In the background is a kupenga (fishing net).

In the early stages of constructing a kupenga, loops are made on a supporting stand. In this instance, the mesh is being gauged by the anthropologist Te Rangi Hīroa (Peter Buck).

Hooks varied in size and shape and were made from wood, bone, stone or shell. Sometimes a gorge was used. This was a sharp piece of bone on a line, which caught in a fish's throat when pulled. To attract kahawai, iridescent pāua shell was used on lures.

Pātiki (flounder) were sometimes caught with barbed spears similar to those used for hunting birds.

Tāruke filled with bait were used to catch crayfish. The pots were made from young mānuka stems, which were bent around a frame of supplejack vine and mānuka, and then tied with flax and vines.

Traditional fishing grounds

All fishing grounds, banks and rocks were specially named. Some were several kilometres out to sea – the historian Rēweti Kōhere of the Ngāti Porou tribe wrote that his ancestors' favourite ground was Hapurapoi, about 12 kilometres north of East Cape. Fishermen used prominent landmarks to identify these spots, taking their bearings by aligning one mountain or peninsula with another:

TE MAHINGA KAI | FOOD GATHERING

This 1850 watercolour by Charles Heaphy depicts a fishing camp, with large tents and a drying rack for the fish. Dominating the background is the cone of Auckland's dormant volcanic island, Rangitoto.

Photographed in 1907, these people are cleaning fish during a fishing expedition at Pārengarenga in Northland. As the large number of children indicates, this type of fishing involved the entire whānau.

From the sea, look at the white cliffs on shore. A vein of quartz can be seen sparkling in the rocks. Now look towards your port side, the island of Murimotu appears to move and join the mainland. No sea-space is seen between. That is your spot.[1]

Most fishing grounds were jealously guarded by tribes, who passed them down through the generations. To define family and hapū rights, they sometimes used rows of stakes, particularly in lakes, estuaries and other shoal waters.

When to fish

Experts knew all the signs for successful fishing, and used a calendar that listed favourable days (see also pages 20–21). This is still in use today. Often, fishing would be directed by chiefs occupying prominent land points, identifying which grounds were to be fished. These experts knew the movements and seasons of the various fish species. Tāmati Poata of the Ngāti Porou tribe recorded that on the East Coast during March, April and May the seasonable fish is tāmure (snapper). In June and July it is the warehou and moki. In August, September and October it is tarakihi, pōrae (trumpeter fish), rāwaru or taipua (rock cod), kehe (marble fish) and kumukumu (gurnard). South Island fishermen would troll for barracouta, catch small sharks in large nets, big sharks with large baited hooks, and conger eels at sea with a bob made of dressed flax around a bait called a whakapuku. Crayfish were caught in open-mouthed net bags called poraka, and whitebait in a koko – a close-weave net.

Photographed in 1902, these fishermen and their families pose behind their catch of tāmure (snapper) at Whangaroa. After drying on the pole, the fish are packed into kete (baskets).

Traditional practices

Religious rites and other marks of respect were integral to the practice of fishing. Karakia (incantations) were offered to Tangaroa, god of the sea, and the other gods, inviting them to send an abundance of fish. Mohi Ruatapu of the Ngāti Porou tribe cites this karakia, chanted to inspire Tangaroa:

> Kuku, kuku ika, kuku wehiwehi,
> Takina ko koe nā, te iho o ika,
> Te iho o Tangaroa –
> Uara ki uta rā, uara ki tai rā.
> *Hold tight, hold the fish, hold tight with fearsome power,*
> *You are led along, the essence of the fish,*
> *The essence of Tangaroa –*
> *Desired on the land, desired on the sea.* [2]

It was common practice to return the first fish that was caught to the sea. Many tribes also had sites on shore where fishermen would place their offerings of fish to Tangaroa, and recite karakia of thanks.

Māori also used a mauri (talisman) to attract fish. At Mōkau Heads in north Taranaki is the historic punga (anchor stone) of the *Tainui* canoe. The stone has long been considered the mauri of the fisheries in that region, assuring a bountiful supply of all varieties of fish. It also served to safeguard the fisheries. Not too far along the beach is Te Naenae, where local fishermen once made offerings of fish to Tangaroa.

The 20th century

Traditional fishing customs were still being followed in the 20th century. This account from the 1950s describes the rituals used for fishing kahawai in the Waiapu River, in the Ngāti Porou tribal district.

> When the net is complete, a fishing line is threaded through the outside loops of the net. This is known as the 'heart of the fishing net'. After this the net is hung up and a weight placed in the bottom of it to help to tighten the mesh ties. Then a length of red mānuka pole is fashioned and some supplejacks. These are dried and made into an oval frame

PROHIBITIONS

Use of the waters was also regulated by customary law and practices. Catching many species was limited by season, as was the use of some fishing grounds. One form of prohibition was the rāhui, set up to conserve endangered species and protect certain fishing grounds from being overfished.

Tapu surrounded almost all aspects of fishing, as the fisheries were so closely linked to the gods. The success of an expedition depended on strict adherence to the religious restrictions that ensured the favour of the gods. It was believed that food, especially if cooked, could pollute the tapu, with distrastrous effects. The tapu remained until it was removed by a tohunga back on shore.

TE MAHINGA KAI | FOOD GATHERING

TRIBAL EXPEDITIONS

Traditional Māori fishing included large-scale tribal expeditions. One expedition in 1855 by the Te Rarawa people, led by the chief Popota Te Waha, involved more than 1000 individuals in 50 canoes, and lasted over two days.

The fish caught from such communal efforts were divided by the leading chief among each whānau. The fish were then either steamed in a hāngī or hung up on a scaffold to dry in the sun, and saved in pātaka (storehouses) for future consumption.

Te Kaha locals prepare fish for a hāngī. This method of cooking is more usually associated with meat and vegetables.

according to the size of the net. At this stage the new net is ready to be taken to the beach where it is fixed on to the framework.

Before entering the water, the fisherman performs a special rite by urinating on the net and sprinkling some too over his body. Only after this ritual will he enter the water. This ritual is still performed today.

When the first fish is caught, the head is broken off so that the blood spills over the net, after which the fish is hung up on a stake well ashore. That particular fish is not eaten. Then one may proceed to fish. Only after performing the above ritual is the tapu of a new net lifted. (With an old net the urination ritual only is performed.) Sharks and other destructive creatures of the sea will not enter the net.

After having fished the required number, the fish must not be scaled at or near the fishing area. Rather this must be done elsewhere. If scaling is to be done at home, then this must be done outside to avoid contamination by cooked food.[3]

Many people believe that fishing was a task for men, while women collected shellfish. However, there is some disagreement about this.

Communal sharing and gifting
Gift exchange

Sometimes fish were caught for gift exchange with inland tribes. Coastal people gave dried fish, dried edible seaweed and shark oil to those who lived in forests, who reciprocated with preserved birds, rats, hīnau berry cakes, and other food from their domain.

Occasionally the gifting of fish took place as part of a feast, which could be particularly grand when different tribes came together. At a feast prepared by Te Waharoa of Ngāti Hauā in 1837, 20,000 dried eels and several tonnes of fish were presented to the guests. In 1844, 9,000 sharks were laid out at a feast given by the great Waikato chief Pōtatau Te Wherowhero at Remuera.

In the South Island, where similar exchanges occurred, an account of the Ngāi Tahu people who lived on Banks Peninsula has been recorded:

At Pigeon Bay they used to catch large numbers of fish which they suspended in the sun to dry. Shark was one of their favourites. It was customary in the 'forties' [1840s] for the Pigeon Bay and Port Levy Maoris to carry tons of these dried fish inland, meeting halfway the Natives from Little River laden with eels. On the summit both parties held a korero, and after exchanging their burdens, returned respectively to their homes.[4]

European contact and impact

Many early European arrivals in New Zealand noted the teeming fish in coastal waters and commented on Māori expertise and industry in fishing. Captain James Cook, when comparing these skills to those on his ship, wrote in 1773: '[W]e were by no means such expert fishers as them, nor were any of our methods of fishing equal to theirs.'[5]

Trade with settlers

As a trading economy developed with the emergent townships, Māori fishing continued during early European settlement. Initially Māori

These sketches from 1864 show fishermen involved in various activities at Onehunga, including two carrying a pole of fish.

supplied nearly all the fish to the settlers of Auckland, Wellington and Otago. Attorney general William Swainson noted that during 1852, 1792 canoes entered the harbour of Auckland, bringing to market 45 tons of fish, along with other produce.

Decline of Māori fishing

During the time of European settlement, Māori society was undergoing major change. Large-scale fishing became less common as tribes lost land adjoining tribal fisheries, and had greater choices for food and work. Contributing to this decline was the growing European focus on commercial fisheries, the decline of fish stocks, and laws that regulated fishing. Those Māori who worked as commercial fishermen were mostly part-timers, supplementing income derived from the land.

Fish remained a part of the Māori diet however – especially at tangi (funerals) and other special gatherings. Customary fishing continued, but on a reduced scale. Māori became increasingly displeased about the decline of their fisheries. In 1991 Mere Hutcheson of Pōrangahau recalled her childhood, when she would gather a wide variety of shellfish such as pūpū, kina, pāua and kuku:

> The old people used to go or send us young ones to the beach … You used to get a lot of those things, but not today. Now we've got no karengo [edible seaweed], it's hard to get kōura [crayfish]. We use to bring all those things home and Mum use to show us how to dry them. When we got a lot of fish we use to wrap it up in karamu [leaves] and put it in the hāngī. That's what they use to do, dry eels and dry crayfish, but not today. As the years went by, everything changed – it's not the same.[6]

THEIRS IS BIGGER THAN OURS

Fishing nets made by Māori could be gigantic. Joseph Banks, on Captain Cook's voyage, noted on 4 December 1769 that Bay of Islands Māori were amused by the small size of the *Endeavour*'s seine net: '[A]fter having a little laught at our seine, which was a common kings seine, [they] shewd us one of theirs which was 5 fathom deep [9 metres] and its lengh we could only guess, as it was not stretchd out, but it could not from its bulk be less than 4 or 500 fathom [720–900 metres].[7]

TE MAHINGA KAI | FOOD GATHERING

Tuangi (New Zealand cockle)

Mātaitai *shellfish gathering*
Mere Whaanga

Archaeologists have found evidence of the extraordinary variety of seafood enjoyed by Māori in the past. Shellfish such as white slipper shell and volute were gathered, along with the more common pāua, pipi and oysters. Traditional harvesting is still practised at favoured sites around the coast.

Shellfish have been an important part of the Māori diet since the first peoples arrived in New Zealand. Harvesting was a seasonal occupation, part of the cycle of food-growing and gathering essential to the community. The harvest was gathered and prepared for three purposes – immediate need, ceremonial occasions such as hui (meetings) and hākari (feasts), and provisions to store for the winter.

Middens (ancient rubbish sites) give us an insight into the range of shellfish that were available. While tuatua, pipi, pāua, pūpū, mussel, cockles, oysters, scallops and mud snails are familiar species still, archaeologists have found the shells of numerous other species in middens. At Māhia there are shells of limpets, whelks, and karaka or ngāruru.

Other species found include black nerita, ostrich foot, white slipper shell, white rock shell, knobbed whelk, volute, freshwater mussel, trough shell, triangle shell, and ringed venus shell. It is not known whether all were eaten. Some, such as slipper shell and nerita, may have been attached to pāua or mussel shells.

Archaeologists have located extensive middens of the shells left from gathering expeditions on beaches in Northland. At Mahakipawa in

These people are gathering shellfish at the outlet of the Manawatū River, near Foxton.

SHELLFISH EATEN BY MĀORI

*Still gathered and eaten today

Common name	Māori name	Common name	Māori name	Common name	Māori name
Toheroa	Toheroa	Blue mussel*	Kuku	Whelk	Kawari
Tuatua*	Tuatua	Scallop*	Tipa	Rock shell	Ngāeo
Pipi*	Pipi	Mud snail*	Whētiko	White rock shell	Hopetea
Pāua, black foot paua*	Pāua	Cook's turban	Karaka, ngāruru	Oyster borer	Kaikai tio
Pāua, yellow foot paua*	Pāua	Cat's eye, bubu*	Pūpū	Horse mussel	Hururoa
New Zealand cockle*	Tuangi	Ringed dosinia	Harihari	Turret shell	Papatai
Rock oyster*	Tio	Trough shell	Kuhakuha	Limpet	Ngākihi, kākihi
Dredge or Bluff oyster*	Tio	Triangle shell	Kaikaikaroro	Shield shell	Rori
Green-lipped mussel*	Kuku	Ostrich foot	Totorere	Freshwater mussel	Kākahi

Pelorus Sound in the South Island, a large midden of whelk and mud snails was discovered. It is estimated that many tonnes of shellfish were processed there, and that, because there were no fish or bird bones, this was a seasonal camp specifically for gathering shellfish.

Sometimes the harvest was cooked in the umu (earth oven). The tuwhatu method involved piling the shellfish in a heap, then burning dry fern on top, or enclosing it with a circle of fire. In the kōhue method, shellfish were placed in a gourd among hot stones. The shells opened and the liquid that came out was used as a medicine.

In 1843 a surveyor described Māori on D'Urville Island gathering mussels, which they cooked in an earth oven. They would then remove the flesh from the shells and string it up to dry in the trees. This method of preservation was also used for other shellfish such as pipi, tuatua and toheroa – the dried flesh was much lighter and easier to carry back to the village, which could be some distance from the shellfish beds.

Collecting kaimoana (seafood) was of great importance to Māori. Even today, it is a highly valued food resource. Continuing the tradition, two young boys collect shellfish in a flax basket in the Bay of Islands.

TE MAHINGA KAI | FOOD GATHERING

Shellfish were an important component of the Māori diet. These three girls from Northland, photographed in the first half of the 20th century, are shelling toheroa meat into tin cans. Their kete are full of shellfish, and they are surrounded by empty shells.

MUDDY WATERS

In Wairarapa, pāua were often put in fresh water for a few days before being eaten. These places were known as wai pāua (pāua water). A man named Te Harara had his harvest stolen from his wai pāua by a local woman. However, she made a large number of footprints around the area, to give the impression that a group of travellers had passed by and taken the shellfish. Her deception worked and she was not, at the time, identified as the thief.

Traditional patterns of harvest

Before going into the sea to gather food, the harvesters would say karakia and prepare themselves for the activity. Some in Māhia would wash with the water from a particular spring before continuing to the nearby bay for their harvest. On their return home, they stopped again at the spring and repeated the washing and karakia ritual.

One elder from the East Coast said they were told to urinate on the basket before going to gather shellfish. A Ngāpuhi elder said the same was done with fishing nets.

Traditional seafood gathering was a serious undertaking, and the sea a place to be respected. Children were told not to yell or scream when visiting the beach. No seafood was opened on the reef or over the shellfish beds, or while one of the party was still in the water.

Women who were menstruating did not go into the water to gather food. This is because of the woman's tapu status at this time, and there is conflict between tapu, food gathering and immersion in water.

Trips were made for a specific purpose, at the appropriate time for the intended harvest. If the trip was to gather pāua, then that was all that was taken. Separate trips would be made at the right time for taking kina or crayfish. Some people still watch for seasonal signs before going out to harvest seafood. For instance, in the Māhia area, the kina is said to be fat when the mānuka is flowering. In other areas the flowering of the kōwhai or pōhutukawa indicate that the time is right. Earlier generations ate everything within the kina shell, but now most of the contents are discarded and only the yellow roe is eaten.

Each family and hapū controlled areas where they gathered seafood. They knew where crayfish frequented tunnels and holes in the rocks, the channels where kina and pāua were numerous, and where the pipi or tuatua bed was at the time for gathering.

If family from elsewhere wanted to collect seafood, they would visit the kaitiaki (guardian) to seek permission. They would often bring an offering that their relatives considered a treat – wild pork from inland, or oysters

TE MAHINGA KAI | FOOD GATHERING

Little Waihī in the Bay of Plenty was known as a place of abundant seafood. Throughout New Zealand various iwi and hapū have traditional shellfish-collecting areas which are highly valued.

from a family in Raglan. The kaitiaki would then suggest the best place to gather shellfish. On their return, the visitors would leave some of their harvest for the kaitiaki.

Food exchange

The exchange of valued foods was a feature of hui. Offerings would include baskets full of pipi, mussels, karengo, crayfish – whatever their traditional food was. The host tribe would also provide an abundance of the foods for which they were known. This still occurs today. When the Ngāti Rongomaiwahine people hold a hui on one of their marae, they usually provide bowls of kina roe, karengo, creamed pāua and mounds of crayfish.

In the traditional Māori economy, tribes would exchange coastal and inland products. Baskets of dried seaweed were carried inland to be traded for forest products such as preserved birds. The people of Rotorua and other inland lakes of the north exchanged large quantities of whitebait and crayfish. Marine crayfish were also fermented or dried and used as an item of trade with inland tribes.

A female elder of the Hauraki area has noted that only certain people were allowed to prepare fish for visiting tohunga – both a mark of respect and also a demonstration of the host's manaakitanga.

Veterans of the Māori Battalion in the Second World War have spoken of the welcome arrival of parcels from home containing dried seafood – a variation in their diets, and also a valued connection with the traditions of home.

RĀHUI – BANS

Rāhui are periods when shellfish must not be taken. They are imposed to allow the seafood to regenerate, or if there has been a drowning in the area. In earlier times the area under rāhui was marked with a wooden post, a stick with seaweed on it, or a piece of the missing person's clothing. Most people will respect rāhui if they know it has been imposed.

TE MAHINGA KAI | FOOD GATHERING

Tuangi, or cockles (left), can be found near pipi beds, or in the mudflats of estuaries.

To prise the harvest from the rocks, this woman (below) is using a tomahawk. Her kete is used to hold the shellfish.

Kuku

PIPI AND KUKU AT WAR

The pipi and kuku (mussels) fought long ago at Onetahua. The pipi dug themselves into the sand, and the kuku attacked. However, when the kuku thrust out their tongues, they became clogged with sand and were defeated by the pipi. That is why pipi still hold the sandy beaches, while the kuku were forced to retreat to Rakahore, the offshore rocks.

Popular shellfish species

When people say they are going out to gather kaimoana, they are often only going for pāua and kina.

Pāua are found in crevices, on the undersides of reef shelves, and clinging to rocks in channels through the reef. They feed on seaweed, and the colours of the shells vary according to the type of seaweed that is most abundant in the area.

The shells were used for the eyes in carvings, and the thick lip of the shell was fashioned into pā kahawai, a fishing lure. They are also used extensively for jewellery.

Some people use the hua (stomach or roe) in pāua fritters, or by itself, but most pāua are taken only for the flesh. Very fresh pāua can be fried immediately, but if they are to be eaten later, they are generally beaten with a steak tenderiser to soften the flesh. A favourite recipe is to combine the minced flesh with a little onion and cream. Whichever recipe is favoured, pāua need very little cooking.

Kina (sea urchins) are found under rocks and rock shelves on the shore below the high-tide mark. They often have small stones, shells and seaweed such as neptune's necklace on their spikes as camouflage against snapper and other predators.

TE MAHINGA KAI | FOOD GATHERING

In the mid-1900s there were significant toheroa populations which were extensively harvested both recreationally and for sale. However, they underwent a massive decline, leading to a total ban apart from the occasional open day. These harvesters (above) were searching for their limit of 10 on an open day. By the 2000s, even these opportunities had ceased and the only harvesting was strictly controlled by tangata whenua.

Toheroa

Kina

The shellfish that are most associated with summer holidays are pipi. They are found in the sandy banks near the mouth of estuaries, and harbours where there is considerable water flow. In earlier times people had specific flax baskets for pipi. Smaller specimens would fall between the woven strips and back into the beds as the basket was gently swirled through the water. Tuangi (cockles) are found near pipi beds, although most are in the mudflats of estuaries rather than the sandier beds in the flowing water preferred by pipi.

Tuatua are larger than pipi and found on sandy beaches. They are usually harvested when there is a very low tide. People feel for the shellfish with their feet, only grasping them with their hands when they have located a group. Kaikaikaroro (triangle shells) prefer similar conditions to tuatua – in the area of breaking surf.

Toheroa was a very popular shellfish species, but they have become so scarce that they are now a protected species and can only be gathered when the Ministry of Fisheries declares a one-day open season at Oreti Beach in Southland.

Mussels (kuku or kūtai) grow in clumps on rocks or wharf piles. The larger ones are usually harvested. Weavers use strong mussel shells to scrape the hard, waxy outer surface of flax to make muka, the stripped

PROVEN WISDOM

It was customary to prohibit opening kina over the beds, because this could cause the remaining kina to move. A scientific study has confirmed that in fact kina can release an enzyme that results in other kina moving away from the area.

149

TE MAHINGA KAI | FOOD GATHERING

This fisherman leans over his canoe with a kapu (mussel dredge) at Lake Rotoiti in the early 1900s. The kapu (below) was used to scoop up kākahi (freshwater mussels).

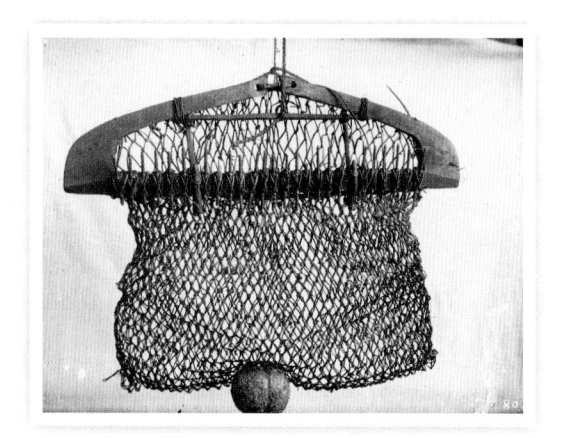

fibre used to weave cloaks. Freshwater mussels (kākahi) were sometimes harvested with a wooden dredge or rake attached to a net. They are found in the mud of lakes, rivers and streams. Although sometimes collected for aquariums, they are rarely gathered for food now.

Tio (native rock oysters) are found in clumps on the rocks in many sheltered harbours and estuaries. The highly prized Bluff oyster is dredged for a short season each year from Foveaux Strait.

Most children enjoy pūpū (cat's eyes), which are found on the rocky shore. They have a round greenish-black shell with a small green and white eye which covers the entrance to the shell. The cooked flesh is extracted with a pin. Whetiko (mud snails) are very like pūpū in appearance. They are found in harbours or on estuarine mudflats. Their shells are lighter in colour and softer than the pūpū, and once cooked the top of the spiral can be cut away and the flesh sucked from the shell.

Crabs were also taken from the reef, along with starfish and octopus.

Kōura

Kōura (red crayfish or red rock lobsters), New Zealand's most common crayfish, were abundant in the Māhia area before the commercialisation of this species. Elders speak of the time when they would gather crayfish for dinner on their way home from school.

The crayfish were easily caught in quite shallow water, and children had no need to dive for them. They would take one for each family member, the size determined by the size of the recipient – a small crayfish would be taken for a young child, and larger ones for the adults. When the crayfish has a soft shell, or the female is carrying eggs, it must be returned to the sea.

Also found in New Zealand, and a traditional food source, is the packhorse crayfish or green crayfish, which is larger than the red species.

TE MAHINGA KAI | FOOD GATHERING

Traditionally kōura (left), or crayfish, were highly prized. Today, the prestige of a hui is often greatly enhanced by the provision of the sought after kōura.

Karengo

The seaweed karengo is another important traditional reef food, harvested in the autumn and winter. It grows on the edge of the reef from the time of the autumn rains. On the eastern coast of the Māhia Peninsula, alongside a small stream that flows out to the beach, is a rock where a quantity of the very first harvest of karengo was left by the kaitiaki whānau (guardian family) of that area. This was part of the ritual that ensured subsequent harvests. Karengo was preserved by drying, and a good harvest would ensure supplies for the year.

Karengo is found on intertidal rocks on exposed coasts, and is collected during autumn and winter. Preserved by drying, it can keep for months.

FRESHWATER CRAYFISH

The freshwater crayfish (above, known as kōura or kēwai) lives in streams, lakes and ponds throughout the country. The smaller species is found in the North Island and in the north-west of the South Island, and the larger variety occurs in the south-east of the South Island and on Stewart Island. They are dull green in colour and only about 125 millimetres long. Traditionally, they were caught by placing a leafy mānuka branch in the water until the kōura crawled in among the leaves and twigs. Then the branch was carefully removed and the catch shaken out on the bank.

Pai Kanohi of the Ngāi Tūhoe tribe sits outside his whare in the early 1900s. Around him are tahā huahua, calabashes for birds preserved in their own fat. These potted birds were a vital part of the Māori diet, particularly as New Zealand had no native land mammals that could be used for meat. They were also traded between some tribes.

Te tāhere manu *bird catching*

Basil Keane

New Zealand's forests provided Māori with food in the form of birds – kererū, kākā, tūī and others. Birds were cooked in a hāngī, or preserved in fat, and their feathers became cloaks or hair ornaments. The bird-catching season was a central part of tribal life, and there were ceremonies to ensure the hunting went well.

The sea and the forest were seen as the two food baskets of the traditional Māori economy. In the forest, birds were important as a supply of protein. Before the arrival of Europeans, New Zealand had no land mammals to use for meat except the introduced kurī (dog) and kiore (rat).

For many tribes, the main fowling season in autumn was a vital part of life. A variety of birds were taken – kererū, kākā and tūī were particularly important. They were often preserved in their own fat. Feathers of different birds were also used for adornment and making cloaks.

The main bird-taking season ran from May to July (autumn–winter). From March, fowlers would look at the birds' food supply in the forest to estimate their likely success in the coming season. As early as April, fowlers would catch weka in the South Island.

In the middle of the season, kākā were fat and seeking food on the ground, and were often caught by hand. Tūī are fat from May to August, and are called kōkō at that time. By late winter (July and August), kererū would be feeding on kōwhai and be unpalatable.

In the South Island, kererū, kākā, kōkō (tūī) and korimako (bellbirds) were all caught in autumn. In the early 2000s, tītī (muttonbirds) were still being taken in autumn from the 36 Tītī Islands off Stewart Island (see page 154).

TE MAHINGA KAI | FOOD GATHERING

Although the main bird-taking season ran through autumn and winter, kererū were caught in summer (December–February) as they ate the ripe berries of the tawa tree. In summer, and also in early winter, kākā were caught using the mutu snare (a perch with a looped rope snare). At this time, other birds are in poor condition.

FOOD OR SPORT?

Like Māori, early European settlers often relied on native birds as a source of food. However, later, Europeans wanted to hunt them as sport.

From 1864, hunting seasons were set in certain areas for kererū and native ducks and in 1865 a law was passed against using snares and traps to catch native birds – shooting was the only approved form of hunting. This restricted traditional Māori fowling methods. In the 1880s and 1890s, the kererū hunting season became an issue. European hunters wanted the season open in early autumn when the kererū was still reasonably agile, making it more suitable as a game bird. Māori hunted the bird for food, not sport, so they wanted it to be fatter. They preferred late autumn and winter. In 1907, preserving native birds after the hunting season was banned to stop large numbers of kererū being stored and sold by hunters. Māori preserved kererū in the birds' own fat for personal use. This was recognised in a 1910 amendment which gave Māori the right to hold potted birds.

Hunters pose by their haul of kererū, around 1900. The birds were an easy target, and large numbers were shot.

153

TE MAHINGA KAI | FOOD GATHERING

TĪTĪ – MUTTONBIRDING

Muttonbirds, or sooty shearwaters, are known to Māori as tītī and they have been regularly harvested for food since early times. How far-reaching this harvest was is still not known, but today muttonbird chicks are still collected by Rakiura Māori on certain islands off the south coast of the South Island. Traditionally the muttonbirds were not only a valuable food source, but also an important trade item, and their harvest was very significant to local hapū.

The harvesting of tītī, known as muttonbirding, is divided into two stages: nanao, when chicks (right) are extracted from their burrows; and rama, when they are caught above ground under torchlight.

Adult tītī returning to their colony in the evening are a spectacular sight.

Pōhā were containers used to preserve birds in their own fat. This one consists of a kelp bag wrapped in tōtara bark inside a flax basket. Pōhā used to preserve tītī were known as pōhā tītī.

Using birds

Birds were usually cooked in a hāngī if they were to be eaten immediately. Otherwise, they were preserved in their own fat. In mid-winter, when Matariki appeared in the sky, signalling the Māori New Year, it was time to cook and preserve birds – a process known as ahi mātiti. This is described in the saying 'Matariki, kua maoka te hinu' (at Matariki, birds are preserved).

The process of preserving birds in their own fat was called tutu. First, they were plucked and cleaned. Larger ones were boned with a shell, a sharp stone flake or even a kākā's sharp, strong beak. Then each bird was put on a spit, and they were cooked together over a fire. The dripping fat was collected in a wooden trough. Later, the cooked birds were potted in tahā (calabashes), pōhā (seaweed containers) or pātua (bark containers). The fat was reheated with hot stones and poured into the containers to cover the birds.

The feathers of birds such as the kiwi and kākāpō were used for making dress capes. The white-tipped black feathers of huia and the white plumes of kōtuku were also used as dress feathers in the hair.

This is a replica of a snare used to catch kākā. As the bird lands the noose is drawn tight, trapping it. The snare, attached to a pole, is then unhooked from the tree and taken down. Then the bird is killed, and the snare is reset and put back on the tree.

Snaring methods: tākiri and tāhei

Snaring with a looped rope was a common method of catching birds. In the tākiri method, a single snare is put on a perch. Birds are caught by the feet in the snare when the fowler pulls an attached cord with a quick tug (tākiri). There are three snares used in this method: the mutu, tumu and pewa.

Mutu

The mutu snare (called tumu or pewa in some areas) was used both on the ground and up in trees. The mutu was made from a single piece of wood, L- or T-shaped, with a horizontal perch and a vertical upright. The mutu was often carved and weathered. A looped snare was draped over the mutu. It was lifted to the tree on a rod and hooked over another rod attached to a branch. When a bird landed on the perch, the looped snare was tugged, trapping the bird against the upright. The fowler then unhooked the mutu, keeping the cord tight, brought the bird down and killed it. The snare was rearranged and the mutu put back up.

The mutu was used in miro, hīnau, maire, kahikatea, tawai, rātā and rimu trees. The word for a tree in which it was used extensively is tūtū.

Tumu

Used by the Ngāti Raukawa tribe, a tumu was a different type of snaring perch, placed on small trees or shrubs. It was not man-made like the mutu – rather, it was a small branch that divided into two branchlets. These were tied together at the end. The branch was left growing on the tree, or cut and reattached to another tree, and a snare-loop was laid on it. A cord tied to this loop led to a shelter where the fowler was hidden. When a bird landed, the fowler pulled the loop, similar to the mutu. The cord had a peg at one end, which was stuck in the ground, tethering the bird. Once most of the snares were full, the fowler would emerge, take the birds and reset the snares.

Pewa

The pewa was used in a similar way to the mutu and tumu. Rather than a single upright perch, it had an upright with a perch lashed to it horizontally and a strut bracing the upright and perch. A lure of ripe berries or nectar-bearing flowers was often tied to the perch to attract birds, and moss or lichen was attached to disguise it.

NEW ZEALAND'S EMU

The kiwi's skin was used to make a cloak known as the kahu kiwi. Its feathers looked like emu feathers, leading some early explorers to state wrongly that emus lived in New Zealand. In 1820, one traveller said, 'The emu is found in New Zealand, though we were never fortunate enough to meet with one.'[8] Another traveller in the 1830s claimed that you could come across an emu in the South Island.

TE MAHINGA KAI | FOOD GATHERING

The tāhei snare (below) consisted of a number of hanging nooses. Fowlers identified trees, streams or pools that were visited by birds. Tūī (right, on a flax bush) were snared on the kōwhai tree in flower, and on smaller trees. Large numbers were often caught, and were described in the saying 'Me te raparapa tuna' (like a row of eels spitted by the fire).

GIVE 'EM A TASTE OF KIWI

Early European explorers, and later settlers, survived by eating native birds – often caught using indigenous methods. Their opinion of kiwi meat varied. Explorer Ernest Dieffenbach said it was quite tasty. On the other hand, the trader Joel Polack thought that the 'flesh is worthless and tough'.[9] Ethnographer Elsdon Best took the middle ground. He said that the kiwi was not tough, tasted fine, but was nowhere near as good as the kererū and tūī.

Tāhei (taeke) method

In the tāhei method the snare was unattended. A row of snares tied with slipknots were attached to a cord, or a rod secured horizontally between branches. The snares were set close to a straight branch or perch. The birds would sit on the branch or perch and be caught by their necks. As they struggled, the slipknot would tighten and catch them.

A tree on which these snares were set was called a rākau tāhei, rākau taeke or taumatua. When the snares were set near water, the water was known as wai tāhei or wai taheke.

Snares were visited once or twice a day. The fowler would gather the caught birds and reset the snares. These unattended snares did not work for kākā, which would rip them apart with their beaks.

Spears, rods, hands and traps

The short spears known as maiere were 3 to 4 metres long. They were used to take birds on shrubs and small trees. Long spears – 6 to 11 metres – were called tao kaihua, taoroa or just tao. They were used on big trees with outspread branches. The spear would rest on the branch and then be pushed rather than thrown at the bird. Because these spears were so long, they were not carried but rather were dragged along by the front end.

Bird spears were made from tawa wood, kāpara (heartwood of rimu or kahikatea) or occasionally aka (stems of climbing plants). They had a barbed point (tara), sometimes detachable. Tara were made from bone (often human), from hardwood or hard parts of tree-fern trunks, or even from stingray spine or pounamu. A tree on which the spear was used was known as a kaihua or rākau wero. Kākā were speared on rātā, kōwhai and tāwari trees.

Tari method

The tari method involved a noose tied with a slip knot on a rod. Fowlers needed to get close enough to slip the noose over the bird's head. They would entice the bird with a small branch or a decoy bird, or by mimicking the bird's call.

To catch a weka, the fowler would rustle a branch in one hand. This brought the bird close enough to put the noose over its head.

Hauhau method

In the hauhau method, the fowler set up a pae kōkō (tūī perch), a 2.5-metre-long rod lashed on a slant to two saplings. The fowler then hid in a shelter. Birds were often attracted with a decoy, or by imitating their call. The fowler would hold the rod against the perch. When a bird landed, it was hit with a mighty blow, using the hauhau manu (bird-striker) – a thick, round rod, about 1.5 metres long. The tūī, hihi, korimako (bellbird), tīeke (saddleback), kōkako, and tātaihore (whitehead) were caught in this way. Sometimes, the perch was set up near the water. When thirsty birds landed on it, the fowler hit them. Another structure consisted of two vertical poles, with a horizontal pole lashed between them about 1.5 metres above the ground.

Hopu kōkō

This method was used on frosty winter nights, from midnight to just before dawn. During the day, fowlers would locate tūī nests and mark the trails using light-coloured rangiora leaves. They could find their way at night, seeing the leaves by the light of a torch. Then they would climb the trees and grab (hopu) the bird (kōkō). The Ngāti Porou tribe called this method rutu (dash down), as the fowler would knock the branch. The birds were often so cold that they simply fell to the ground.

In winter, Māori set traps and hunting platforms in miro to catch kererū that came to feed on the tree's seeds. The birds were easy to spear or trap after they had gorged on the seeds.

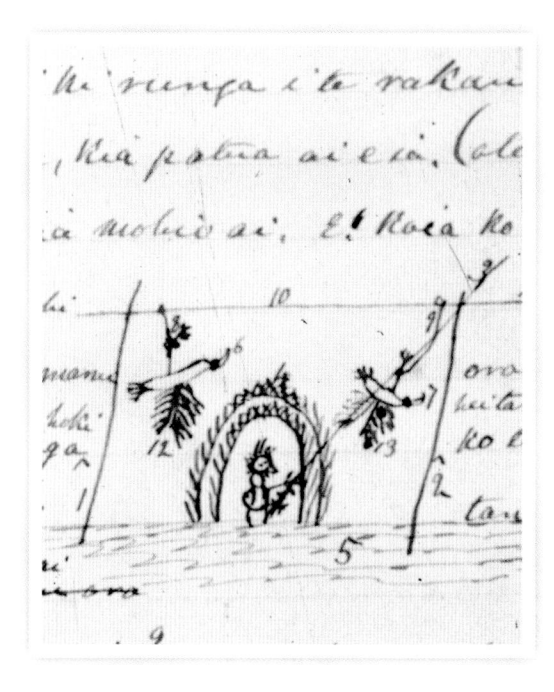

This sketch was drawn by Te Arawa elder and scholar Te Rangikāheke in a manuscript about fowling. It depicts a fowler holding a stick and hiding in a temporary hut. Two decoy birds, described by Te Rangikāheke as manu tīoriori (song birds) are attached to the perch. The decoys attract other birds, and when they alight on the perch the fowler knocks them off with his stick.

MOTHER KNOWS BEST

A legend tells how Māui was bird-spearing with his brothers. But every time they speared a bird, it escaped, as there was no barb on the spear. Māui told his mother, Taranga, how hopeless the expedition had been, so she advised him to fashion a point with barbs. He did and was able to spear birds successfully. This explains the origin of the tara kāniwha (barbed point).

TE MAHINGA KAI | FOOD GATHERING

William Fox's 1846 picture 'In the Aglionby or Matukituki (Matakitaki) Valley, looking into the Otapawa (Matiri)' shows the Māori guide Kehu snaring a weka. He holds a tari (slip noose on rod) and entices the weka with a decoy – a shorter stick with a bunch of feathers attached. Kehu imitated a bird call at the same time, so the weka would think the feathers were a bird. The method was successful, and was one of many used by Kehu to feed himself and the party he was guiding.

Traps

Māori also used a number of traps. The puaka was a spring snare (tāwhiti) inside an enclosure. The bird would walk over the snare, release the spring and be caught. The korapa, a small U-shaped net, was a trap for karuwai (robins). Bait was scattered close by, and the trap was pulled down on a karuwai when it arrived.

Attracting birds

Fowlers often attracted birds by imitating their cries. To lure the kiwi, the fowler put a finger in his mouth and mimicked its call. A leaf used when imitating a call was called a pepe. A flax leaf was used to call weka, while tūī were lured with a leaf from the manono or the patatē. The Ngāti Porou tribe used pāpā, whangewhange or māhoe leaves. Fowlers put a leaf (doubled or flat) between their lips and made a chirping sound by breathing in. When hunting with dogs, fowlers often lured ground birds such as weka and kiwi by imitating their calls. The fowler would then release the dog, which seized the bird. The dog was controlled by

TE MAHINGA KAI | FOOD GATHERING

This sketch showing the taki or decoy technique was made by Tāmati Ranapiri of Ngāti Raukawa. The bird at the bottom of the pole is a decoy. The fowler is hidden in the hut. At the top of the taki is the kākā that has been attracted by the decoy. Ranapiri noted that this method did not catch as many birds as the mutu snare.

This waka kererū (pigeon trough) was photographed at Ruatāhuna in 1899. The trough was filled with water, and kererū would come to drink. Snares were set on either side of the trough, and when the birds tried to drink they were caught.

THE BIRD WHISPERER

European trader Joel Polack told of seeing a fowler catch a kererū by using a leaf to imitate its call. The bird heard the call and came to the fowler, who lulled it to sleep and then caught it. Polack's description has been derided by a number of writers, but no doubt call-leaves were very effective. In the 1800s, Major J. L. C. Richardson saw his Māori guide pluck a leaf after hearing a bird twitter. The guide imitated the bird, and eventually one flew close enough for him to grab it.

a rod attached to its collar. Rattles were also attached to its neck, so it could be followed when released.

Taki means to entice. In this method, a pet kākā was used as a decoy to attract other kākā. A fowler would lash a pole to two trees, about 2 to 3 metres high. Another pole was placed on an angle against the first. It was secured by tying the upper end, or grounding the lower end.

The decoy parrot was tied to the base of the pole. It was trained to scratch around and screech to attract other birds. The fowler would hide near the pole, behind a screen of tree-fern fronds. When a wild kākā got close it was hit with a stick, caught with a noose or grabbed.

The waka manu, also known as a waka kererū, was a wooden trough filled with water and left in a tree or on its trunk. When the birds became used to the trough, snares were set. Waka manu were often used in miro trees, as birds feeding on miro berries got thirsty. They would drink from the trough and become caught in the nooses. The troughs were often quite long – around 1.5 metres.

TE MAHINGA KAI | FOOD GATHERING

A RITUAL MEAL

Tamarau Waiari, a leader and priest of the Tūhoe tribe, explained how the first birds they caught were ceremonially cooked and eaten. 'Women and food were prohibited from the whare mata until the rau huka ceremony was performed, freeing the hut and people from restriction. The readied snares would be taken and set on various trees. When the first birds were caught, they were cooked in the rau huka oven and eaten by the priest, thereby freeing all people from restriction.'[10]

Spiritual aspects

In Māori tradition, the health and vitality of the birds and trees in the forest is the result of the forest's mauri. Mauri could be represented by a talisman, also called a mauri. This was usually a stone that was hidden in the forest. It was seen as a place for the atua (gods and spiritual beings) that protected the forest. The tohunga who placed the mauri often released a lizard at that spot to guard the mauri.

Generally, ceremonies relating to the forest were carried out at the site of the mauri. If the trees or birds became less fruitful, a charm (whakaara) was said to reawaken the mauri. In the ceremony of uruuru whenua, a small branch was placed near the mauri, to placate the spirits or gods. The first bird caught in the fowling season was offered to the forest mauri.

Sometimes a tohunga would carry out a ceremony to make a particular tree attractive to birds, so they could be caught. He would say a karakia over a bird caught in the tree, to make the tree tapu. The tohunga would hide the bird, or part of it, which now represented the life force of the tree.

Like all activities in Māori society, fowling was affected by tapu. A tapu on a waterway could prevent any use of it – drinking, bathing, fishing or using a canoe. A forest, or part of a forest, might be under a tapu which stopped anyone going into it. However, tapu might simply prevent birds being caught. At the whare mātā (place where fowling and fishing equipment was made), women and cooked food were not permitted. If tapu was breached in any way, the gods would be offended and their help withdrawn.

The fowling season was opened with the ahi taitai ceremony. The first birds caught were offered to the gods. They were cooked in the ceremonial oven, and lifted the tapu from the forest and the whare mātā.

Rāhui was a form of tapu. A rāhui could prohibit the taking of birds, for instance from a tree, a grove or an entire forest. It could also refer to particular birds – for example ducks in moulting season. A rāhui was often indicated by a post (pou rāhui), sometimes painted red. Clothing, a lock of hair, or a fern might be tied to a stake to signal a rāhui. In other cases, a chief would note that an area had been placed under a rāhui, and word of mouth would let people know the place was tapu.

Unlucky signs were known as pūhore. Certain words were banned when fowling. The remedy for pūhore was to set a post (tuāpā), sometimes painted red, in the ground. It was not tapu. Fowlers going out would take a small branch, touch their spear or basket of snares with it, then toss it down at the base of the post. They would then say a karakia.

This whakapakoko (carved figure) was used to warn people against trespassing on lands where they might breach rāhui – a ban against entering a place, or taking certain things, such as birds from a forest. Posts, clothing or a lock of hair were also used to let people know of a rāhui.

TE MAHINGA KAI | FOOD GATHERING

These footprints of a large moa were exposed in August 1912 when a flood on the Manawatū River swept away the blue clay that had covered and preserved them. They show that the moa had three strong front-pointing toes and, unlike most other ratites, a small rear toe.

MOA

When moa bones were first discovered by Europeans in New Zealand in the 1830s, the birds were declared a scientific marvel. A number of species – some very large and some small – once roamed the country, but probably became extinct about 500 years ago. Much about them remains a mystery. For years, people have hunted for more clues, or a glimpse of any survivors. During the first century or so after their arrival in New Zealand from Polynesia (1250–1300 AD), Māori extensively hunted moa as a ready source of food. Hundreds of archaeological sites ranging from single-kill locations to vast middens up to 100 hectares across have shown the great significance of moa in their diet. Moa bones were carved into fish hooks and pendants, and the skins and feathers were made into clothing. In the archaeological record, Māori use of moa began about 650–700 years ago, but moa remains do not appear in middens later than 1550 AD. There have been a number of claimed historic sightings of the bird, but none held up to scrutiny. Having survived in New Zealand for millennia, with only the giant eagle as a predator, moa were almost certainly extinct by the time of European colonisation, in the early 1800s. Direct hunting and the modification of their habitat led to their rapid demise. Perhaps because the bird had long disappeared, the name 'moa' does not appear to have been widely used by Māori by the time Europeans arrived, and there were few traditional stories about them. The name was first heard by the missionaries William Williams and William Colenso on the East Coast in January 1838, and thereafter became commonly used.

Trevor H. Worthy

Te hopu tuna *eeling*

Basil Keane

Eels were a vital food for Māori, who caught them using weirs built on rivers, or with traps, nets, spears and bait. Large numbers of eels were captured on their yearly migrations to the sea, and live eels were kept in cages or ponds as a ready food supply.

Shortfin eels (above) are one of the two freshwater eel species native to New Zealand, and also occur in Australia, New Caledonia, Lord Howe Island, Norfolk Island and Fiji. They live mainly in rivers near the coast.

The word tuna refers to eels – specifically freshwater eels. In some contexts it can also refer to conger eels and other fish that look like eels. Tuna were an important food for Māori – especially freshwater eels and eel-like piharau (lampreys).

The origins of tuna are explained in several traditions. In one tradition, Tuna came from Puna-kauariki, a spring in the highest heavens. The families in the spring were Para (frostfish), Ngōiro (conger eel), Tuna (freshwater eel) and Tuere (hagfish or blind eel). The waters of the heavens dried up, and this group made their way down to Papatūānuku. Tuna remained in fresh water, but Para, Ngōiro and Tuere all went to the sea.

In another story, Tuna, a giant eel, frightened the wives of the demigod Māui. As punishment, Māui cut Tuna in half. One half landed in the sea and became the conger eel. The other half fell in a river and turned into the freshwater eel.

Tuna: eel species and other eel-like species

New Zealand has two native species of freshwater eel. The longfin eel has a long dorsal (back) fin. It is unique to New Zealand and is found in rivers and streams well inland. The shortfin eel has a short dorsal fin. It does not live as far inland as the longfin eel.

There are over 100 different tribal names for freshwater eels, describing

TE MAHINGA KAI | FOOD GATHERING

In one South Island tradition, Māui fought Tuna, a supernatural giant eel, because it had frightened his wives, Hine-tū-repo and Hine-te-ngahere. Māui cut Tuna in half. One part became the sea-dwelling conger eel and the other a freshwater eel.

Rangi Goodman (below, left) and Don Edwards hold a monster longfin eel, caught by their friend Warren Kennedy, from the Wainuiomata River in 1965.

Māui attacks Tuna

AOTEAROA NEW ZEALAND $1·00

The head of a female longfin eel still living in its freshwater home is blunt with a bulbous dome behind the eyes. When the eel migrates to spawn in tropical sea water, the head becomes sleeker as muscle is lost. The eyes and pectoral fins also enlarge. The eel will not feed again, and dies after spawning.

their different colours and sizes. The ngōiro (called kōiro in the South Island) is the conger eel. It lives in the sea and grows up to 1.8 metres long. Ngōiro were caught using a 'bob' – a lure made from flax tangled around bait. The tuere or napia is the hagfish, which lives in the sea. It is sometimes called the blind eel, as it has no eyes, or the snot eel because it exudes blue slime when threatened. Tuere are not eels, or even true fish, as they have no spine. They grow up to a metre long and are good eating once the slime has been removed.

The para or frostfish is thin and long – 90 centimetres to 1.5 metres. It resembles an eel, but is silver, with scales. Para live in the sea, and often wash ashore in clear, frosty weather – hence their English name. They are said to taste delicious. The piharau or lamprey is a slime-covered creature that looks like an eel but lacks bones. Piharau are sometimes called lamprey eels, korokoro or kanakana. Like eels, they spend time in rivers and the sea. They spawn in rivers before dying.

EEL WELLBEING

The number and health of eels in a river were believed to be protected through mauri – talismans, usually stones. These were placed near eel weirs, often at the base of the posts at the downstream end.

163

TE MAHINGA KAI | FOOD GATHERING

Pā tuna *eel weirs*

The pā tuna was a common device for catching eels in rivers, streams and the outlets of lagoons and lakes. Weirs were used in autumn, to catch eels as they headed downstream to spawn in the sea. Fences in the water guided the eels into a net and then into a hīnaki (eel pot). Pā tuna were useful when rivers were in flood or flowing heavily.

Eels run mostly at night, so people sometimes stayed up to empty the hīnaki as they filled.

Pā tauremu

Most pā tuna were pā tauremu – two fences that funnelled the eels into a hīnaki. The fences were made of strong stakes (usually mānuka) driven into the river bed, with mānuka brush or bracken fern between the posts. Water could get through, but the eels, coming downstream in large numbers, could not. The two fences were set in a V shape – upstream they were wide apart, but downstream the gap between them narrowed, and a pūrangi (net) guided the eels into a hīnaki.

Pā auroa *the Whanganui eel weir*

A different type of weir was used on the Whanganui River because of the large amount of driftwood in the river. The pā auroa was a single fence, built almost parallel to the current at the top of a rapid. As eels came downstream, the fence guided them into a net attached to the end post and another single post opposite. Pā auroa had to be very strong to withstand floods.

Loss of eel weirs

In the 19th century, European settlers removed pā tuna to make rivers more navigable, leading to conflict with Māori. In the 1880s, there were more than 350 pā tuna and 92 utu piharau (lamprey weirs) in the Whanganui River. Between 1886 and 1888 over 500 tribal members petitioned the government to save their weirs – but by the turn of the century, almost all were gone.

This is a small pā tuna of the pā tauremu type at Ngutuwera on the Moumāhaki River. Eel weirs were used in autumn, to catch eels on their way downstream to spawn.

Ngōiro (conger eels, below) live in the sea, and can weigh up to 16 kilograms.

The piharau (or lamprey, right) is popularly known as the lamprey eel. It looks like an eel, but has no backbone. Māori valued them as food.

TE MAHINGA KAI | FOOD GATHERING

Paratene Ngata of the Ngāti Porou tribe (left) is weaving a hīnaki. He is being observed by anthropologist Te Rangi Hīroa (Peter Buck), right, with notebook.

Pū toke (bait pots) were put inside hīnaki. They were a similar shape to hīnaki, and made of the same materials. This pot is 25 centimetres long.

Hīnaki *eel pots*

The hīnaki was a basket-like pot that was set in open water with bait, or used at pā tuna. Intricately woven, the best-made hīnaki were works of art.

Ordinary hīnaki (called hīnaki tukutuku) had one entrance. When they were set without a weir, the entrance faced downstream. The eels would smell the bait, and swim upstream to find it. The hīnaki was anchored with stones and tied to a stake, a tree or a pole driven into the stream bed.

A large type of hīnaki, called hīnaki tarino, was used in the Waikato River and its tributaries. The hīnaki waharua had an entrance at each end – waharua means 'two mouths'. They were set in deep rivers or in lagoons. Temporary waharua were sometimes made of flax leaves and used in the Manawatū River. Neither of these were used with eel weirs.

The entrance to the hīnaki – called the akura – had a circle of sticks inside. These pointed inwards, touching in the centre, so the eel could push through to enter, but could not get back out. Other hīnaki stopped the eel escaping with a small bag-like net inside the akura.

Bait

Hīnaki were used with bait – often worms, or even birds. Bait was put in a small pot called a pū toke, which looked like a miniature hīnaki, or a small flax bag called a tōrehe. At other times it was tied inside the hīnaki. The Ngāti Porou people would thread earthworms on a string and tie them to a piece of flax flower stalk, which floated inside the trap.

Hīnaki at eel weirs were used without bait.

Making hīnaki

Hīnaki were often made from stems of mangemange, which only grows in the north. Mangemange is strong and flexible, and if hīnaki were being carried far, they could be soaked in water, pressed flat, stacked and lashed to poles. When they were untied, they sprang back to their original shape.

Around Ōtaki, north of Wellington, hīnaki were made from the aerial roots of kiekie and the stems of aka-tororaro, a climbing plant. Supplejack was also used, but it was a poor substitute. Temporary hīnaki were sometimes made from flax.

NO WAY OUT

In one story, Māui improved the design of the hīnaki. When his brothers tried to catch eels, the eels went into the hīnaki, ate the bait, then turned around and went back out. Māui invented the akura – a funnel of sticks that join at an apex. The eel can get in, but if it tries to get out it faces a cluster of pointed sticks.

This watercolour by T. W. Downes shows a giant eel being lured out of a stream with a bird on a stick. Ordinary eels were also caught by dangling bait from a rod. This method was called toi, and used a bob made from worms threaded on flax, or spiders in a bag.

MARAMATAKA

Like all fishing, eeling was controlled by the maramataka (lunar calendar). One maramataka shows the first six and last seven nights of the moon as best for catching eels by torch light. Moonlit nights were poor for eeling.

Eel spears are called matarau. Their points were made from hardwood – particularly māpara, the heart-wood of the kahikatea.

Other ways to catch eels

Eels feed mainly at night, so people hunted them in the dark, using a torch flare (rama) and a spear or hand-net. This method was called rama tuna.

Māpara, the hard heartwood of the kahikatea, was made into torches. Kauri gum, found in the far north, burns easily, so it was used with dried flax leaves for torches. In the South Island they were made from bundles of dry, finely split mānuka or supplejack.

The kōrapa was a net used by the Ngāti Porou tribe. It was a hoop net on a straight handle, used to scoop up eels at night. When the eel was caught, the handle was lifted and the eel slid into an attached net bag.

Matarau or eel spears were commonly used. The shaft was around a metre long, and it often had seven points, including the sharpened shaft. A single-pointed spear was known as a taotahi, or pātia in the South Island. The spear's points were usually made from hardwood, especially māpara, or sometimes whalebone.

With patu tuna (eel striking), fishers used a thin rod to kill eels in shallow water, often at night by the light of a torch. A companion would string the eels together and drag them along.

Bobbing for eels

Another common way of catching eels was bobbing, called toi. A bob was made by threading flax or cabbage-tree leaf fibres through worms or grubs. The bob was tied to a rod, usually of mānuka. When the eel's teeth caught on the fibres, the person bobbing would swing it ashore. Eels are largely nocturnal and avoid light – so eel-bobbing was done at night, or sometimes in the day when the water was muddy or discoloured. A made-up eel bob is called mōunu (bait) or tui (to thread). Tui toke is a bob made from earthworms, while tui huhu is made from huhu grubs. In Ōtaki, spiders were put in a small flax bag. In the South Island, noke waiū (big white worms) were used with wīwī (split flax and rushes). Today, bobs are made from worms sewn together.

TE MAHINGA KAI | FOOD GATHERING

This utu piharau (lamprey weir) is on the banks of the Whanganui River, shown here in the late 1800s. Lamprey weirs were built around March, before winter rains swelled the river.

KARAKIA

A number of karakia (charms) were associated with eeling – including one for the first eels caught in a season. This is a simple karakia to encourage eels into a hīnaki:

Tēnā te puna kei Hawaiki,
Te pū kei Hawaiki,
Te puna kei Rangiriri.
The source is at Hawaiki,
The origin is at Hawaiki,
The source at Rangiriri.[12]

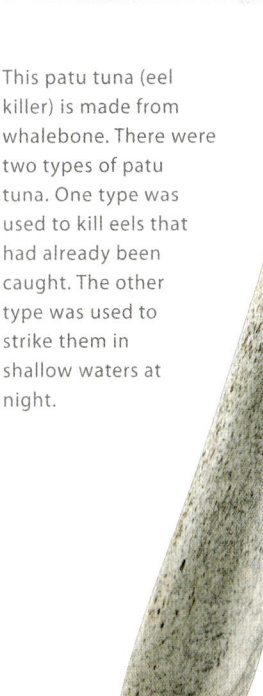

Teone (Hōne) Taare Tīkao, a South Island elder, described how conger eels were caught by bobbing:

> The conger-eel (koiro) at sea could be caught with a bob called whaka-puku. This was made of whitau (dressed flax) tangled round a bait, which can be left all day or night. The only fish to tackle it is the koiro, as others cannot eat it, but koiro bolts it down and then finds he can neither digest nor spew it out, so he is held a prisoner until the fisherman comes.[11]

Catching eels by hand

Rapu tuna was another common method. Rapu means to seek. Fishers would search for eels with their hands or feet under banks or stones, or in muddy places. In the takahi tuna method, a group would stand in a semicircle in the water. One person would stamp to scare the eels out of their hiding places, and another would grab them.

Catching piharau

The piharau or lamprey lives in fresh water and the sea. Piharau resemble eels, but have no bones. Prized by Māori, they are also called korokoro or kanakana. The utu piharau or lamprey weir was a straight fence placed across a river or stream, leaving an opening at one side. A net was set just downstream, leading into a hīnaki. Piharau would swim along the fence to the opening, and be swept by the current into the net and hīnaki. Lamprey weirs were known as pā kanakana in the South Island.

The whakaparu piharau was a type of weir, made of stones and lined with ferns and grass. The whakapua was a bracken mat pegged to the river bed. When enough piharau were caught, it was rolled up and taken ashore.

As piharau worked their way up waterfalls, they were knocked off with a fern or nīkau leaf and put in a bucket. They were also caught in small hīnaki. Piharau are mentioned in the proverb 'Ka kitea a Matariki, ka rere te korokoro' (when Matariki is seen, the lamprey migrate). Matariki is the Pleiades constellation, which rises in the pre-dawn sky around June, signalling the Māori New Year – and the running of the piharau.

This patu tuna (eel killer) is made from whalebone. There were two types of patu tuna. One type was used to kill eels that had already been caught. The other type was used to strike them in shallow waters at night.

TE MAHINGA KAI | FOOD GATHERING

These tuna fillets (right) are drying on a tīrewa (rack) at Wairewa (Lake Forsyth), just south of Banks Peninsula. Once dried, eels could last for months.

Live eels were sometimes caught and kept in a korotete, an eel cage (below). They were stored in running water and fed with potatoes and other food until needed.

Cooking, preserving and storing eels

In the kope or kōpaki method, eels were wrapped in leaves of rangiora, raurēkau or green flax and roasted over glowing embers.

The tāpora method involved packing eels into a small basket and covering them with pūhā leaves and young fronds of mauku, which were cooked and eaten with the eels.

Eels were a valued food source in traditional Māori society. They were often preserved, and were then called tuna pāwhara or tuna maroke. The backbones, heads and tails were removed and the eels were hung out to dry – or partially cooked on a grating of green sticks over a fire. Curing them like this would preserve them for months, and they were hung in a shed or packed in baskets. For eating, they were softened by steaming in a hāngī.

Keeping live eels

Live eels were kept in water in a hīnaki or a korotete (eel cage) – a special pot similar to a hīnaki, often made from mangemange stems. In Ōtaki, north of Wellington, these cages could hold up to 300 eels. Cages were put in a stream, and tied to a stake or tree. The eels were fed potatoes and other food.

The Ngāti Kuru-mokihi people of Tūtira in Hawke's Bay built whare tuna – shelters in the water for eels. These were over 4 metres long, 1 metre wide and half a metre high, made of mānuka lashed with flax. The downstream end was blocked and weighted with stones, and the top was open. The shelter was filled with waterweed, rimurimu. Eels gathered there of their own accord, and were removed as needed.

Ponds or lagoons that had no outlet to the sea were sometimes deliberately stocked with eels.

Matamoe and haumate tuna (two types of eel) were put into a lagoon that used to exist in Miramar, Wellington. The Ngāti Porou tribe sometimes dammed a stream and stocked it with eels, taking them as the need arose.

FIRST FRUITS

The first eel caught at a weir was put aside as an offering to the gods – a tradition when fishing or gathering food. When a youth caught eels for the first time, the catch was cooked on a sacred fire (ahi parapara) for a feast.

168

TE MAHINGA KAI | FOOD GATHERING

These ditches have been dug at the end of Wairewa (Lake Forsyth) to catch eels as they migrate to the sea. Teone (Hōne) Taare Tīkao, an elder of the Ngāi Tahu tribe, described how this method was used in the South Island: 'When the great eel migrations (heke-tuna) were on you could catch them in surprising numbers by two or three ways. One way was to make canals or drains from the waterways for a chain or two through the sand or shingle with a hole (parua) at the end, and sometimes the eels could be scooped out in thousands.'

Eel migrations *heke tuna*

Each year, adult eels head out to sea to spawn. Māori often caught them in large numbers as they migrated.

In Wairarapa, migrating eels pass through Lake Wairarapa into tidal Lake Ōnoke, then head past a gravel spit and out to sea. Tame Saunders, a Wairarapa elder, described in 1965 how the different types of eels came down in the same order: first the hao (king eels, about 30 centimetres long), then the riko (greenish-backed eels, about a metre long), then the paranui (dark, with thick skins), and finally the kōkopu tuna (up to 1.8 metres long and weighing just under 30 kilograms).

Around the time of the eel run, the mouth of Lake Ōnoke would close, blocking the eels' access to the sea. They were caught by setting a large number of nets and hīnaki in the lake, with a single channel between them. The eels would swim down the channel, reach the spit, turn back and be caught. The traps were set just before sunset, and removed in the early hours of the morning.

Tame Saunders described catching eels at Lake Wairarapa using a technique called kōumu:

> Another method of catching these tunas is to dig a large pit in the sand, about 10 yards from the end of the lake. A ditch is then dug from the lake to the pit, and as soon as the water starts to run into it, the eels swim into the pit. When the pit is full of eels the far end of the ditch is closed up, and the eels are left high and dry.[13]

South Island eel migrations

Eels were caught at Te Waihora (Lake Ellesmere) by the kōumu method. Long channels about a metre wide were dug through the gravel between the lake and the sea. Water flowed in, and the eels followed. Then the entrance to the channel was blocked with stones, or with net traps called kōhau.

At nearby Wairewa (Lake Forsyth), eels cross the shingle bar at Birdlings Flat in autumn. They are caught and stored for eating later – a traditional harvest that continues today.

OPENING THE LAKES

Before European settlement, Lakes Wairarapa and Ōnoke often flooded when Lake Ōnoke's mouth was closed. European settlers, particularly farmers, wanted to keep the mouth permanently open to reduce flooding. Māori opposed this out of concern that it would decrease the take of eels. In 1896 the lakes were gifted to the Crown by Wairarapa Māori. Lake Ōnoke was eventually kept open to the sea.

TE MAHINGA KAI | FOOD GATHERING

Ngā tupu mai i Hawaiki *plants from Polynesia*
Louise Furey

This 1907 painting by Gottfried Lindauer shows Māori men digging a kūmara garden with kō (digging sticks). These kō have the teka, an attached foot tread.

When the ancestors of Māori crossed the ocean to New Zealand, they brought plants from Polynesia to cultivate in their new home. Kūmara became a staple food, and hue were used to store water and food. But other plants did less well in the cooler climate.

From Polynesia to New Zealand

When Europeans arrived in New Zealand, six introduced cultigens (cultivated plants that have no known wild ancestor) were being grown by Māori.

They were: kūmara (sweet potato), hue (bottle gourd), aute (paper mulberry), taro, uwhi (yam), and tī pore (Pacific cabbage tree).

These plants were brought from Polynesia by the ancestors of Māori when they arrived in New Zealand from around 1250–1300 AD. Other food crops, such as arrowroot, banana, breadfruit, coconut and sugar cane, may also have arrived on the voyaging canoes, but could not be grown in the new country's cooler climate. Some plants may have been introduced to New Zealand more than once, possibly coming from different island groups.

Polynesians cultivated a number of plants which their ancestors had taken eastwards across the Pacific from Asia. Taro was most commonly grown on islands with a high rainfall, like Samoa. Yams fared better in places with separate wet and dry seasons, like Tonga. Breadfruit and bananas were the main crop in the Marquesas Islands and southern Cook Islands. Polynesians linked the calendar year and rituals to the annual growth cycles of these crops.

This woman is using a timo or grubber in the 1900s. These tools would have been used in much the same way before European arrival.

Taumata atua (resting place of gods) were stone figures that represented Rongo (left). They were believed to preserve the mauri (life force) of the kūmara crop.

This taputini kūmara is one of four varieties that may date from before European arrival in New Zealand – the others are rekamaroa, hutihuti and houhere. The kūmara brought to New Zealand from Polynesia were smaller than the kūmara sold in shops today.

Kūmara

Unlike the Polynesians' other cultigens, kūmara is indigenous to South America and did not come across the Pacific from the west. Archaeological research on the settlement of Polynesian island groups and their horticultural history points to kūmara arriving in Polynesia between 900 and 1100 AD. The seafaring Polynesians had large, double-hulled sailing canoes, and the navigating skills and ability to travel across large areas of ocean from one island group to another. It seems likely that some travelled to South America, and returned to Polynesia with kūmara.

There were a number of domesticated crop plants in South America, so the question of why the Polynesian visitors chose kūmara to take home is intriguing. Archaeologist Helen Leach has suggested that kūmara was adopted because of the similarity of its leaf shape and tubers to the yam (already grown in Polynesia). Unlike yams, however, kūmara could be grown year-round, and could be reproduced by planting rooted cuttings instead of tubers. Kūmara was a minor crop on most islands – it became dominant only on Rapa Nui (Easter Island) and in New Zealand. Growing practices and rituals associated with yams were transferred to kūmara. Linguistics and archaeology suggest that the Society Islands, or Mangaia in the Cook Islands, may have been the source of the kūmara varieties.

CANOE IMPORTS

There are different traditions about the arrival of cultivated plants in New Zealand. The *Horouta* canoe is said to have brought the kūmara, taro, hue and uwhi. Ngāti Whātua believe that Kui, a wife of the ancestor Tumutumuwhenua, introduced taro and hue. In another tradition, the *Tainui* waka arrived carrying hue, aute and kūmara.

TE MAHINGA KAI | FOOD GATHERING

This aerial view shows a pā site which includes gardens and stone-row boundaries, in the Wairarapa. The stone rows may have been used to define land-use rights.

The hue (Polynesian bottle gourd) was used in a number of ways in New Zealand. Smaller fruits were eaten, while larger hue were used to hold water or preserved food.

Adapting to New Zealand

In Polynesia, it was common to plant kūmara and yams on mounds. Gourds and taro were grown in shallow hollows to retain moisture. Polynesians built stone walls and rows for shelter and as boundaries around the gardens. They also used fences and shallow ditches.

These methods were brought to New Zealand, where the Polynesian colonists quickly learned to adapt their planting regimes and techniques to the cooler climate. The growing season was restricted to the warmer months, and they added coarse sand and gravel to soil – probably to improve drainage, increase the temperature and extend the period of plant growth. This was particularly important from Marlborough south to Banks Peninsula (the southern limit of kūmara growing).

The planting, tending and harvesting of the main crop, kūmara, was accompanied by many rituals, believed to ensure plentiful results. Traditional kūmara plants were different from modern varieties – they were bushy, with few runners, and long, thin tubers. These early varieties had white skin and white flesh, or red skin and purple flesh. Tubers were planted in puke (mounds) in spring and the crop harvested in autumn before the first frosts. Early European visitors described in detail the ordered and tidy state of the kūmara gardens.

After harvest, the kūmara were sorted to remove any damaged tubers, and placed in storage pits designed to maintain an even temperature and high humidity through winter. This helped preserve the tubers to be eaten in winter and spring, and the seed tubers to be planted for the next year's crop.

Hue

Hue were once believed to have originated in South America. But DNA research in the early 2000s suggests that the gourds grown in Polynesia and New Zealand are a hybrid of American and Asian species. Scientists think that gourds were either deliberately introduced from Asia and America, or may have floated across the sea to Polynesia and then been grown from the seeds inside.

Hue was grown primarily for its fruit, which were made into containers when mature. In summer, the small immature fruits were eaten. Gourd plants were grown in hollows, as they preferred moist soil, and the trailing plants may have been grown up stakes. In 1769, William Monkhouse, surgeon on James Cook's ship the *Endeavour*, reported gourd plants being grown over houses at Anaura Bay on the East Coast. In Māori tradition, the hue originated with Pū-te-hue, a child of the god Tāne.

Taro

Taro was grown for its starchy tuber. It was considered a kai rangatira (food for important people). Early explorer William Colenso named 10 varieties from Northland, some of which were only eaten on particular occasions, and another nine from the East Coast

AUTE

Aute is a shrub or small tree that is abundant throughout Polynesia but does not appear to have thrived in New Zealand. The plant was a valuable source of tapa cloth in Polynesia. Bark was stripped from the stem, beaten and felted with a wooden beater on a hard surface. Only small quantities of cloth were made in New Zealand – it was observed in the Bay of Islands in 1769, worn as small rolls in earlobes. Tapa beaters are reported from as far south as Taranaki, which may indicate the southern limit of aute cultivation.

and Hawke's Bay. Like kūmara, these varieties were distinguished by size, sweetness and colour.

Taro needs plenty of moisture, and microfossil analysis of peat soils in Northland has shown that taro was grown in swamps with elaborate drainage networks to maintain appropriate conditions. These sites, which are similar to the Polynesian wetland ditch-and-irrigation systems, were no longer in use by the late 18th century. Only dry-land taro gardens were reported by early European observers, who saw taro being grown in hollows or on flattened areas.

Uwhi

Very little is known about uwhi cultivation in New Zealand. A growing period of eight months or more is needed for the tubers to reach maturity (compared to five months for kūmara). As a result, yams could not be grown in many areas, and yields may have been low. Eighteenth-century European visitors saw yams growing in gardens in Northland, and in Tolaga and Anaura bays on the East Coast. The plants have a twining habit and, like kūmara, were planted on puke (mounds). However, introduced vegetables – especially potatoes – later replaced yams.

Tī pore

Tī pore (Pacific cabbage tree) was grown primarily for its tap root, which, after bruising and steaming in a hāngī (earth oven), was sweet and edible. The central shoot and stem pith could also be eaten. Tī pore is now extinct in the wild in New Zealand, but grows well on Raoul Island in the Kermadecs, where it may have been introduced during Polynesian voyages south to New Zealand. The shrub-like plant was reproduced vegetatively, but took several years to reach maturity. It seems to have been grown only in the Far North of New Zealand. Polynesian settlers assigned the name tī to the native New Zealand cabbage trees (which are in the same genus). They cooked the root in a similar way, but did not cultivate the plants.

The tī pore (Pacific cabbage tree) was introduced into New Zealand in the waka (canoe) migrations of the 13th century. It was grown for its taproot, which was cooked in a hāngī (earth oven).

Kiore *Pacific rats*

Bradford Haami

Kiore travelled across the Pacific to New Zealand in the canoes of Polynesian seafarers, the ancestors of Māori. These hardy rodents found plenty to plunder in their new home – and became a threat to many native plants and animals.

Kiore or Pacific rats (*Rattus exulans*) are found throughout Asia and the Pacific. They are believed to have originated in South-East Asia, and dispersed through the Pacific in the canoes of Polynesian seafarers. The Polynesian ancestors of Māori arrived in New Zealand around the 13th century with kiore on board.

Kiore are small for a rat – about 11–13 centimetres long excluding the tail, and 60–80 grams in weight. They are brown, with a grey-and-white underside. Kiore is the usual name given to this species in New Zealand, although other names have also been used: maunga-rua is a 'large rat'; tāpapa a 'well-grown rat'; torokaha a 'big buck'; toko-roa a 'light-coloured rat'; while hāmua refers to a rat considered an ill omen that was seldom eaten.

Habitat and diet

During the day, kiore stay in holes in the ground or in hollow tree trunks, emerging at night to feed. Māori trapped kiore in winter, when the rats were in prime condition – in summer they were thin. When kiore fattened and their fur changed colour, it indicated plentiful forest berries and the approach of spring. Hīnau berries were their favourite food, as signalled in the proverb, 'Mā wai e kai te hīnau, te kame a te kiore' (for whom is the hīnau, it is food for the kiore). They were also known to eat miro, tawa, tawai, karamū, taraire, kohekohe, pūriri and patatē berries. The tāwhara fruit of the kiekie plant was another favourite. It was common to tie kiekie leaves over the fruit to stop kiore eating it before it could be harvested.

Kiore also ate the eggs and chicks of birds, as well as lizards, frogs and insects. They contributed to the extinction of a number of species.

Decline

Norway rats (*Rattus norvegicus*) were introduced by Europeans in the 18th century, and ship rats (*R. rattus*) in the 19th century. Māori names for these rats included pou-o-Hawaiki and muritai. Their introduction, together with that of the mouse, led to a decline in kiore numbers because of competition for resources. By the early 1920s kiore were considered extinct. However, some survive in Fiordland, on Stewart Island and on several offshore islands.

A northern tribe, Ngāti Wai, sees itself as kaitiaki (guardian) of kiore. Ngāti Wai and a number of Māori believe there are historic and cultural reasons these rats should survive. However, kiore are not protected by law, and evidence of their predation on endangered native birds, lizards and insects have seen them eradicated from Crown-owned islands by the Department of Conservation. The department recognises that kiore may be of cultural interest, and consult with tribes before carrying out eradication programmes.

Traditions

The whakapapa of kiore is associated with kūmara. Rongo-māui stole celestial kūmara from his older brother, Whānui (the star Vega), and brought them back to earth in his scrotum. He impregnated his wife Pani, who gave birth to earthly kūmara. She cooked them to break the tapu from their celestial origin. But the demigod Māui had watched Pani giving birth to the kūmara, and told the people they were eating her impurities. In shame she fled to the underworld of Mataora with her youngest daughter, Hinemataiti ('the small-eyed girl'). Hinemataiti was to become the ancestor of kiore. And just as her father Rongo-māui had stolen kūmara from the sky, Hinemataiti stole them from Pani while they were overwintering in underground storage pits. Some tribes believe Hinamoki is the father of kiore. Hinamoki is also the name given to a type of rat.

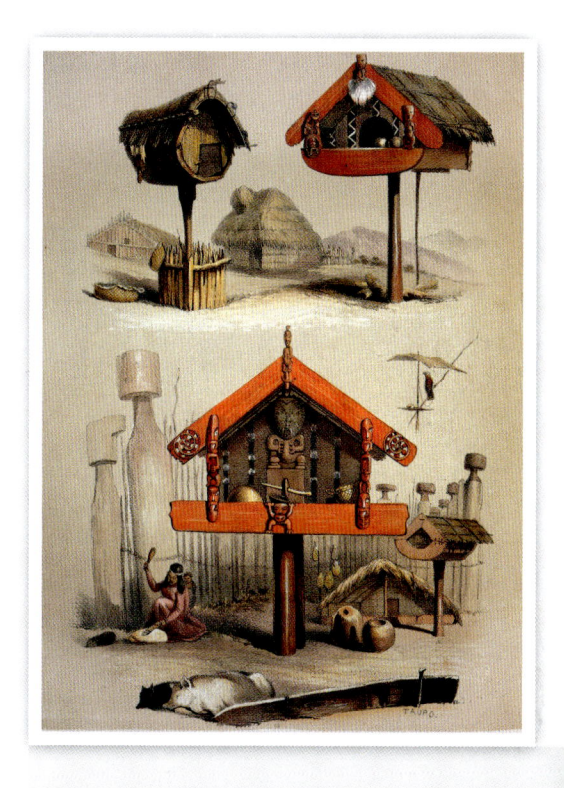

STOP, THIEF!

Elevated platforms and storehouses were used to stop kiore stealing food. People building them were warned, 'He pou pai ka eketia e te kiore, he pou kino e kore e eketia' (an attractive or carved post will be climbed by kiore, an ugly, uncarved one won't). Carved posts supporting storehouses or stages provided footholds for kiore. The saying was also a warning that the conspicuous display of wealth encouraged thieves.

The fruit of the kiekie is known as tāwhara. It was a favourite of kiore, and when the fruit was abundant it was a good time to catch these rats for food.

TE MAHINGA KAI | FOOD GATHERING

These kiore were photographed on Little Barrier Island (Hauturu). Kiore arrived in New Zealand with the Polynesian ancestors of Māori, around the 13th century. Kiore are bigger than mice, but smaller than other rats.

RATS IN RESEARCH

Kiore might be small, but they loom large in scientific research. Ancient Polynesian voyages have been traced by analysing the DNA of kiore from different Polynesian islands. In New Zealand, carbon dating of the bones of kiore, and the seeds and snail shells kiore gnawed, tells us that Māori ancestors arrived around the 13th century.

The traditions of the *Aotea*, *Horouta* and *Māmari* canoes mention that kiore were passengers on their voyages to New Zealand. Carvings on a window frame of Te Ōhākī marae at Ahipara depict the story of Ruanui's kiore. Ruanui was captain of the *Māmari* canoe. On arriving in Hokianga Harbour, he released his kiore onto an island now called Motukiore (rat island).

Kiore are remembered in the names of people, houses, landscapes, plants and animals. Nihootekiore (rat's tooth) and Motukiore (rat island) are places, Hine-kiore (rat girl) is a name, and tūtae-kiore (rat excrement) is a plant. Kiore is the name of a star cluster, while kiri-kiore (rat skin) and Pū-kiore (rat's nest) are patterns in carvings and tattoos.

Kiore feature in proverbs, songs and dance. 'Ko tini o para kiore' (a swarm of rats) refers to a heavily populated area. 'Honoa te hono a te kiore' (gather as rats do) was used by the Ngāi Tūhoe ancestor Karetehe to rally warriors who were facing defeat. His warriors knew to group together like rats and run straight through enemy ranks.

Hunting and eating kiore

Kiore were an important source of protein for Māori. Because the rats did not carry transmissible diseases, they presented little or no threat to human health. Tribes set rāhui (restrictions on killing) or created forest reserves so kiore could breed, and in the right season they were harvested for food. These reserves were owned by specific iwi and hapū, and were jealously guarded. Special permission was needed for strangers wanting to harvest the animals.

Kiore hunting was well organised. Ara kiore (rat tracks) in the forest or on hillsides, no matter how steep the gradient, were lined with tāwhiti kiore (unbaited traps) and pokipoki (baited traps). Paepae-kiore (pit traps) were dug in a way that made it hard for kiore to escape.

TE MAHINGA KAI | FOOD GATHERING

Tawiti kiore (rat trap).

This trap is the taupopoki. A kiore would go part way through the loop to reach the bait. The rat would pull at the bait, releasing the stick that stopped the loop from springing up.

This pit trap is known as a rua torea. Kiore walked across the stick to the bait and slipped into the pit, where they were collected by a trapper.

This portable trap is the tāwhiti makamaka, made of mānuka bark, aka pirita (supplejack) and muka (flax fibre). A kiore would chew through the cord to reach the bait. When the cord snapped, the bent stick would spring up and snare the rat in a loop inside the trap.

Once caught and killed, kiore were skinned and roasted over a fire or pre-cooked in a hāngī. They were placed in gourds in their own hinu (fat), which acted as a preservative once set. Kiore huahua (preserved rat) was saved as a delicacy for visitors.

Feasts and exchange

Because kiore were a special delicacy, they were a form of currency at many ceremonial occasions. The custom of kaihaukai (feast gifts) was carried out at food feasts between coastal and interior tribes, where preserved rat was served. Sometimes battles between warring factions were played out with reciprocal feasts. The open display of food indicated a tribe's mana, and the lesser opponent had to pay homage to the victor in some form.

One great feast, called Ngā-tau-tuku-roa, was hosted by the central Hawke's Bay chief Te Rehunga in response to a taunt. At the feast he served kiore preserved in fat. His opponent, Tama-i-waho, paid homage to his mana and gifted lands to Te Rehunga. He confirmed the contract with food, and placed kiore huhuti (plucked rats) on hills to mark the boundaries of the gift. The name Takapau was given to this area, after the sacred mat on which Te Rehunga's feast was presented.

A WEAKNESS FOR RATS

Although appreciated as an energy-giving food, kiore were used as a metaphor for weakness. A weak person was said to have 'he uaua kiore' (sinews of a rat), compared with a strong person's 'he uaua parāoa' (sinews of a whale). A person whose boasts exceeded his abilities might hear the saying, 'He nanakia aha tō te kiore nanakia?' (How fierce is the kiore?)

One of the oldest artefacts discovered in New Zealand is this carved wooden dog. It was found in Monck's Cave, on Banks Peninsula.

Kurī *Polynesian dogs*

Basil Keane

A vital source of protein and fur, the sturdy kurī was also a favoured pet of Māori chiefs. Ancient accounts tell of dogs turned to stone, ghostly barking, and supernatural beings in the form of kurī.

Kurī were Polynesian dogs which gradually died out in New Zealand. They were descended from the dogs brought to New Zealand from Polynesia, on the ancestral canoes of the Māori people in the 13th century. Kurī became bigger and more active than dogs on other Polynesian islands. Their average weight was between 13 and 15 kilograms.

Kurī were small, long-haired dogs about the size of a border collie. They had a small head, pricked ears, a terrier-like snout and a powerful jaw. The shoulders and neck were heavy, the legs were short, and the tail was bushy. Some were black, some white, and others a combination with patches or spots. Some had yellow coats.

The kurī was also known as gurī by Māori in the South Island. Another name, pero, made some believe that kurī had been introduced by Spanish settlers, as perro is Spanish for dog. 'Kararehe' was later used by Māori to refer to any four-legged animal. The term 'Māori dog' probably arose from 'kurī māori'. But this actually means '[any] ordinary dog'.

TE MAHINGA KAI | FOOD GATHERING

This stuffed kurī is at the Museum of New Zealand Te Papa Tongarewa, in Wellington. The first Polynesians to settle in New Zealand brought the dogs with them on voyaging canoes.

AUAU!

Kurī, like other Polynesian dogs, did not bark, but howled. The sound was described as a 'long, melancholy howl', like that of a fox. The Māori word for its howl was 'auau', while the bark of the European dog was 'pahupahu'.

Food source

Wherever Polynesian explorers travelled they would take dogs, pigs, chickens and rats. All except the kiore were domesticated, and they were all eaten. However, only kurī and kiore arrived in New Zealand. With no pigs – a source of protein in Polynesia – kurī became an important substitute. In early Māori settlements, kurī probably had greater access to food, including moa and seals, than at later times. They were probably also more plentiful in the early days, which would explain why such a high percentage of dogs slaughtered for food were young. Their meat would have been tastier, and there would have been less need to retain breeding stock. During the later settlement period, kurī were fed mainly on fish, and slaughtered dogs were more likely to be adults. In the South Island, kurī were said to have been castrated to fatten them more quickly for eating.

It is unclear when kurī died out. Although scientists travelling with Captain James Cook saw the dogs throughout New Zealand (on voyages between 1770 and 1779), they probably became rare through cross-breeding with introduced dogs, and then disappeared altogether.

Kurī flesh was considered a delicacy. A number of places were named for feasts where dog meat was on the menu. Hikawera, in Hawke's Bay, a chief at Waiohiki, ordered 70 dogs to be slaughtered to feed travellers. The scraps were thrown in the river – hence its name, Tūtaekurī, meaning dog offal. The place where the animals were cooked on this occasion was called Te Umukurī (kurī oven).

The kurī supporting the figures on this wooden bowl is Pōtaka Tawhiti – one of the most famous dogs in Māori tradition. It belonged to Houmaitawhiti, a chief in the Polynesian homeland of Hawaiki. Another chief, Uenuku, ate the dog. He was found out by Tamatekapua, Houmaitawhiti's son, when the dog's spirit howled from inside his stomach. Conflict followed, leading Tamatekapua to make the long journey to Aotearoa in the *Te Arawa* canoe.

TE MAHINGA KAI | FOOD GATHERING

Because it took a great deal of labour to produce a dogskin cloak (kahu kurī), these garments were highly prized, and worn by rangatira (chiefs).

This carved taiaha (fighting staff) is decorated with white hair (known as awe) from a kurī. The hair was used to distract an opponent, because it would move as the weapon was wielded.

From Curio Bay in the South Island, this necklace is made from kurī bones. The dogs' bones were also used to make awls and pendants.

Found at Jackson Bay on the South Island's West Coast, these fish-hook points were made from the jawbones of kurī.

DOG FOR DINNER

On his 1769 voyage, Captain James Cook spoke of a kurī tasting almost as good as lamb. Sydney Parkinson, an artist on the voyage, compared it to coarse beef. An early explorer, Thomas Brunner, got so low on food he was forced to eat his dog Rover. This didn't seem to distress him too much, as he noted that the flavour was very tasty, somewhere between mutton and pork. Māori gave him the nickname Kai Kurī (dog eater).

Uses of kurī

Dog skins were used to make kahu kurī (cloaks), and a garment to ward off weapons. This was known as 'he tāpahu o Irawaru' (the protective cloak of Irawaru, god of dogs). The dog's long, bushy tail was shaved for its hair, from which circlets for mourners were made, or to adorn weapons. Its bones were made into awls, pendants and necklaces, while the jaw and teeth were used for fish hooks. The teeth were also used as ear pendants.

Traditional accounts describe kurī being used for hunting. Tūrongo, a Tainui chief, left his dog with his wife Mahinaarangi, from the East Coast, to guide her and catch game when she journeyed to his home. Tara, son of the explorer Whātonga, had a kurī that was also a renowned hunter.

In the 1800s, kurī were used for catching kiwi, kākāpō, weka, pūkeko and māunu (moulting ducks). The fowler would often lure a kiwi by imitating its cry. As it came close, the fowler would release the dog, which he led on a rope, or give it enough slack to catch the bird. The Ngāi Tahu scholar Hōne Taare Tikao described how kurī were used to catch pūkeko, which are not good flyers. To flush out the birds, the people would beat the swamp during

TE MAHINGA KAI | FOOD GATHERING

Kurī appear (bottom right) in this painting of a kāinga (village), at Maurea on the banks of the Waikato River. It was painted by George French Angas in 1847.

a strong north-west wind, and the birds would tire of flying against the wind. At this point, the dogs would catch them.

Kurī were sacrificed on ceremonial occasions. Tohunga would sacrifice a dog to appease Tūmatauenga, the god of war, or other gods. Dogs were also used as a tapu food for tohunga. In the 1830s at Mangakāhia, when a high-born woman was to get a moko, one of the last kurī in the district was killed as tapu food for the tattooer.

Wild kurī

Some traditional accounts refer to wild kurī. At Waitomo there is a cave named Ruakurī (dogs' den). Attacked there by wild kurī, a fowler and his companions organised large snares near the cave to capture them.

Wild or pestering dogs were also trapped in a tāwhiti (spring trap). The place name Tāwhitikurī (found throughout the country) indicates sites where this happened. A South Island custom was to tether a female dog that was in heat, and capture the wild dogs that were drawn to her.

In post-European times, feral packs of kurī–European dog cross-breeds were shot on sight and gradually exterminated.

COVER-UP

One northern tribe got their name from using dog skins as a ruse in battle. Unable to defeat a fortified pā, they made the likeness of a stranded whale out of dogskin cloaks. The besieged people, coming out to harvest this bounty, were quickly overcome by the tribe, which was known as Ngāti Kurī from then on.

181

This vibrant rainforest illustrates the Māori term matomato. It has two meanings: green, and growing vigorously. When the forest is matomato it shows its mana (spiritual power).

Kaitiakitanga *guardianship and conservation*

Members of the Ngāti Whātua tribe plant native trees at Bastion Point in July 2004. This was part of a Ngāti Whātua project, Ko te Pūkaki, which aims to re-establish their forest. Over 15,000 trees and shrubs had been planted over the previous three years.

Kaitiakitanga means guardianship and protection. It is a way of managing the environment, based on the Māori world view.

A kaitiaki is a guardian. This can be a person or group that cares for an area such as a lake or forest. They are given that role by the local tribe.

In the Māori world view, people are closely connected to the land and nature. Kaitiakitanga is based on this idea of humans as just another species in the natural world.

Traditional practices

In the past, people followed traditional practices when they were hunting, fishing, growing or finding food. These helped them to care for the environment.

They included:
- temporary bans (rāhui) on taking food from an area
- using the lunar calendar (maramataka) to decide when to plant and harvest
- taking only what was needed
- hunting and fishing only for food, not as sport

The peninsula at Maketū was named by Te Arawa chief Tamatekapua after the bridge of his nose. Chiefs often claimed land by naming it after parts of their body, making it tapu.

- using bird snares at the right time – for example, not when the birds were breeding
- using loosely woven baskets for gathering shellfish so the young fell through and continued to grow.

Mana, tapu and mauri

Mana means spiritual power. If a forest has mana, it will have plenty of flowers, fruit and birds.

Tapu can mean spiritual restriction. Sometimes rāhui are needed to help the mana of the forest. A rāhui might stop people taking birds, fish or fruit from a certain area, or at a certain time.

Mauri means life force. This must be protected in forests, rivers, gardens, lakes and the sea. Special mauri stones, which tohunga (priests) said prayers over, were used to preserve this force.

Kaitiakitanga today

Today there is growing interest in kaitiakitanga. Iwi are recovering traditional knowledge about their environment, and using it as part of the management of tribal land.

- The Ngāi Tahu tribe are guardians of pounamu (greenstone) in the South Island.
- The Te Ati Awa ki Taranaki tribe made a claim to the government to stop pollution in their fishing areas.
- Four tribes (Ngati Kahungunu, Rangitāne, Muaūpoko and Ngāti Raukawa) have come together to stop the Manawatū River being polluted.
- The Te Rarawa people are working to save the kukupa (wood pigeon).

Kaitiakitanga is one way Māori today still share the value their ancestors placed on the natural world, and so embody the traditional saying:

Ka puta ki te whaiao, ki Te Ao Mārama.

Emerge from the dim light of morning to the bright light of day.

Customary fishing officers Maadi Te Kahu (left) and Renee Randall play an important role in assisting modern-day kaitiaki (guardians). Officers were recruited by the Ministry of Fisheries in 1999 to help enforce customary fishing regulations.

Glossary of Māori words

aho line
ariki chief, leader, first-born
aruhe fern root
ātahu love charm
hākari feast
hāngī earth oven
Haumia-tiketike, Haumia-tikitiki god of fern root and uncultivated foods
hei tiki neck pendant
heru comb
hīnaki trap
hinātore moonlight
hōanga sandstone
hui meeting
iwi tribe
kaharoa seine net
kahu huruhuru feather cloak
kahu kiwi kiwi-feather cloak
kaihaukai present of food
kaitiaki guardian
kāpia kauri gum
kapua cloud
karakia prayer
karengo edible seaweed
kaumātua elder
kaupapa platform, plan, proposal
kete basket
kihikihi cicada
kiore Pacific rat
kō digging stick
kōanga spring
kōauau flute
koko close-weave net
kōkōwai red ochre
kōrari flax stalk
kōrero say, story
koru tree-fern shoot
kūmara sweet potato
kupenga net
kurī Polynesian dog
māhē stone sinker
māheuheu weed
maihi bargeboard
mākutu magic art
mana status
manaakitanga hospitality, respect, care
marae tribal forum, meeting place
marama moon
maramataka Māori lunar calendar
matarau eel spear
matau hook
matira fishing net
matua parent

māunu moulting duck
mauri life force
mihi greeting
moko facial tattoo
namu sandfly
namu poto small sandfly
naonao midge
ngahuru autumn
ngāwhā hot spring
pā fortification, eel weir
pakake whale motif
pākau fin, kite
pākērangi flax garment
Papatūānuku earth mother
pare lintel
pātaka storehouse
pātia fishing spear
patu short hand club
patu muka stone flax pounder
pātua food container
patupaiarehe, tūrehu, pakepakehā fairy-like being
peketua, weri centipede
pepe-te-nuinu butterfly
pia, ware gum
pito umbilical cord
pō darkness, the night
pōhoi feather ball worn in the ear
pōito float
ponaturi sea fairy
pora, pūreko rough mat
poraka mussel dredge
pounamu greenstone
poupou carved post
pōwhiri formal welcome
puia geyser
pungapunga pollen
pūngāwerewere spider
pūtōrino flute
rā sun
rāhui ban, prohibition
rangi sky
Ranginui sky father
raumati summer
rō stick insect
Rongo god of kūmara, cultivated foods and peace
taewa potato
tahā hinu small gourd vessel
tahā huahua, pātua container for holding preserved birds
takurua winter
Tāne god of the forest

Tangaroa god of the sea
tangata whenua people of the land
tangi funeral
taniwha supernatural creature
taonga treasure
taoroa long bird spear
tāruke fishing pot
tātai genealogy
tātaka huhu beetle larvae
taurapa stern post
Tāwhirimatea god of the wind
tāwhiti spring trap
tekoteko carved gable figure
teretere gecko
tipua supernatural creature
tīrewa rack
tititorea stick game
titoko ika hand net
tohunga priest, expert
toki adze
tokotoko walking stick
tongi saying
tūā charm or spell
Tūmatauenga god of humankind and war
tumu stump
tupuna ancestor
ua rain
umu earth oven
waeroa mosquito
waiariki hot spring
waiata song
waka canoe
waka huia treasure box
waka kōiwi burial chest
waka taua war canoe
whai string game
whaikōrero speech making
whakairo carve, wood carving
whakapapa genealogy
whakataukī proverb
whānau family
whao chisel
whare rūnanga, wharenui meeting house
whata platform
whē caterpillar
whetū star

Glossary of species names

aka pirita	supplejack, *Ripogonum scandens*
aute	paper mulberry, *Broussonetia papyrifera*
hakurā, iheihe	Gray's beaked whale, *Mesoplodon grayi*
hāpuku	groper, *Polyprion oxygeneios*
harakeke	flax, *Phormium tenax*
heketara	(a tree), *Olearia rani*
hihi	stitchbird, *Notiomystis cincta*
hīhue	Sphinx moth, *Agrius convolvuli*
hīnau	(a tree), *Elaeocarpus dentatus*
hopetea	white rock shell, *Dicathais orbita*
hue	bottle gourd, *Lagenaria siceraria*
huhu	(a beetle), *Prionoplus reticularis*
huia	(an extinct bird), *Heteralocha acutirostris*
huruhuru whenua	shining spleenwort, *Asplenium oblongifolium*
kahawai	(a fish), *Arripis trutta*
kaikaikaroro	triangle shell, *Spisula aequilatera*
kaikōmako	(a tree), *Pennantia corymbosa*
kākā	(a parrot), *Nestor meridionalis*
kākahi	freshwater mussel, *Hyridella menziesi*
kākāpō	(a parrot), *Strigops habroptilus*
kākara	knobbed whelk, *Austrofucus glans*
kānuka	(a tree), *Kunzea ericoides*
karaka	(a tree), *Corynocarpus laevigatus*
karaka, ngāruru	Cook's turban, *Cookia sulcata*
kareao	supplejack, *Ripogonum scandens*
kārearea	New Zealand falcon, *Falco novaeseelandiae*
kāreke	marsh crake, *Porzana pusilla*
karoro	black-backed gull, *Larus dominicanus*
kātote	soft tree fern, *Cyathea smithii*
kauri	(a tree), *Agathis australis*
kawekaweau	large gecko, *Hoplodactylus delcourti*
kehe	marble fish, *Aplodactylus arctidens*
kēkerewai	green mānuka beetle, *Pyronota festiva*
kererū, kūkupa	New Zealand pigeon, *Hemiphaga novaeseelandiae*
kiekie	(a vine), *Freycinetia banksii*
kina	sea urchin, *Evechinus chloroticus*
kiokio	(a fern), *Blechnum novae-zelandiae*
kiore	Pacific rat, *Rattus exulans*
kiwi	(a bird), *Apteryx* species
koekoeā	long-tailed cuckoo, *Eudynamys taitensis*
kōhūhū	(a tree), *Pittosporum tenuifolium*
kōmiromiro	tomtit, *Petroica macrocephala*
kōpuru	(a liverwort), *Lophocolea semiteres*
kōtuku	white heron, *Egretta alba modesta*
kōura, kēwai	freshwater crayfish, *Paranephrops planifrons*, *P. zealandicus* (larger variety)
kōwaowao	hound's tongue fern, *Phymatosorus pustulatus*
kōwhai	(a tree), *Sophora* species
kūaka	godwit, *Limosa lapponica*
kuhakuha	trough shell, *Mactra discors*
kuku, kūtai	green-lipped mussel, *Perna canaliculus*
kūmara	sweet potato, *Ipomoea batatas*
kumukumu	gurnard, *Chelidonichthys kumu*
kuruwhengu	Australasian shoveler, *Anas rhynchotis*
māhoe	whiteywood, *Melicytus ramiflorus*
maire	(a tree), *Nestegis cunninghamii*
mamaku	tree fern, *Cyathea medullaris*
mangemange	(a climbing fern), *Lygodium articulatum*
mānuka	(a shrub), *Leptospermum scoparium*
maomao	pink maomao, *Caprodon longimanus*
mataī	(a tree), *Prumnopitys taxifolia*
matamoe	shortfin eel, *Anguilla australis*
matangārahu	black nerita, *Nerita atramentosa*
matapōuri, pāpango	New Zealand scaup, *Aythya novaeseelandiae*
mātātā	fernbird, *Bowdleria punctata*
matuku	bittern, *Botaurus poiciloptilus*
miro	(a tree), *Prumnopitys ferruginea*
moho pererū	banded rail, *Gallirallus philippensis*
moki	(a fish), *Latridopsis ciliaris*
moko kākāriki	green gecko, *Naultinus grayii*
mokomoko	skink, *Oligosoma* and *Cyclodina* species
mokopāpā, moko tāpiri	Pacific gecko, *Hoplodactylus pacificus*
neinei	grass tree, *Dracophyllum latifolium*
ngōiro, kōiro	conger eel, *Conger verreauxi*
ongaonga	tree nettle, *Urtica ferox*
ōrea	longfin eel, *Anguilla dieffenbachii*
paikea	southern humpback whale, *Megaptera novaeangliae*
pakake	minke whale, *Balaenoptera acutorostrata*
para	frostfish, *Lepidopus caudatus*
parāoa	sperm whale, *Physeter macrocephalus*
patatē	seven-finger, *Schefflera digitata*
pātiki	flounder, *Rhombosolea plebeia*
pāua	abalone, *Haliotis iris*
pawharu	packhorse crayfish, green crayfish, *Sagmariasus verreauxi*
pepetuna, pūriri	pūriri moth or ghost moth, *Aenetus virescens*
piharau	lamprey, *Geotria australis*
pikopiko	common shield fern, *Polystichum richardii*
pipi	(a shellfish), *Paphies australis*
pīpīwharauroa	shining cuckoo, *Chrysococcyx lucidus*

Glossary of species names (continued)

pōhutukawa	(a tree), *Metrosideros excelsa*	**tī-kouka**	cabbage tree, *Cordyline australis*
ponga	silver tree fern, *Cyathea dealbata*	**tī pore**	Pacific cabbage tree, *Cordyline fruticosa*
pōpokotea	whitehead, *Mohoua albicilla*	**tīeke**	North and South Island saddleback, *Philesturnus rufusater* and *P. carunculatus*
pōrae	trumpeter fish, *Latris lineata*		
poroporo	(a shrub), *Solanum laciniatum*	**tio**	rock oyster, *Saccostrea cucullata*
puahou	five-finger, *Pseudopanax aboreus*	**tītiti pounamu**	rifleman, *Acanthisitta chloris*
puawānanga	(a vine), *Clematis paniculata*	**tītoki**	(a tree), *Alectryon exelsus*
pūhā	sowthistle, *Sonchus* species	**toheroa**	(a shellfish), *Paphies ventricosa*
pukatea	(a tree), *Laurelia novae-zealandiae*	**tohorā**	southern right whale, *Eubalaena australis*
pūpū	cat's eye, *Turbo smaragdus*	**tōrea**	pied oystercatcher, *Haematopus ostralegus*
pūpū-rore	volute, *Alcithoe arabica*	**toroa**	great albatross, genus *Diomedea*
rangiora	(a shrub), *Brachyglottis repanda*	**tōtara**	(a tree), *Podocarpus totara*
rārahu, rauaruhe	bracken fern, *Pteridium esculentum*	**totorere**	ostrich foot, *Struthiolaria papulosa*
rātā	northern and southern rata, *Metrosideros robusta*, *M. umbellata*	**tuangi**	cockle, *Austrovenus stutchburyi*
		tuangi haruru	ringed venus shell, *Dosinia anus*
raukawa	(a tree), *Pseudopanax edgerleyi*	**tuatara**	(a reptile), *Sphenodon punctatus*, *S. guntheri*
raupeti	black nightshade, *Solanum nigrum*	**tuatua**	(a shellfish), *Paphies subtriangulata*
raupō	bulrush, *Typha orientalis*	**tuere, napia**	hagfish, *Eptatretus cirrhatus*
raurēkau	(a shrub), *Brachyglottis repanda*	**tūī**	(a bird), *Prosthemadera novaeseelandiae*
rāwaru, taipua	rock cod, *Lotella rhacinus*	**turiwhatu**	dotterel, *Charadrius obscurus*
rengarenga	(a lily), *Arthropodium cirratum*	**tūtaeruru**	grass grub beetle, *Costelytra zealandica*
rereti, mouku	hen and chicken fern, *Asplenium bulbiferum*	**ūpokohue**	pilot whale, *Globicephala melaena*
rimu	(a tree), *Dacrydium cupressinum*	**uwhi**	yam, *Dioscorea* species
riroriro	grey warbler, *Gerygone igata*	**warehou**	(a fish), *Seriolella brama*
rō	stick insect, *Clitarchus hookeri*	**wētā punga**	giant weta, genus *Deinacrida*
ruru	morepork, *Ninox novaeseelandiae*	**whai**	stingray, *Dasyatis thetidis*
takahē	(a bird), *Porphyrio hochstetteri*	**whekī**	rough tree fern, *Dicksonia squarrosa*
tākapu	gannet, *Morus serrator*	**whekī-ponga**	brown tree fern, *Dicksonia fibrosa*
tāmure	snapper, *Pagrus auratus*	**whetiko**	mud snail, *Amphibola crenata*
tara	tern, *Sterna striata*		
taraire	(a tree), *Beilschmiedia tarairi*		
tarakihi	(a fish), *Nemadactylus macropterus*		
taramea	spear grass, *Aciphylla* species		
tarāpunga	red-billed and black-billed gull, *Larus novaehollandiae*, *L. bulleri*		
tarata	lemonwood, *Pittosporum eugenioides*		
taro	(a vegetable), *Colocasia esculenta*		
tātaramoa	bush lawyer, *Rubus* species		
tawa	(a tree), *Beilschmiedia tawa*		
tawhai, tawai	beech, *Nothofagus* species		
tētē whero	brown teal, *Anas chlorotis*		

Note: many of these species have more Māori names than are given here, and occasionally one generic name had been given to several species. Sometimes different names applied in different seasons, for example the names for bird species when they were fat and ripe for hunting in winter. Some birds have different male and female names. Names vary from tribe to tribe and there are dialectal variations. The natural world is a vivid reference for metaphorical imagery and some species have many names, for example the bellbird has 27 Māori names.

End notes

Part 1 Ranginui *the sky*

1. Adapted from Elsdon Best, *The Maori division of time*. Dominion Museum monograph no. 4. Wellington: Government Printer, 1986, pp. 18–19 (originally published 1922).
2. *The Maori division of time*, p. 20.
3. Adapted from *The Maori division of time*, pp. 34–35.
4. Elsdon Best, *The astronomical knowledge of the Maori*. Wellington: Government Printer, 1986, p. 47 (originally published 1922).
5. Harry Dansey, 'Matariki'. *Te Ao Hou* 61 (December–February 1967/68): 15–16.
6. 'Sacred funeral: Tangi for Te Puea.' *Te Ao Hou* 3 (Summer 1953): 5.
7. A. T. Ngata, *Ngā mōteatea*. Part I. Wellington: Polynesian Society, 1970, pp. 236–237 (originally published 1958).
8. Quoted in Elsdon Best, *Maori religion and mythology*. Vol 1. Wellington: Te Papa, 1995, p. 389 (originally published 1924).
9. Tuta Nihoniho, 'Uenuku or kahukura, the rainbow god of war.' *Te Ao Hou* 26 (March 1959): 50–53.

Part II Papatūānuku *the land*

1. Taimoana Tūroa, *Te takoto o te whenua o Hauraki: Hauraki landmarks*. Auckland: Reed, 2000, p. 45.
2. Ngārongo Iwikātea Nicholson, personal communication, 2003.
3. Carmen Kirkwood, *Tawhiao: king or prophet*. Huntly: MAI Systems, 2000, p. 138.
4. Michael Reilly and Jane Thomson, eds, *When the waves rolled in upon us: essays in nineteenth-century Maori history*. Dunedin: University of Otago Press, 1999, frontispiece.
5. George Grey, *Ngā mahi ā ngā tūpuna*, 4th ed., edited by H. W. Williams. Wellington: A. H. & A. W. Reed, 1971, p. 16–17 (originally published 1928).
6. *Te Toa Takitini* 90 (1 February 1929): 931.
7. New Zealand Ministry of Education, *Te Wharekura* 58 (1999).
8. *Te Pipiwharauroa* 149 (September/Mahuru 1910): 11.
9. Rihi Puhiwahine, 'Ka eke ki Wairaka', *Ngā mōteatea*, Part 1, edited by Apirana T. Ngata. Auckland: Polynesian Society, 1928, pp. 150–151.
10. J. M. McEwan, *Rangitane: a tribal history*. Auckland: Reed Methuen, 1986, p. 1.

Part III Tangaroa *the sea*

1. Te Ahukaramu Charles Royal, *Native traditions by Hūkiki te Ahu Karamū o Otaki, Jany 1st 1856*. Ōtaki: Te Wānanga-o-Raukawa, 2003, pp. 25–27.
2. Grey, George, *Polynesian mythology and ancient traditional history of the New Zealand race*. http://www.nzetc.org/tm/scholarly/tei-GrePoly-c1-1.html page 5 (last accessed 6 September 2010).
3. Translated from the *Journal of the Polynesian Society* 37 (1928): 261.
4. A. T. Ngata, *Ngā mōteatea*. Part I. Wellington: Polynesian Society, 1970, pp. 126–127 (originally published 1958).
5. *Te Pipiwharauroa* 116 (1907): 9.
6. Provided by Tūpara Tokoaitua in 1895. In A. W. Reed, *Reed book of Māori mythology*, revised by Ross Calman. Auckland: Reed, 2004, p. 491.
7. Quoted in Gerard Hutching, *The natural world of New Zealand*. Auckland: Viking, 1998, p. 206.

Part IV Te Waonui-a-Tāne *the forest*

1. James Cowan, 'The patu-paiarehe: notes on Maori folk-tales of the fairy people.' *Journal of the Polynesian Society* 30 (1921): 96–102; 142–151.

Part V Mahinga kai *food gathering*

1. *Report of the Waitangi Tribunal on the Muriwhenua fishing claim* (Wai 22). Wellington: The Tribunal, 1989, p. 35.
2. Anaru Reedy, ed., *Nga korero a Mohi Ruatapu: the writings of Mohi Ruatapu*. Christchurch: Canterbury University Press, 1993, pp. 70; 174.
3. Koro Dewes, 'Fishing for kahawai in the Waiapu River.' *Te Ao Hou* 23 (1958): 16–17.
4. *The Ngāi Tahu Sea Fisheries Report* (Wai 27). Wellington: The Waitangi Tribunal, 1992, 3.7.2.
5. J. C. Beaglehole, ed., *The journals of Captain James Cook on his voyages of discovery*. Vol. 2. Cambridge: Hakluyt Society, 1961, p. 169.
6. Quoted in Mira Szaszy, *Te timatanga tātau tātau: early stories from founding members of the Māori Women's Welfare League*, edited by Anna Rogers and Miria Simpson. Wellington: Māori Women's Welfare League and Bridget Williams, 1993, p. 55.
7. Banks's journal: daily entries. 4 December 1769 http://southseas.nla.gov.au/journals/banks/17691204.html (last accessed 24 August 2010).
8. Quoted in Elsdon Best, *Forest lore of the Maori*. Wellington: Te Papa Press, 2005, pp. 165–6 (originally published 1942).
9. *Forest lore of the Maori*, p. 170.
10. Tamarau Waiari, quoted in *Forest lore of the Maori*, p. 408.
11. Teone Taare Tikao, *Tikao talks: ka taoka tapu o te ao kohatu: treasures from the ancient world of the Maori*. Auckland: Penguin, 1990, p. 138 (originally published 1939).
12. Elsdon Best, *Fishing methods and devices of the Māori*. Wellington: Te Papa Press, 2005, p. 131 (originally published 1924).
13. T. V. Saunders, 'The eels of Lake Wairarapa.' *Te Ao Hou* 51 (June 1965): 37.

Bibliography

Andersen, Johannes C. *Māori life in Ao-tea*. Christchurch: Cadsonbury, 2000 (originally published 1907).

Andersen, Johannes C. *Myths & legends of the Polynesians*. New York: Dover, 1995 (originally published 1928).

Atkinson, I. A. E., and D. R. Towns. 'Kiore.' In *The handbook of New Zealand mammals*, edited by Carolyn M. King, 159–174. Auckland: Oxford University Press, 2005.

Ballard, C., and others, eds. *The sweet potato in Oceania: a reappraisal*. Pittsburgh: Dept. of Anthropology, University of Pittsburgh; Sydney: University of Sydney, 2005.

Barlow, Cleve. *Tikanga whakaaro: key concepts in Māori culture*. Auckland: Oxford University Press, 1994.

Best, Elsdon. *Fishing methods and devices of the Māori*. Wellington: Te Papa, 2005 (originally published 1924).

Best, Elsdon. *Forest lore of the Maori: with methods of snaring, trapping, and preserving birds and rats, uses of berries, roots, fern-root, and forest products, with mythological notes on origins, karakia used, etc.* Wellington: Te Papa, 2005 (originally published 1942).

Best, Elsdon. *Māori agriculture: the cultivated food plants of the natives of New Zealand: with some account of native methods of agriculture, its ritual and origin myths*. Wellington: Te Papa, 2005 (originally published 1925).

Best, Elsdon. *Māori religion and mythology: being an account of the cosmogony, anthropogony, religious beliefs and rites, magic and folk lore* of the Maori folk of New Zealand. 2 vols. Wellington: Te Papa Press, 2005 (originally published 1924).

Best, Elsdon. *The astronomical knowledge of the Māori genuine and empirical: including data concerning their systems of astrogeny, astrolatry and natural astrology, with notes on certain other natural phenomena*. New ed. Christchurch: Kiwi Publishers, 2002 (originally published 1922).

Best, Elsdon. *The Māori*. Christchurch: Kiwi, 2002 (originally published 1924).

Best, Elsdon. *Tuhoe, the children of the mist*. 4th ed. Auckland: Reed, 1996 (originally published 1925.

Brougham, Aileen E., and A. W. Reed. *The Reed book of Maori proverbs = Te kohikohinga whakatauki a Reed*. Auckland: Reed, 1999.

Buck, Peter. 'Fishing'. In *The coming of the Maori*. Wellington: Maori Purposes Fund Board, 1950.

Clark, G. 'Kuri.' In *The handbook of New Zealand mammals*, edited by Carolyn M. King, 256–260. Auckland: Oxford University Press, 2005.

Cowan, James. *Fairy folk tales of the Maori*. Auckland: Whitcomb & Tombs, 1925.

Crowe, Andrew. *Which native tree?: a simple guide to the identification of New Zealand native trees*. Auckland: Penguin, 1999.

Crowe, Andrew. *Which native fern?: a simple guide to the identification of New Zealand native ferns*. Auckland: Viking, 2001.

Crowe, Andrew. *Which native forest plant?: a simple guide to the identification of New Zealand native forest shrubs, climbers and flowers*. Auckland: Viking, 1994.

Firth, Raymond. *Economics of the New Zealand Maori*. Wellington: Government Printer, 1972 (originally published 1929).

Grace, John Te H. *Tuwharetoa: a history of the Maori people of the Taupo district*. Auckland: Reed, 1992 (originally published 1959).

Grey, George. *Polynesian mythology and ancient traditional history of the New Zealand race: as furnished by their priests and chiefs*. Hamilton: University of Waikato Library, 1995 (originally published 1885).

Guthrie-Smith, W. H. *Tutira: the story of a New Zealand sheep station*. Auckland: Godwit, 1999 (originally published 1921).

Haami, Bradford. *Cultural knowledge and traditions relating to the kiore rat in Aotearoa. Part 1: a Maori perspective*. Science and Mathematics Education Papers. Hamilton: University of Waikato, 1993.

Hakaraia, Libby. *Matariki: the Māori New Year*. Auckland: Reed, 2004.

He Korero Purakau mo nga taunahanahatanga a nga tupuna: Place names of the ancestors, a Maori oral history atlas. Wellington: New Zealand Geographic Board, 1990.

Henderson, J. McLeod. *Ratana: The origins and the story of the movement*. Wellington: Polynesian Society, 1963.

Hohepa, Bill. *How to catch fish, and where*. Auckland: Sporting Press, 1997.

Horrocks, M. 'Polynesian plant subsistence in prehistoric New Zealand: a summary of the microfossil evidence.' *New Zealand Journal of Botany* 42 (2004): 321–334.

Hyland, Rikihana. *Illustrated Maori myths and legends*. Auckland: Reed, 2003.

Ihimaera, Witi. *The whale rider*. Auckland: Reed, 2002.

Leach, Helen. *1,000 years of gardening in New Zealand*. Wellington: Reed, 1984.

McKinnon, Malcolm, ed. *Bateman New Zealand historical atlas: ko Papatuanuku e takoto nei*. Auckland: David Bateman in association with Historical Branch, Department of Internal Affairs, 1997.

Marsden, Māori. 'God, man and universe: a Maori view.' In *Te ao hurihuri: aspects of Maoritanga*, edited by Michael King, 118–138. Auckland: Reed, 1992.

Marsden, Māori. *The woven universe: selected writings of Rev. Māori Marsden*, edited by Te Ahukaramū Charles Royal. Ōtaki: Estate of Rev. Māori Marsden, 2003.

Matariki, he maramataka Māori, 2004/2005 Aotearoa–Pacific year: a bilingual journal/diary in Māori & English, with Māori fishing and planting guides. Auckland: Matakite, 2004.

Mead, Sidney Moko, ed. *Te Māori: Maori art from New Zealand collections*. Auckland: Heinemann, 1984.

Miller, David. 'The insect people of the Maori.' *Journal of the Polynesian Society* 61 (1952): 1–61.

Morton, Harry. *The whale's wake*. Dunedin: University of Otago Press, 1982.

Nahe, Hoani. 'Maori, tangata maori.' *Journal of the Polynesian Society* 3 (1894): 27–35.

Ngata, P. 'Nga mahi hi ika a te Maori.' *Te Maori* 2, no. 1 (December 1970–January 1971): 13.

Orbell, Margaret. *A concise encyclopedia of Māori myth and legend*. Christchurch: Canterbury University Press, 1998.

Orbell, Margaret. *Birds of Aotearoa: a natural and cultural history*. Auckland: Reed, 2003.

Orbell, Margaret. *The illustrated encyclopedia of Māori myth and legend*. Christchurch: Canterbury University Press, 1995.

Orbell, Margaret. *The natural world of the Maori*. Rev. ed. Auckland: David Bateman, 1996.

Pond, Wendy. 'Parameters of oceanic science.' In *Science of Pacific Island peoples: fauna, flora, food & medicine*, edited by John Morrison and others, 109–123. Suva: Institute of Pacific Studies, 1994.

Reed, A. W. *Reed book of Maori exploration: stories of voyage and discovery*. Rev. ed. Auckland: Reed, 2006.

Reed, A. W. *Reed book of Māori mythology*. Revised by Ross Calman. Auckland: Reed, 2004.

Reilly, Michael, and Jane Thomson, eds. *When the waves rolled in upon us: essays in nineteenth-century Maori history*. Dunedin: University of Otago Press, 1999.

Riley, Murdoch. *Maori bird lore: an introduction*. Paraparaumu: Viking Sevenseas, 2001.

Riley, Murdoch. *Māori healing and herbal: New Zealand ethnobotanical sourcebook*. Paraparaumu: Viking Sevenseas NZ, 1994.

Roberts, Mere. *Scientific knowledge and cultural traditions. Part 2: a Pakeha view of the kiore rat in New Zealand*. Science and Mathematics Education Papers. Hamilton: University of Waikato, 1993.

Roberts, Mere, and others. 'Whakapapa as a Maori mental construct: some implications for the debate over genetic modification of organisms.' *The Contemporary Pacific* 16, no. 1 (Spring 2004): 1–28.

Royal, Te Ahukaramū Charles. *Native traditions by Hūkiki te Ahu Karamū o Otaki, Jany 1st 1856*. Ōtaki: Te Wānanga-o-Raukawa, 2003.

Salmond, John T. *New Zealand native trees*. Auckland: Reed, 1994.

Tomoana, P. H. 'Ko nga tau, ko nga marama, ko nga ra me nga po pai, whai kai, kore kai ranei i runga i a te Maori korero.' *Te Kopara* 71 (October 1919).

Tomoana, P. H. *Te aroha o Rangi-nuikia Papa-tua-nuku o te tau*. Hastings: Hart & Co., 1921.

Te Tumu korero. Ngāruawāhia: Turongo House, 1983.

The lore of the whare-wānanga. Written down by H. T. Whatahoro from the teachings of Te Matorohanga and Nepia Pohuhu; translated by S. Percy Smith. 2 vols. Christchurch: Kiwi, 1998 (originally published 1913–15).

Thornton, Agathe. *The birth of the universe – Te whānautanga o te ao tukupū: Māori oral cosmogony from the Wairarapa*. Auckland: Reed, 2004.

Tikao, Teone Taare. *Tikao talks: ka taoka o te ao kohatu*. Auckland: Penguin, 1990 (originally published 1939).

Tūroa, Taimoana. *Te takoto o te whenua o Hauraki: Hauraki landmarks*. Auckland: Reed, 2000.

Wakefield, Edward Jerningham. *Adventure in New Zealand*. 2 vols. London: John Murray, 1845.

Whaanga, Mere. *The legend of the seven whales of Ngāi Tahu Matawhaiti: te pakiwaitara o ngā tohorā tokowhitu a Ngāi Tahu Matawhaiti*. Auckland: Scholastic, 2005.

White, John. *The ancient history of the Maori, his mythology and traditions*. 13 vols. Hamilton: University of Waikato Library, 2001.

Picture credits

Maps and diagrams are copyright to Te Ara – the Encyclopedia of New Zealand.

ANZ	Archives New Zealand – Te Rua Mahara o te Kāwanatanga
ATL	Alexander Turnbull Library – Te Wharepukapuka o Alexander Turnbull
AWMM	Auckland War Memorial Museum – Tāmaki Paenga Hira
DOC	Department of Conservation – Te Papa Atawhai
GNS	GNS Science – Te Pū Ao
LINZ	Land Information New Zealand – Toitū te Whenua
NSIL	Natural Sciences Image Library
NZP	New Zealand Post
PC	Private collection
TA	Te Ara – the Encyclopedia of New Zealand
TP	Museum of New Zealand Te Papa Tongarewa

Cover
Front cover: (top) photograph by V. Piskunov/istock; (middle) photograph by Brady Dyer/istock; (bottom) Oneclearvision/istock; back cover: (top) NSIL, Bi0204Rbt. tif, photograph by G. R. Roberts; (bottom) GNS, 19989, photograph by Lloyd Homer

Introductory pages
2 Te Herenga Waka Marae, Victoria University of Wellington, photograph by Andy Palmer; 4 PC, photograph by Simon Nathan

Te ao mārama – the natural world
6–7 photograph by Joe Gough/Shutterstock; 8 LINZ, carving by Rangi Hetet; 9 DOC, 10054029, photograph by Philippe Gerbeaux

Part I Ranginui – the sky
10–11 photograph by Phillip Bartlett/istock; 12 photograph by Martin Maun/istock; 13 (top) National Library Gallery, artwork by Cliff Whiting; 13 (bottom) NZP; 14 TP, ME 15027, sculpture by Jim Wiki; 15 photograph by Robert Simon/istock; 16 (top) Starry Night Photography, photograph by Chris Picking; 16 (bottom) NZP; 17 (top) photograph by V. Piskunov/istock; 17 (bottom) ATL, 1/2-003184; F; 18 (left) AWMM, photograph by Dianne Nothcott; 18 (right) ATL, Northwood Collection (PAColl-3077), 1/1-006265-G; 19 ATL, Northwood Collection (PAColl-3077), 1/1-006273-G; 20 (top left) ATL, Polynesian Society Collection, MSPapers-1187-184-004; 20 (top right) Starry Night Photography, photograph by Chris Picking; 20 (bottom) Ocean Wildlife, photograph by Ross Armstrong; 21 (top) ATL, Tourist and Publicity Department Collection, 1/2-040047-F; 21 (bottom) PC, photograph by Nick Roskruge; 22–23 Carter Observatory, photograph by Mark Cannell; 23 (bottom) TP, I.004228; 24 Astronomy New Zealand, image by Richard Hall; 25 (left) *Hawke's Bay Today*, 14 June 2004; 25 (right) AWMM, C1414, photograph by Bob Maysmor; 26–27 *New Zealand Herald*, 2 February 2005, photograph by Richard Robinson; 27 Metservice New Zealand, artwork by Cliff Whiting; 28 GNS, CN45245/24; 29 (top) ATL, New Zealand Railways Collection (PAColl-5167), 1/2-023706-G; 29 (bottom) NSIL, In2939Smn.jpg, photograph by Peter E. Smith; 30 (top left) PC, photograph by Christina Troup; 30 (top right) PC, photograph by Christina Troup; 30 (bottom) photograph by Phillip Bartlett/istock; 31 PC, photograph by Christina Troup; 32 Shutterstock; 33 NSIL, En0752LC8. jpg, photograph by John Hunt; 34 NSIL, En0075LC1.tif; 35 PC, photograph by Carl Walrond; 36 (top) DOC, 10052003, photograph by Peter Simpson; 36 (middle) photograph by Don Komarechka/istock; 36–37 Archives/istock; 36 (bottom) NSIL, DSCF8627.jpg, photograph by Peter E. Smith; 37 (bottom) photograph by Thomas Hruschka/Shutterstock

Part II Papatūānuku – the land
38–39 GNS, 41063, photograph by Lloyd Homer; 40 AWMM; 41 TA, photograph by Jock Phillips; 42 Ministry for Culture and Heritage, hand-coloured lithograph by John Bevan Ford; 43 (top) ATL, E. R. Williams Collection, G-140365-1/2; 43 (bottom) TP; 44 ATL, A. P. Goodber Collection, G-953-1/2-APG, photograph by A. P. Godber; 45 (top) GNS, CN28727/3, photograph by Lloyd Homer; 45 (bottom) Auckland Art Gallery – Toi o Tāmaki, photograph by Josiah Martin; 46 (top) PC, photograph by Christina Troup; 46 (bottom) *New Zealand Herald*; 47 ATL, William James Harding Collection (PAColl-3042), 11-000013-G, photograph by William James Harding; 48 PC, photograph by Kynan Gentry; 49 DOC, 10054005, photograph by Philippe Gerbeaux; 50 Scholastic New Zealand Ltd, Annie Rae Te Ake Ake, *Myths and legends of Aotearoa*. Auckland: Scholastic, 1999, acrylic on paper by Angus Kerr; 51 PC, photograph by Richard Chambers; 52 GNS, Extremophile photo collection, DCP-1370, photograph by Bruce Mountain; 53 (left) photograph by Jesse Baget/istock; 53 (top right) photograph by Natalia Minton/istock; 53 (bottom) ATL, PAColl-6406-01; 54 (top) Bateman, photograph by Russell McGeorge; 54 (middle) ATL, Cowan Collection (PAColl-3033), 1/2-066389-F; 54 (bottom) NZP; 55 GNS, CN43650/23, photograph by Lloyd Homer; 56 Taupō Museum of Art and History; 57 (top) GNS, CN26492/15, photograph by Lloyd Homer; 57 (bottom) Waikato Museum of Art and History; 58 GNS, 12936, photograph by Lloyd Homer; 59 (top) Bateman, photograph by Rafael Valentino; 59 (bottom) GNS, 22841/18, photograph by Lloyd Homer; 60 GNS, 9147/22, photograph by Lloyd Homer; 61 (top) DOC, 10060684, photograph by Sietse Bouma; 61 (bottom) DOC, 10047681, photograph by Lisa Forester; 62 (top) TA, photograph by Jock Phillips; 62 (bottom) PC, photograph by Simon Nathan; 63 Museum of Wellington City and Sea; 64 Bateman, photograph by Russell McGeorge; 65 (top) TA, photograph by John Wilson; 65 (bottom) Te Herenga Waka Marae, Victoria University of Wellington, photograph by Andy Palmer; 66 (top) GNS, CN9167/9, photograph by Lloyd Homer; 66 (middle) Tinakori Gallery, sculpture by Lewis Gardiner; 66 (bottom) PC, photograph by Simon Nathan; 67 PC, photograph by Simon Nathan; 68 (top) TP, I.007751; 68 (middle) TP, B.000881; 68 (bottom) CM, E163.254; 69 (top) PC, photograph by Bruce McFadgen; 69 (bottom left) AWMM; 69 (bottom right) TP, F. 004312/1

Part III Tangaroa – the sea
70–71 photograph by Patricia Hofmeester/istock; 72 (left) Bateman, photograph by Russell McGeorge; 72 (right) AWMM; 73 (top) TA, photograph by Jock Phillips; 73 (bottom) Puke Ariki – Taranaki Museum & Library, A77.330, carving by Tuiti-Moeroa; 74–75 photograph by Patricia Hofmeester/istock; 76 (left) TP, I.006367; 76 (right) Te Herenga Waka Marae, Victoria University of Wellington, photograph by Leanne Tamaki; 77 (top) TA, photograph by Jock Phillips; 77 (bottom) DOC, 10047807, photograph by Chris Rudge; 78 New Zealand Whale and Dolphin Trust, photograph by Steve Dawson; 79 The Roving Tortoise, photograph by Tui de Roy; 80 (top left) DOC, 10049662, photograph by Andy Cox; 80–81 TP; 80 (bottom) Paikea, Waipapa Marae, University of Auckland, photograph by Melanie Lovell-Smith; 82 (top) Bateman, photograph by Russell McGeorge; 82 (middle) *New Zealand Herald*, 1 December 2004; 82 (bottom) ATL, Northwood Collection (PAColl-3077), 1/2-051326-F; 83 (top) Whale Watch Kaikoura Ltd; 83 (bottom) ATL, Dominion Post Collection (PAColl-7327), EP/1996/0832/9A; 84 NZP, artwork by D. F. Kee; 85 AWMM; 86 (left) NZP; 86 (right) NZP; 87 (top) ATL, A-076-012, watercolour by Thomas William Downes; 87 (bottom) Whanganui Regional Museum, WR/S/17c; 88 ATL, C-075-013; 89 Auckland City Libraries – Tāmaki Pātaka Kōrero, Sir George Grey Special Collection, 7-A3159; 90 TP, MA_1.018357; 90–91 Mark Brimblecombe Photographer; 92 Waiatarua Publishing Co Ltd, Ron Bacon, *Tāmure me te taniwha*. Auckland: Waiatarua, 1996, pp. 12–13; 93 (top) PC, photograph by Basil Keane; 93 (bottom) ATL, Northwood Collection (PAColl-3077), 1/2-03000-F; 94 DOC, 10031460, photograph by Dick Veitch; 95 (left) ATL, A. P. Goodber Collection, PAColl-3039-1-012; 95 (right) DOC, 10047443; 96 TA, Walter Buller, 'A list of the lizards inhabiting New Zealand, with descriptions.' *Transactions and proceedings of the New Zealand Institute*, 1870, Vol. 3. Wellington: James Hughes, 1871, plate 2; 97 (top) NSIL, DSCG4229Smd.jpg, photograph by Peter E. Smith; 97 (middle) TA, Elsdon Best, *The Maori*. Wellington: Board of Maori Ethnological Research for the Author and on behalf of the Polynesian Society, 1924, p. 277; 97 (bottom) Tinakori Gallery, sculpture by Manos Nathan

Part IV Te Waonui-a-Tāne
98–99 GNS, 19989, photograph by Lloyd Homer; 100 ANZ, AAQA 6500 Col 1500, photograph by John Johns; 101 DOC, 10059548, photograph by Catherine Tudhope; 102 (top) NSIL, Gy0014smt, photograph by Peter E. Smith; 102 (bottom) PC, photograph by Richard Chambers; 103 (top)

PICTURE CREDITS

PC, photograph by Richard Chambers; 103 (middle) TA; 103 (bottom) Graham Meadows Photo Library, photograph by John Salmon; 104 (top) TA, photograph by Alastair McLean; 104 (bottom) DOC, 10060387, photograph by Catherine Tiffen; 105 (top left) AWMM; 105 (right) Te Herenga Waka Marae, Victoria University of Wellington, photograph by Miranda Wells; 106–107 photograph by Duncan Babbage/istock; 107 (top right) DOC, 10031106, photograph by Dick Veitch; 107 (bottom) AWMM; 108 (left) DOC, 10046841, photograph by Rod Morris; 108 (right) PC, photograph by Richard Chambers; 109 (top) TA, photograph by Carl Walrond; 109 (bottom) PC, photograph by Richard Chambers; 110 (top right) PC, photograph by Richard Chambers; 110 (top left) DOC, 10056882, photograph by Dick Veitch; 110 (bottom right) photograph by Irina Yun/Shutterstock; 110 (bottom left) TA, photograph by Melanie Lovell-Smith; 111 (top left) DOC, 10049474; 111 (top right) TP, I.006539; 111 (bottom right) PC, photograph by Simon Nathan; 112 (left) TA, photograph by Jock Phillips; 112 (right) Landcare Research – Manaaki Whenua, photographs by Robert Lamberts and Sue Scheele; 113 (left) TA, photograph by Alastair McLean; 113 (top right) PC, photograph by Peter Johnson; 113 (bottom) PC, photograph by Jeremy Rolfe; 114 (top left) TA, Elsdon Best, *Forest lore of the Maori*. Wellington: Dominion Museum, 1942; 114 (top right) DOC, 10059173; 114 (bottom) PC, photograph by Simon Nathan; 115 (left) PC, photograph by Iona Wassilieff; 115 (right) TA, photograph by Emily Tutaki; 116 (left) TP, MA_F.006611/01-09; 116 (right) ATL, PUBL-0014-27, hand-coloured lithograph by George French Angas; 117 (top left) DOC, 10029510; 117 (top right) DOC, 10053925, photograph by Ross Henderson; 117 (bottom left) DOC, 10059516, photograph by Tui De Roy; 117 (bottom right) ATL, PUBL-0026-19, hand-coloured lithograph by John Gould; 118 (top left) DOC, 10038053, photograph by Peter Blok; 118 (right) photograph by K. B. Browne/Shutterstock; 118 (bottom) NSIL, AWC 4231.jpg, photograph by Peter Righteous; 119 (top) photograph by Irina Yun/istock; 119 (middle left) Nga Manu Images, photograph by David Mudge; 119 (middle right) DOC, 10028777, photograph by M. F. Soper; 119 (bottom) *New Zealand Herald*, photograph by Greg Bowker; 120 (top left) DOC, 10023530, photograph by Mike Aviss; 120 (top right) NSIL, Bi0207RBt.tif, photograph by G. R. Roberts; 120 (bottom) DOC, 10031093, photograph by Rod Morris; 121 (top left) NSIL, Bi0204Rbt.tif, photograph by G. R. Roberts; 121 (top right) PC, photograph by Richard Chambers; 121 (bottom) *New Zealand Herald*, 22 December 2004, photograph by Alan Gibson; 122 (top) DOC, 10031416, photograph by Dick Veitch; 122 (bottom) NSIL, DSC11401Smd.jpg, photograph by Peter E. Smith; 123 (top left) DOC, 10033123, photograph by M. F. Soper; 123 (top right) PC, photograph by Christina Troup; 123 (middle right) PC, photograph by S. R. Chambers; 123 (bottom) PC, photograph by Richard Chambers; 124 (left) photograph by V. M. Jones/istock; 124 (right) DOC, 10033821, photograph by Dave Crouchley; 125 (top) PC, artwork by John Bevan Ford; 125 (middle left) DOC, 10059691, photograph by Rachael McClellan; 125 (middle right) DOC, 10055744, photograph by Greg Lind; 125 (bottom) photograph by mikeuk/istock; 126 NSIL, In0451Mrt.tif, photograph by John Marris; 127 (top) NSIL, In0645Mrt.tif, photograph by John Marris; 127 (middle) Landcare Research – Manaaki Whenua; 127 (bottom) McGraw-Hill Education, Mona Riini and Robert Jahnke, *Te timatanga o te ao: nga kete wananga*. Auckland: Shortland, 1992; 128 (top) DOC, 10048548; 128 (middle) DOC, 10032253, photograph by Rod Morris; 128 (bottom) PC, photograph by Andrew McLachlan; 129 (left) DOC, 10032088, photograph by Rod Morris; 129 (right) AWMM; 130 (left) DOC, 10033131; 130 (right) DOC, 10032176, photograph by Rod Morris; 131 (top left) PC, photograph by Steve Trewick; 131 (top right) National Library of New Zealand, artwork by Cliff Whiting; 131 (bottom) TP; 132–33 photograph by Luis Santos/istock; 133 (top middle) NZP; 133 (right) TP, B.024928; 134 Jade and Bone, graphic by Brian Flintoff; 135 (top) TA, Makereti Papakura, *The old-time Maori*. London: Gollancz, 1938, plate 13; 135 (bottom left) ATL, MNZ-2424-1/2-F; 135 (bottom right) GNS, 17584-17, photograph by Lloyd Homer

Part V Te mahinga kai
135–36 photograph by Matthew Gough/Shutterstock; 138 (left) TP, ME023196; 138 (right) ATL, 1/2-078253-F; 139 (top left) TP, I.006400; 139 (top right) ATL, 1/4-012590-F, photograph by James Macdonald; 139 (bottom right) ATL, 1/2-038203-F, photograph by W. R. Reynolds; 140 (top) ATL, C-025-002; 140 (bottom) Christchurch City Libraries, PhotoCD 8 IMG0053; 141 AWMM; 142 ATL, John Pascoe Collection, 1/4-001074-F, photograph by John Dobrée Pascoe; 143 ATL, B-045-001, watercolour by Edward Arthur Williams; 144 Ngāi Tahu Seafood Limited; 145 (top) ATL, Adkin Collection, PA1-f-005-424; 145 (bottom) Destination Northland; 146 ATL, Northwood Collection (PAColl-3077), 1/1-026522-G; 147 TA, photograph by Jock Phillips; 148 (top left) photograph by Bridget Lazenby/istock; 148 (bottom left) photograph by Peter Seager/istock; 148 (right) ATL, 1/2-008468-G, photograph by Frank J. Denton; 149 (left) ATL, Dominion Post Collection (PAColl-7327), EP/1969/4132A/38; 149 (top right) ATL, Dominion Post Collection (PAColl-7327), EP/1968/4058; 149 (bottom) DOC, 10048319, photograph by Paddy Ryan; 150 (top) ATL, PA1-f-179-51-2, photograph by Thomas Pringle; 150 (bottom) TP, B.000801; 151 (top left) DOC, 10051853; 151 (top right) PC, photograph by Malcolm Francis; 151 (bottom) PC, photograph by Iona Wassilieff; 152 ATL, 1/2-019482-F; 153 (top) PC, photograph by Christina Troup; 153 (bottom) Nelson Provincial Museum, Tyree Studio Collection, 176893/3; 154 (top) PC, photograph by Darren Scott; 154 (middle right) PC, photograph by Darren Scott; 154 (bottom left) TP, MA_1.004217; 155 TP, MA_B.000957; 156 (left) TA, Elsdon Best, *Forest lore of the Maori*. Wellington: Dominion Museum, 1942; 156 (right) PC, photograph by Christina Troup; 157 (top) Auckland City Libraries – Tāmaki Pātaka Kōrero, GNZ MMSS 118/1.A11475; 157 (bottom) ATL, B-023-018, photolithograph after a drawing by Russell Stuart Clark; 158 ATL, B-113-008, watercolour by William Fox; 159 (top) Polynesian Society Collection, 80-115-12/6, pencil sketch by Tamati Ranapiri; 159 (bottom) TP; 160 AWMM; 161 (left) TA, K. Wilson, 'Footprints of the Moa.' *Transactions of the Royal Society of New Zealand 45* (1912) plate 2; 161 (right) TP, watercolour by Paul Martinson; 162 DOC, 10049724, photograph by Stephen Moore; 163 (top left) NZP, 1994 series regarding Māui; 163 (top right) NSIL, DSCF9226Smd, photograph by Peter E. Smith; 163 (bottom) ATL, EP-Zoology-Eels-01; 164 (top) TA, T. W. Downes, 'Notes on eels and eel-weirs (tuna and pa tuna).' *Transactions and proceedings of the Royal Institute of New Zealand 50* (1918). Wellington: Govt Printing Office, pp. 296–316; 164 (bottom left) PC, photograph by Jim O'Brien; 164 (bottom right) DOC, 10049717, photograph by Stephen Moore; 165 (top left) ATL, Ramsden Papers, 1/2-037930-F, photograph by James Ingram McDonald; 165 (right) TP; 166 (top) ATL, A-076-016, watercolour by Thomas William Downes; 166 (bottom) TP; 167 (top) ATL, 1/1-000483-G; 167 (bottom) TP; 168 (top) Wairewa Runanga Group, photograph by Iaean Cranwell; 168 (bottom) TP, I.005554; 169 Landcare Research – Manaaki Whenua; 170 Auckland Art Gallery – Toi o Tāmaki, oil painting by Gottfried Lindauer; 171 (top left) TP, MA_A.000002; 171 (top right) The Open Polytechnic of New Zealand – He Wharekura-tini Kaihautu o Aotearoa, photograph by Graham Harris; 171 (bottom left) TP, MA_1029479; 172 (top) DOC, 10051760, photograph by Kevin Jones; 172 (bottom left) University of Auckland, photograph by Mike Burtenshaw; 172 (bottom right) TP, MA_1004189; 173 (top) TP; 173 (bottom) DOC; 174 DOC, 10033847, photograph by Dick Veitch; 175 (top) ATL, PUBL-0014-30, lithograph by George French Angas; 175 (bottom) DOC, 10054851; 176 DOC, photograph by Rod Morris; 177 (top left) University of Waikato, illustrations prepared for White's *Ancient history of the Maori*. Wellington: Government Printer, 1897, p. 75; 177 (right) TP, ME023624; 177 (bottom) TA, Elsdon Best, *The Maori*. Wellington: Board of Maori Ethnological Research and on behalf of the Polynesian Society, 1924, p. 501; 178 Canterbury Museum, E158.356; 179 (top) TP, MA_1006390; 179 (bottom) Otago Museum; 180 (top left) TP, MA_1047091; 180 (middle) TP, MA_1036464; 180 (top right) Otago Museum; 180 (bottom right) Otago Museum; 181 ATL, PUBL-0029-033, tinted lithograph by George French Angas

Kaitiakitanga
182 (top) NSIL, Ec0040Rbt, photograph by G. R. Roberts; 182 (bottom) Ngāti Whātua o Ōrākei; 183 (top) TA, photograph by Jock Phillips; 183 (bottom) ATL, EP/1999/3746/35, photograph by Craig Simcox

Index

A
adornment 82, 116, 148, 180 *see also* feathers, hei tiki
adzes (toki) 66, 68
Ahipara 176
Ahuahu (Great Mercury Island) 58
Ahuriri (Napier) 63, 65, 90, 91
Akaroa 65, 133
akeake (tree) 26
albatross (toroa) 60, 118
Alexandrina, Lake 35
amokura (red-tailed tropic bird) 42
Anaura Bay 172, 173
ancestors 9, 29; shaping of the land 48; used to claim links to land 57
Angas, George French 116
āniwaniwa *see* rainbow
Antares *see* Rehua
Ao-kehu (taniwha) 90, 92
Aoraki Mt Cook 30, 49, 54
Aotea (canoe) 61, 64, 176
Aotea Harbour 57, 61
Aotearoa 62; naming of 30
Arahura River 66, 93, 133
Ārai-te-uru (canoe) 49
Āraiteuru (taniwha) 86
Arcturus *see* Ruawāhia
argillite 66, 68
aruhe (fern root) 19, 113, 114, 115, 130; origins of 114
Ātiamuri 58
Atutahi (also Atuatahi, Autahi, Canopus) 15, 16
Auckland 61, 63
aute (paper mulberry) 112, 170, 173

B
banded rail (moho pererū) 118
Banks Peninsula 65, 142, 178
Banks, Joseph 143
bans, temporary *see* rāhui
barracouta 140
Barrett, Dicky 83
basalt 66
Bastion Point 182
Bates, Henry S. 54
Bay of Islands 129, 143, 173
Bay of Plenty 17, 40
beech (tawai, also tahwai) 108, 174; black, mountain (tawhairauriki) 108; red, hard (tawhairaunui) 108; silver (tawhai) 108
beetles 127, 128; green mānuka 29
bellbird (korimako) 123, 152
berries, edible 108 *see also* trees, fruiting
Best, Elsdon 18, 23, 92, 156
bird catching 152–160; decoys 117; preserving 23, 152, 153, 154; snares 153, 155–156, 157, 158, 159, 183
Birdlings Flat 169
birds 94, 116–125; associated with death 118ñ119; containers for cooking and preserving 117, 152, 154; names 124–125; in predicting the weather 121; in sayings, metaphors and stories 122–123; in signs and predictions 119 *see also* individual species
bittern (matuku) 118, 119
black nerita 144
blackfish (ūpokohue) 79
blowflies (rango) 127
blue duck (whio) 125
bowenite 66
bracken fern 114–155, 130, 131; harvest and preparation 115 *see also* aruhe (fern root)
brown teal (tētē whero) 125
Brunner, Lake 133
Brunner, Thomas 180
Buller, Walter 96
Busby, Hekenukumai 25
bush lawyer (tātaramoa) 104
bush wren (hurupounamu) 121
butterflies (pepe, pepe-te-nuinui) 127, 128

C
cabbage tree (tī-kouka) 102, 103, 111; dwarf (tī rauriki) 111; mountain (tī tōī) 111; Pacific (tī pore) 170, 173
canoe: explorations 57–61; navigation 16; traditions 57
Canopus *see* Atutahi
Cape Colville 133
Cape Kidnappers 81
Cape Palliser 63
Cape Rēinga *see* Te Rēinga
carving, origins of 76–77, 127
Castlepoint *see* Rangiwhakaoma
caterpillars (whē) 64, 129, 130
cat's eye (pūpū) 143, 144, 145, 150
centipedes (peketua) 127, 129
Chatham Islands (Wharekauri) 26, 35, 83
cicada (kihikihi) 29
cloaks: dogskin 180; feather 116, 152; kiwi feather 117, 155
clothing 105, 112, 134 *see also* cloaks
clouds 30ñ33; names for 30; reading 32
cockle (tuangi) 144, 145, 148, 149
Colenso, William 112, 161, 172
Collingwood 93
comets 17
conger eel (ngōiro, kōiro) 140, 162, 163, 164, 167
conservation *see* kaitiakitanga
containers: bark (pātua) 154, calabashes (tahā) 154; hinu 114; huahua 23, 152; seaweed (pōhā) 154
Conway, Denis 127
Cook Strait 83, 86
Cook, Captain James 34, 142, 179, 180
Cook's turban (karaka, ngāruru) 138, 145
cooking 54, 145, 154, 168, 177 *see also* hāngī, umu
Coromandel Peninsula 46
Cowan, James 132
crabs 150
crayfish (kōura) 140, 146, 147, 150; freshwater (kōura, kēwai) 147, 151; pots 138, 139
creation tradition 8, 13, 14, 40, 41, 74–75
cuckoo, long-tailed (koekoeā) 121
Curio Bay 180

D
D'Urville Island 145
dew 36
Dieffenbach, Ernest 156
dogs, Polynesian *see* kurī
dotterel (turiwhatu) 120
Downes, T. W. 87, 166

E
earth mother *see* Papatūānuku
East Coast 63, 146, 161, 172
Edwards, Don 163
eeling 21, 162–169
eels (tuna) 94, 142: cooking, preserving and storing 168–169; longfin 162, 163; migrations 169; shortfin 162; snot 163
Ellesmere, Lake (Waihora) 46, 55, 169
Endeavour 143, 172
Europeans 142, 143, 153, 161, 164, 172, 173, 175, 181
exploration by Māori 56–66

F
fantail (pīwakawaka, tīrairaka, tīwaiwaka, tīwakawaka) 119
Farewell Spit 66
feathers: for adornment 116, 152, 154; albatross 118; for capes 154 *see also* cloaks
Feilding 64
fern root *see* aruhe
fernbird (mātātā) 118
ferns: common shield (pikopiko) 115; hen and chickens (mouku) 115; hound's tongue (kōwaowao) 115; kiokio 115; silver (ponga) 109 *see also* ground ferns, tree ferns
fertility 16, 23
Fiordland 175
fire-making 17, 18, 108
fish 94, 128, 179; attracting 141; communal sharing and gifting 142; hooks 138, 139, 180 *see also* individual species
fishing 138–143: moon as guide for 21
flax (harakeke) 9, 105, 111, 112, 139, 165, 168; fibre 138; for nets 138; garments (pākērangi) 134; leaves 166; mountain (wharariki) 111, 112; swamp (harakeke) 112 *see also* muka
flint 66
Flintoff, Brian 134
flounder (pātiki) 139
flowering plants 110
flutes 133, 134
food, storing *see* pātaka, preserving under bird catching, eels, kiore
Ford, John Bevan 42, 125
forest: lore 106–115; mythology 100–107
Forsyth, Lake (Wairewa) 21, 55, 168, 169
Foveaux Strait 82
Fox, Major *see* Taranui, Te Pōhika
Fox, William 158
frost 36
frostfish (para) 162, 163
Fyfe, George 83

G
gannet (tākapu) 118
Gardiner, Lewis Tamihana 66
geckos 94, 95 97, 129; common green (moko kākāriki) 106; kawekaweau 94, 95, 97; Pacific (moko tāpiri, mokopāpā) 95, 96, 97, 106
genealogies 47 *see also* whakapapa
geothermal activity 46, 52–54, 57
geysers 46; Waikite 53
giant eagle 161 *see also* Haast's eagle
gift exchange 142
Gilroy, Paddy 83
giraffe weevil 127
Gisborne *see* Tūranganui
glacial lakes, formation of 54
god stick 72, 171
gods: of cultivated foods *see* Rongo; of forests *see* Tāne; of peace *see* Rongo; of thunder *see* Whaitiri (goddess); of uncultivated foods *see* Haumiatiketike; of war *see* Tūmatauenga; of the winds *see* Tāwhirimātea

191

INDEX

godwit (kūaka) 118, 119
Goodman, Rangi 163
Gould, John 117
gourds (bottle) 43, 138, 172; for preserving birds 23 *see also* containers, hue
grasshoppers (kāwhitiwhiti) 127
Greening, Happy Jack 83
greenstone trails 67 *see also* pounamu
grey duck (pārera) 123
grey warbler (riroriro) 121
Grey, George 75
Grey's beaked whale (hakurā, iheihe) 79
ground ferns 114–115
guardianship *see* kaitiakitanga
gulls 119: black-backed (karora) 119–120; black-billed and red-billed (tarāpunga) 120
gum 103, 114; kauri 108; pūhā 115
gurnard (kumukumu) 140

H

Haast's eagle (Te Pouākai) 124, 125
Haberfield, William 83
hagfish (napia, tuere, blind eel) 162, 163
Hāhuru 81
hail 36
hair oil 114
haka 122
Hākarimata mountain 57
Halbert, Thomas 83
hāngī (earth oven) 142, 154, 173, 177
hāpuku (fish) 138
Hapurapoi 139
harakeke 111, 112; symbolism of 103; medicinal properties 112 *see also* flax
harrier (kāhu) 122
harvest: by lunar calendar 18, 19; and Matariki 25
Hatupatu 93
Haumapuhia (taniwha) 55
Haumiatiketike (Haumia) 8, 13, 114, 130, 131; whakapapa 131
Haunui 64
Hauraki (tribe) 62, 63
Hauraki region 42, 68, 85, 86, 92, 123, 147
Hauturu (Little Barrier Island) 107
Hawaiki 50, 52, 54, 62, 66, 81, 86, 87, 118, 129, 170, 179
Hawke's Bay 36, 41, 173, 177, 179
Heaphy, Charles 140
heavens, creation of 13, 14
Heberley, Jacob 43
hei tiki 68
Heketangawainui 73
Hērangi, Te Puea 33
Heretaunga (Hastings area) 88
Hetet, Rangi 8
Hikawera (chief) 179
Hikurangi mountain 38–39, 49
hīnaki (eel pot or trap) 88, 138, 139, 164, 165, 167
Hinamoki 175
hīnau (tree) 113, 174; food from 113
Hine Te Apārangi 62
Hineāmaru 64
Hinekau-i-rangi 58
Hine-kōrako 88
Hinemarino 57
Hinemataiti 175
Hinemataroa 60
Hinemoa 52
Hine-nui-te-pō 119
Hinepeke 130
Hinepūkohurangi 9
Hineteiwaiwa 80
Hine-te-ngahere 163

Hine-tū-repo 163
Hīroa, Te Rangi (Peter Buck) 138, 139, 165
Hokianga 95, 97
Hokianga Harbour 62, 64, 86, 176
Horouta (canoe) 57, 58, 171, 176
Horowhenua 51
horse mussel (hururoa) 145
hot springs 53
Hotupuku (taniwha) 92
Hoturoa 46, 57
Hotuwaipara 59
Houhora mountain 62, 82
Houmaitawhiti 179
Huata, Te Rangi 25
hue (bottle gourd) 170, 171, 172 *see also* gourds
Hughes, John 83
huhu beetle 128
huia (bird) 116, 117, 118, 154
Huiarau Range 61
Humuhumu (taniwha) 92
hunting *see* bird catching
Hūtana, Ihaia 50
Hutcheson, Mere 143
Hutt Valley 59

I

Īhenga 58, 133
Ikatere 8, 96
insects 94, 97, 126–131 *see also* individual species

J

Jackson Bay 180
Jahnke, Robert 127
Jervois, Governor General Sir William 43
jewellery *see* adornment
Jupiter (Pareārau) 16, 17

K

Kae 79, 80
kahawai (fish) 76, 138, 139, 141
kahikatea (tree) 108, 166
Kahukura 134
kahukura (butterfly) 129
Kahumatamomoe 57, 58
Kahungunu 46, 97
Kahupekapeka 57
Kahurere 57
Kahutiaterangi 80, 87
Kaiapoi 65, 68
kaikōmako (tree) 108
Kaikōura 65, 83
Kaikōura Whale Watch 83
Kaimai Range 57, 63
kaimoana *see* fishing, shellfish gathering
Kāingaroa Plains 58, 92
Kaipara 61, 92
Kaitangata 95
kaitiaki (guardians) 53, 124, 151; taniwha as 91
kaitiakitanga (conservation, guardianship) 182–183
Kaiwhare (taniwha) 92, 93
kākā (bird) 109, 117, 152, 153, 155, 156
kākāpō (bird) 117, 154, 180
Kākaramea mountain 89
kākāriki (bird) 124
Kakepuku mountain 57
Kanohi, Pai 152
kānuka (tree) 109
Kapiti Coast 42
Kapowairua Bay 63
karaka berries 113
karakia (charms) 76, 84, 92, 93, 141, 146, 160, 167
Karamea 128
karamū (plant) 174

Kareariki 93
Karekare (Auckland) 32
karengo (seaweed) 147, 151
Karetehe 176
Karikari 82
Karitoki (chief) 90
Kaūpokonui 24
kauri (tree) 101, 108; and the whale 79; gum 166
Kawautahi, Lae 87
Kāwhia 43, 57, 61
kea (bird) 124, 125
Kehu 158
Kennedy, Warren 163
kererū (kūkupa, New Zealand pigeon) 8, 117, 152, 153, 156, 157, 159; hunting 157
Kermadecs 173
Kerr, Angus 50
kete (woven basket) 111, 141, 148
Keteketerau 81
Ketemaringi 115
Kewa 15
kiekie (plant) 111, 165, 174, 175
kina (sea urchin) 110, 143, 146, 148, 149
kingfisher (kōtare) 123
kinship 8, 46, 134
kiokio (fern) 115
kiore 108, 120, 152, 174–177, 179; hunting, eating and preserving 176–177; in sayings and proverbs 175, 176; traps for 176, 177, 181; whakapapa of 175
kites (pākau) 25
kivi (bristle-thighed curlew) 124
Kiwa 58
kiwi 117, 124, 154, 158, 180; eating 156; for cloaks 155; meat 117
knowledge, creation of 14, 126, 127
kō (digging sticks) 170
Ko te Pūkaki 182
kōauau (flute) 133, 134
kohekohe (tree) 174
Kōhere, Rēweti 34, 139
kōhūhū (tree) 108
kōkako (bird) 122
kōkō 152
kōkōwai (red ochre) 54, 135
Koperu 64
kōrapa 166
koru (new shoots) 109, 115
kōtuku (white heron) 118, 154
kōura *see* crayfish
kōwhai (tree) 28, 110, 146, 156
Kūhā, Matiti 20
Kui 171
kuku (also kūtai) *see* mussel
kūkupa *see* kererū
kūmara 18, 21, 110, 123, 130, 170, 171, 172, 175
Kupe 30, 50, 57, 62, 63, 76, 86, 114
Kurahaupō (canoe) 59, 64
Kuramārōtini 30
Kurangaituku 93
Kurawaka 41
kurī (Polynesian dog) 152, 178–181; as food source 179–180

L

Lake ..., *see* name e.g., Alexandrina, Lake
lakes, southern 54–55, 65
lamprey (piharau, kanakana, korokoro) 162, 163, 167; weirs 164, 167
land: and human body 45; importance of 9, 40–41; loss of 47; naming 45; ownership 56; and people 46; shaping of 48–55; and women 42

INDEX

landforms, explaining origins of 46
laughing tiutiu (tiutiu kata) 120
Leach, Helen 171
life force *see* mauri
life, cycles of 23
lightning 35; and death 35
Lima, Manuel 83
limpet (kākahi, ngākihi) 144, 145
Lindauer, Gottfried 170
Little Akaloa 122
Little Barrier Island (Hauturu) 176
Little River 142
Little Waihī 147
lizards 94, 96, 128, 130; fear of 97; as kaitiaki 97 *see also* geckos, skinks, tuatara
Love, Jacky 83
lunar calendar 18–21, 182
Lysnar, W. D. 95
Lyttelton Harbour 133

M

Mahakipawa 144
Māhia 60, 144, 146, 150
Māhia Peninsula 57, 59, 81, 82, 151
Māhinaarangi 103, 180
māhoe (tree) 108, 158
Māhū 55
Māhuhu (canoe) 92
Mahuika 108
maire (tree) 103
Mākaro (Ward Island) 57, 63
Maketū 45, 57, 58, 138, 183
mamaku (tree fern) 109
Māmari (canoe) 86, 176
mana 42, 56, 177, 182, 183
mana whenua 43, 47
manaakitanga 147
Manaia 129
Manawapōuri (Manapōuri) 54
Manawatū Gorge 55
Manawatū River 59, 64, 145, 165; creation of 55
Mangakāhia 181
Māngārara (canoe) 96, 129
Mangatī river 61
mangemange (plant) 105, 165
Mangō 96
Mangōnui 90
mantis, male (rōtane) 130
mānuka (tree) 109, 139, 146, 151, 166, 177
Manukau Harbour 58, 93
maomao (fish) 29
Māori: Battalion 147; exploration 56; fishing 138; New Year 16, 22, 154 *see also* Matariki; star names 16; story of creation 36
Maraenui 83
marakihau (taniwha) 73
marama *see* moon
maramataka (lunar calendar) 18–21, 166, 182
marble fish (kehe) 140
Marcury (Whiro) 16
māripi (shark-tooth knife) 90, 92
Marlborough Sounds 86
Marokopa 61
Marquesas Islands 170
Mars (Whero) 16
Marsden, Maori 14
marsh crake (kāreke) 119
Massey University 21
Mataatua 17, 81
Mataatua (canoe) 60, 61
mataī (tree) 109
mātaitai *see* shellfish gathering
Matanginui 64
Mataora 175

Matariki 22–25, 154, 16; (the Pleiades) 16, 22
Matatā 81
Mataura 92
Matauri Bay 62
Matawhaorua (canoe) 86
Matiu (Somes Island) 57, 63
mats, rough (pora or pūreke) 134
Mauao 133
Māui 12, 15, 16, 40, 63, 108, 117, 118, 122, 124, 157, 162, 165, 175; death of 119; and place names 49
mauku (fern) 168
Maungakawa Range 89
Maungapōhatu 60, 61
Maungatautari 42
mauri (life force) 81, 106, 107, 160, 163, 171, 183; to attract fish 141; kaitiaki of 97; stone 107, 183
McLean, Donald 74
meteors 17
middens 144, 145
midges (naonao) 127
Milford Sound 66
Milky Way 22
minke whale (pakake) 79
Miramar 168
miro (tree) 109, 115, 157, 174
Miru 97, 135
Mirupōkai 60
mist 37
moa 107, 123, 161, 179
Moawhango River 57
Moehau 46, 135
Moekau 61
Mōkau Heads 141
moki (fish) 29, 140
moko 105, 181
Moko-hiku-waru 97
Mokoia Island 52, 120
mokomoko *see* skinks
Monkhouse, William 172
months 18–19 *see also* lunar calendar
moon 15, 16; phases of 20 *see also* lunar calendar
Moremore 90, 91
morepork *see* ruru
Moriori people 35
Morris, William 83
mosquitoes (waeroa) 127, 129, 130–131
moths (pepe) 127, 128, 130
Mōtū River 58
Motueka 54
Motukiore (rat island) 176
Moumāhaki River 164
mountains: battle of 50, 51; conceptualisation of 41
Moutohorā (Whale Island), Bay of Plenty 82, 107
Mt Albert Research Centre 127
Mt Victoria, Wellington 87
Muaūpoko 183
mud snail (whetiko) 144, 145
muka (flax fibre) 112, 149, 177 *see also* flax
Muriwai (Coopers Lagoon) 55
Muriwhenua 81
mussel (kūtai, kuku) 144, 145, 147, 148, 149; freshwater 144, 145, 150; shells 149
muttonbirding 154
muttonbirds (tītī) 152, 154
Mutuwhenua 20

N

Nahe, Hoani 134
Naihera, Wī 47
Namuiria 126

Napier *see* Ahuriri
Nathan, Manos 97
Native Land Court 47
navigation, canoe 16
Nelson 54, 65
nets: eeling 166; fishing 134, 138, 139, 140; and tapu 138
New Zealand falcon (kārearea) 120, 121, 122
New Zealand pigeon *see* kererū
Ngāhue 66
Ngāi Tahu 21, 34, 35, 36, 47, 83, 142, 169, 183
Ngāi Tara 59
Ngāi Tūhoe 9, 18, 55, 112, 152, 176 *see also* Tūhoe
Ngake (taniwha) 63, 86–87
Ngāpuhi 62, 63, 93, 120, 146
ngārara *see* reptiles
Ngārara Huarau 89, 96
Ngāruawāhia 44
Ngata, Paratene 165
Ngāti Apa 64, 65
Ngāti Apakura 33
Ngāti Awa 15, 130
Ngāti Hako 42
Ngāti Hau 89
Ngāti Hauā 142
Ngāti Hauiti 64, 65
Ngāti Haumia 83
Ngāti Hikairo 43
Ngāti Hine 64
Ngāti Kahu 62, 63
Ngāti Kahungunu 15, 19, 20, 45, 46, 50, 51, 81, 130, 183
Ngāti Korakorako 134
Ngāti Kura 134
Ngāti Kurī 62, 83; origins of name 81, 181
Ngāti Kuru-mokihi 168
Ngāti Maniapoto 8, 51, 112
Ngāti Maru 134
Ngāti Mutunga 138
Ngāti Naho 93
Ngāti Pikiao 138
Ngāti Porou 33, 34, 35, 44, 49, 51, 76, 81, 88, 96, 112, 114, 129, 132, 139, 140, 141, 157, 158, 165, 166, 168
Ngāti Rāhiri 63
Ngāti Rāhiri-tumutumuwhenua 63
Ngāti Ranginui 65
Ngāti Rangiwewehi 89
Ngāti Raukawa 42, 43, 74, 89, 103, 155, 159, 183
Ngāti Rongomaiwahine 147
Ngāti Ruanui 62, 63
Ngāti Tamaterā 86
Ngāti Toa 42, 45
Ngāti Toarangatira 49, 51
Ngāti Tūrehu 134
Ngāti Tūwharetoa 8, 9, 29, 51, 52
Ngāti Wai 83, 175
Ngāti Wairangi 67
Ngāti Whātua 9, 92, 127, 171, 182
Ngāti Whitikaupeka 65
Ngātoroirangi 46, 52, 53, 54, 57, 58
Ngāuruhoe mountain 51
Ngāwhā 93
Ngongotahā mountain 133
Ngutuwera 164
nights of the month *see* lunar calendar
Nihoniho, Tuta 33, 35
nīkau palm 111
Ninety Mile Beach 63
Niua (taniwha) 86
Northland 41, 57, 59, 60, 115, 144, 146, 172, 173
Nukupori 134
Nukutaimemeha (canoe) 49

193

INDEX

O
obsidian 66
octopus 94, 150
Ōhau 54, 64
Ōhinemutu 45
Ōhiwa Harbour 58
Ōhopa 86
Ōkatia 55
Ōkoriwa (Palliser Bay) 59
Ōkūrei peninsula 45
Ōmāpere, Lake 86, 93
Onehunga 143
Onetahua 148
Onetapu 54
ongaonga (tree nettle) 104
Ōngare Point 72
Ōnoke, Lake 169
Ōpepe 56
Ōpihi River 84
Opo 86
Opononi 86
Ōpoutere 82
Ōrākei Kōrako 53, 54
Ōreti Beach 149
ostrich foot (totorere) 144, 145
Ōtaki 165, 166, 168
Ōtarahioi 61
Ōtautahanga pā 89
owl: laughing (whēkau) 120; morepork see ruru
oyster (tio) 144, 145, 146, 150; native rock (tio) 145, 150
oyster borer (kaikai tio) 145

P
pā see weir
Pacific rat see kiore
packhorse crayfish (also green crayfish) see kōura
Paekākāriki 83
Pahīatua 64
Pāhua 66
Paikea 80, 81, 87
Pākehā 135; whalers 83 see also Europeans
pakepakehā see patupaiarehe
Pane-iraira (taniwha) 87
Panguru mountains 86
Pani 175
Pānia 90, 91
Pāoa 57, 58, 123
pāpā (plant) 158
Papakura, Mākereti 135
Papatūānuku 8, 12, 13, 15, 23, 36, 37, 40, 41, 42, 43, 47, 73, 74, 96, 114, 162; whakapapa 41
paper mulberry see aute
Parangārehu (Fitzroy Bay) 59
parapara (plant) 114
Pārengarenga 140
Parihaka 17
Pari-ka-whiti 89
Pariwhero 96
Parkinson, Sydney 180
pātaka (storehouses) 142, 175
patatē (tree) 108, 174
Pātea River 62
patupaiarehe 114, 132; encounters with 134
pāua 143, 144, 145, 146, 148; shell 139, 148
Pekahourangi 62
Pekehaua (taniwha) 92
Pelorus Jack 86
pendants 180 see also adornment
penguin, Fiordland crested (pokotiwha) 125
peruperu 29
pets 120; birds 117

pied oystercatcher (tōrea) 121
Pigeon Bay 142
pigeon trough 159
Piha 92, 93
Pīhanga 36, 50, 51
piharau see lamprey
Piki 87
pilot whale (ūpokohue) 79, 82
Pio, Hamiora 15
piopio (New Zealand thrush) 120
pipi 144, 145, 146, 147, 148, 149
pipit (pīhoihoi) 122
Pire, Rangihuna 24
Pirongia 57, 115
Pitaka 92, 93
piupiu 112
place names 45, 56
placenta, significance of 43
planets 16–17
planting: crops 24, 170–173; moon as guide for 21
plants: in cultivation 170–173; flowering 110; fruiting 113–114; scented 103; symbolism of 102–105; for weaving 111, 112 see also trees, individual species names
Pleiades see Matariki
Poata, Tāmati 159
pōhoi see feathers
pōhutukawa (tree) 110, 146
pointer stars 16
Polack, Joel 156, 159
Polynesia 9, 40, 56, 112, 129, 172, 173, 178; fishing equipment from 138; plants from 170–173
Polynesian bottle gourd see gourds, hue
Polynesian dog see kurī
Polynesian rat see kiore
Polynesians 171
ponaturi (sea fairies) 134
ponga (silver fern) 109
Pōrangahau 46, 143
Porirua Harbour 60
poroporo (tree) 113
Port Levy 142
Pōtae, Hēnare 76
Pōtaka Tawhiti 179
Pōtatau Te Wherowhero 142
Pōtoru 93
pou (also poupou) 8, 65, 105
pou rāhui 105
Pou-mātangatanga 83
pounamu 66, 67, 68, 156, 183; whakapapa of 67
Poutini 66
Poutoru 93
preserving: food 21, 145, 153, 154, 168
prohibitions on fishing 141 see also rāhui
Puanga (Rigel) 16, 23, 24, 110
puawānanga (plant) 110
pūhā (plant) 108, 115, 168
Puhi 60
Puhiwahine, Rihi 52
pūhore 160
Pūkaki 54
Pūkaki, Lake 54
pukatea (tree) 102
pūkeko (bird) 123, 180
Puke-o-Kahu mountain 57
Pukerua Bay 64
Puketoi Range 55
Puna-kauariki 162
Punga 8, 73, 94, 95, 126; offspring of 95
pūngāwerewere (spiders) 128, 129, 130
Pūrākau 61
Pureora 57, 58, 115
pūriri (tree) 115, 130, 174

pūriri moth (pepetuna, ghost moth) 130
Putauaki mountain 50
Pū-te-hue 172
pūtōrino (flute) 133, 134
Pūwhenua 133

Q
quail, New Zealand (koreke) 122

R
Raglan 57, 147
Rāhiri 63
rāhui 141, 147, 160, 176, 182, 183
rain 32–33; and death 33
rainbow 37
Rākaihautū 46, 54, 65
Rakataura 57
rākau tipua (enchanted logs) 92 see also taniwha
Ranapiri, Tāmiti 159
Randall, Renee 183
Ranginui 8, 12, 13, 14, 15, 23, 26, 36, 37, 40, 41, 73, 74, 96, 114
rangiora (plant) 157, 168
Rangitāne 55, 59, 183
Rangitātā 2
Rangi-te-wanawana 127
Rangitīkei River 60, 64
Rangitoto (Auckland) 46, 115, 140
Rangitoto (D'Urville Island) 66
Rangiwhakaoma (Castlepoint) 17, 59
Rāninikura 63
Raoul Island 173
Rapa Nui (Easter Island) 171
rarauhe see bracken fern
Rarotake 114
Rarotimu 114
Rātā 107, 128, 129
rātā (tree, vine) 110, 156; northern 110
rats: Norway 175; ship 175 see also kiore
Raukatauri 80
raukawa (plant) 103
Raukūmara Range 58
raupō (plant) 113
Raureka 67
Rehua (Antares) 16, 28, 29, 110
Reipae 57
Reitū 57
Remuera 142
reptiles 94–97, 129; giant 89
rereti (fern) 115
Reretua 59
Rētāruke River 87
Richardson, Major J. L. C. 159
rifleman (tītiti pounamu) 125
right whale see southern right whale
rimu (tree) 108, 109, 110
rimurimu (seaweed) 168
ringed dosinia (harihari) 145
ringed venus shell 144
Riukaramea (canoe) 90
rō (stick insect) 127, 131
robin (pītoitoi, karuwai) 124, 158
rock cod (taipua, rāwaru) 140
rock shell (ngāeo) 145
Rokohouia 65
Rona 12, 16
Rongo 8, 13, 171
Rongokako 46
Rongomāui (also Rongo-māui) 130, 175
Rotoaira, Lake 116
Roto-a-Tara 88
Rotoiti 54
Rotoiti, Lake 58, 150
Rotorua 53, 54, 58, 92, 133, 147
Rotorua, Lake 52, 58

194

Ruahine Range 64
Ruamano 81, 86
Ruanui 176
Ruapehu mountain 51, 64
Ruatāhuna 159
Ruataniwha plains 88
Ruatapu 80, 81
Ruatapu, Mohi 76, 141
Ruatepupuke 76–77
Ruawehea 42
Ruawharo 81
ruru (morepork) 120

S
saddleback (tīeke) 125
Samoa 170
sandflies (namu) 127, 129, 130–131
Saunders, Tame 169
sayings (whakataukī) 23: birds in 122; trees and plants 103
scallop (tipa) 144, 145
scamperdown whale (hakurā, iheihe) 79
scaup (pāpango) 124
sea birds 118
sea urchin *see* kina
seals 179
Sealy Range 30
seasons 19, 28–29
seed, edible 109
shag, spotted (kawau pāteketeke) 122
sharks 94, 140, 142; as taniwha 90–91
shellfish gathering (mātaitai) 144–150
shield shell (rori) 145
shining cuckoo (pīpīwharauroa) 121
shining spleenwort (huruhuru whenua) 115
shooting stars *see* meteors
shoveler (kuruwhengu) 124
Sirius (Takurua) 16, 29
skinks (mokomoko) 94, 95, 97
sky father *see* Ranginui
sleet 36
snapper (tāmure) 140, 141
snow 36
sooty shearwaters 154
Southern Alps 54, 67, 68; formation 49
Southern Cross 16
southern humpback whale (paikea) 79
southern right whale (tohorā) 78, 79, 80
spears: for eels 166; for fishing 138, 139; for hunting birds 113, 156, 157
Spencer, James 83
sperm whale (parāoa) 79, 82, 83
spider, Nelson cave 128
spiders 97, 129 *see also* pūngāwerewere
spirits 16, 77, 118, 119, 120, 128, 130, 160
spiritual restriction 183 *see also* rāhui, tapu
starfish 150
stars 15, 16
Stewart Island 49, 152, 175
stick games (tititorea) 135
stilt, pied (poaka) 123
stingray 94; spine of 156
stitchbird (hihi) 124
stone: figures 171; Māori use of 68–69; resources 66–69; stone-row boundaries 172; trading 66
storehouses *see* pātaka
storms 35
string games (whai) 135
sun 15–16: god *see* Te Rā
supernatural creatures 84 *see also* Ngārara Huarau, patupaiarehe, ponaturi, taniwha
supplejack (aka pirita) 92, 133, 139, 141, 165, 166, 177, 185

Swainson, William 143

T
taewa (potato) 21
Tahanga 66
Tahurangi 134
taiaha 180
Taihape 64
Taikehu 83
Tainui 57
Tainui (canoe) 42, 46, 57–61, 66, 81, 83, 87, 141, 171
Tairea (canoe) 66
Takaaho 79
takahē (bird) 124
Takapau 177
Takauere (taniwha) 93
Takere-piripiri 89
Tākitimu (canoe) 81, 86, 87
Tākitimu Range 133
Tākou Bay, Northland 60
Takurua (Sirius) 16, 29
Tama 92
Tamaāhua 66
Tamaariki 83
Tama-i-waho 177
Tamatea 2, 57, 64–65
Tamatea-pōkaiwhenua 46
Tamatekapua 45, 46, 58, 179, 183
Tamatekapua meeting house 95
Tāminamina (taniwha) 89
Tāmure 92, 93
Tāne 13, 14, 41, 75, 96, 100, 101, 106, 107, 114, 117, 126, 127, 128, 130, 172; symbolism of 102
Tāneatua 60
Tāne-kino 88
Tāne-mahuta (also Tānemahuta, Tāne Mahuta) 8, 26, 101, 102, 108
Tangaroa 8, 13, 26, 49, 72, 73, 74, 75, 79, 94, 95, 128, 141; offspring of 96
tangata whenua 9, 43
tangi (funeral) 117, 143
taniwha 55, 63, 66, 73, 81, 84–93 *see also* individual names
tapa cloth 112, 173
Tapsell, Phillip 83
tapu 118, 120, 138, 141, 142, 146, 160, 175, 181, 183
Tapuwaeputuputu (canoe) 114
Tara 59, 88, 118, 180
Taraia 81
taraire (tree) 115, 174; food from 113
tarakihi (fish) 140
Taramainuku 58
Taranaki 50, 59, 173
Taranaki (Egmont) mountain 17, 61
Taranga 117, 157
Taranui, Te Pōkiha 138
Tararua Range 59, 64; naming of 45
tarata (plant) 108
Tarawera mountain 58
Tarawera River 58, 59
taro 123, 170, 171, 172–173
Tauhara 50, 58
Tauira tribe 83
Taumarunui 87
Taupiri 33
Taupō 9, 53, 56
Taupō, Lake 52, 58, 60
Tauranga 63
Tauranga tribes 64
Taurenga (taniwha) 88
Tautoki 59
Tautoru (Orion's Belt) 16

tawa (tree) 104, 113, 156, 174; food from 113
Tāwhaki 123, 134
tāwhara (fruit of kiekie) 174, 175
Tāwhiao 44, 105
tāwhiri (plant) 103
Tāwhirimātea 13, 23, 114, 128
Tāwhitikurī 181
Te Ahukaramū, Hūkiki 43, 74
Te Āhuru 15
Te Aitua, Pita 87
Te Aorangi (Feilding) 64
Te Āpiti (the Manawatū Gorge), creation of 55
Te Ara-a-Kewa (Foveaux Strait) 82
Te Ara-a-Paikea (Māhia Peninsula) 82 *see also* Māhia Peninsula
Te Aratiatia 58
Te Arawa 13, 45, 46, 52, 53, 57, 66, 120, 157, 183
Te Arawa (canoe) 45, 46, 52, 58, 66, 179
Te Aroha 57, 63, 115, 133
Te Āti Awa 43, 62
Te Āti Awa ki Taranaki 183
Te Āti Haunui-a-Pāpārangi 62
Te Aupōuri 14, 62
Te Awanga 83
Te Hāpuku 79
Te Harara 146
Te Herenga Waka marae 2, 65, 76, 105
Te Heuheu 9
Te Heuheu Tūkino II, Mananui 89
Te Hoata 46, 52, 53, 54
Te Huhu 35
Te Hurinui Jones, Pei 51
Te Ika-a-Māui (the fish of Māui) 49
Te Ikaroa (the Milky Way) 15
Te Kaha 142
Te Kahu, Maadi 183
Te Kaiwhakaruaki 93
Te kōhatu o Hatupatu 93
Te Kūiti 115
Te Manuhauturuki 76
Te Mata Peak 46
Te Mimi-a-Homaiterangi geyser 54
Te Moana-o-Raukawa (Cook Strait) 86 *see also* Cook Strait
Te Naenae 141
Te Ngārara Huarau 89, 96
Te Ōhāki marae 176
Te Pāteanui-a-Turi 61
Te Pipiwharauroa newspaper 86
Te Pō 13
Te Puea Hērangi 44
Te Pupū 46, 52, 53, 54
Te Pūwhakahara 79
Te Rā 12, 15, 17, 23, 28
Te Rangihaeata 45, 49
Te Rangikāheke 89, 157
Te Rangikāheke, Wiremu Maihi 13
Te Rarawa 35, 62, 142, 183
Te Rauparaha 42, 51
Te Rehunga 177
Te Rēinga (Cape Rēinga) 77, 118, 119
Te Rēinga falls 88
Te Tahi-o-te-rangi 81, 87
Te Tai Poutini (the South Island's West Coast) 83
Te Tau-a-Porirua 88
Te Tihi-o-Manono 14
Te Toa Takitini newspaper 50
Te Toi-o-ngā-rangi 14
Te Toki a Tapiri (canoe) 129
Te Waha, Popota 142
Te Waharoa 142
Te Wai Pounamu (South Island) 54
Te Waiiti River 61

INDEX

Te Wairoa 63
Te Waiū-o-Te-Tohorā 82
Te Wākā Māori o Niu Tirani newspaper 88
Te Wano 33
Te Whakaruaki 96
Te Whānau-ā-Apanui tribe 83
Te Whanganui-a-Tara *see* Wellington
Te Whatanui 42
Te Whatu-i-apiti 51
Tekapo (Takapō) 54
terns (tara) 118
thermal wonders *see* geothermal activity
thunder 35
Tia 58
Tikao, Teone (Hone) Taare 35, 167, 169, 180
Tīkapa (the Firth of Thames) 85
tī-kōuka *see* cabbage tree
Tinirau (whale) 79, 80
tipua 92, 93
Tītapu 118
tītī *see* muttonbirds
Titi Islands 152
Tītīraupenga 58, 115
titoki (tree) 130: berries 114
toetoe grass 113
Tōhē 63
toheroa (shellfish) 145, 146, 149
tohunga (priests) 34, 81, 87, 90, 106, 107, 147, 160, 181, 183
Toka, Henare 127
Tokomaru Bay 63, 73
Tolaga Bay 34, 173
tomtit (kōmiromiro) 120
Tonga 170
Tongariro mountain 9, 36, 46, 50, 51, 52, 53, 57, 60, 65
Tonihi 135
tools 66, 68, 180: tūwiri (drills) 68; stone 68; grubber 171
tōtara (tree) 108; symbolism of 102
traps *see* bird catching, eeling, kiore
tree ferns 109, 156
tree nettle *see* ongaonga
trees 108–109, 110, 111; fruiting 113–114 *see also* individual species
triangle shell (kaikaikaroro) 144, 145
trough shell (kuhakuha) 144, 145
trumpeter fish (pōrae) 140
Tuariki 91
tuatara 94, 95, 96, 97, 129; origins of 89
tuatua (shellfish) 144, 145, 146, 149
Tuhiraki (Mt Bossu) 65
Tuhirangi (taniwha) 86
Tūhoe 37, 44, 130, 133, 160 *see also* Ngāi Tūhoe
Tūhua (Mayor Island) 66
Tūhuruhuru 80
tūī (bird) 28, 119, 152, 156, 157, 158
tukutuku panel 8, 105
Tūmatauenga (Tū) 13, 26, 75, 126, 131, 181
Tumutumuwhenua 171
tuna 162–169 *see also* eel
Tūnui 81
Tūpari 95
Tuputupu-whenua 9
Tūranganui (Gisborne) 58, 63
tūrangawaewae 44, 45
Tūrangi 52
tūrehu *see* patupaiarehe
Tūrei, Mohi 51, 88, 132
Turi 61
Tūrongo 103, 180
turret shell (papatai) 145
Tūtaekurī 179
Tūtaeporoporo (taniwha) 90, 91, 92
Tūtakangahau 18

Tūtānekai 52
Tū-tangata-kino 97
Tutarakauika (whale) 81, 87
Tūtaua (enchanted log) 92
Tūteahuru 130
Tū-te-kawa 67
Tū-te-wanawana 95, 96
Tūtewehiwehi (Tū-te-wehiwehi) 8, 96
Tūtira 168
turu (plant) 113; extracting juice from 113
Tutunui 79, 80

U
ua *see* rain
Uenuku 37, 80
Uenuku (chief) 179
umbilical cord, significance of 43
umu (earth oven) 145 *see also* cooking
Ureia (taniwha) 85
Urenui river 61
Urewera ranges 9, 37, 60, 133
Uruao (canoe) 54, 65
urukehu (red-heads) 132, 134, 135
uwhi (yam) 170, 171, 173

V
Vega *see* Whānui
Venus (Kōpū) 16, 17
Volcanic Plateau 52; stories of origins 46
volute 144
voyaging canoes 128

W
Waiapu 138
Waiapu River 58, 141
Waiari, Tamarau 160
Waihī 89
Waihora (Wiahola) *see* Ellesmere, Lake
Waihou 86
Waihuka 81
Waikanae 64
Waikaremoana, Lake 55, 92
Waikato 57, 81, 92, 133, 142
Waikato River 57, 58, 165
Waimā 114
Waimakariri River 31
Waimamaku 97
Waimana River 61
Waimangu 53
Waimārama 86, 89
Wainuiomata River 163
Waiohiki 179
Waiōmio 64
Waipā 133
Waipapa 88
Waipawa Plains 64
Waipoua Forest 101, 108
Wairaka 64
Wairarapa 59, 63, 64, 89, 126, 146, 169, 172
Wairarapa, Lake 64, 169
Wairewa *see* Forsyth, Lake
Wairoa 88, 133
Wairoa River 58, 88
Waitaha 81
Waitaha tribe 46, 65, 124
Waitaiki 66
Waitākere Ranges 133
Waitara 61, 73
Waitohi 42
Waitomo 181
waka: huia 116; kererū 159; kōiwi (burial chest) 97; taua (war canoes) 108
Wakatipu, Lake 54
Wānaka, Lake 12, 54

Wārahi 87
warehou (fish) 140
water: categories of 77; names for 72; source of life 76
weather 26–37
weaving, plants for 111, 112
weirs, for eels and lampreys 138, 163, 164, 167
weka (bird) 123, 152, 157, 158, 180
Weller, Edward 83
Wellington 63, 77
Wellington Harbour 57, 59, 63; creation of 86
wētā (insect) 126, 127
Whāingaroa (Raglan) 57
Whaitiri (goddess of thunder) 36, 95
Whaiwhaiā (enchanted log) 92
Whakaari 46, 52, 53, 81, 87
whakapapa 47, 130; of fish and other underwater species 73; Papatūānuku and Ranginui 41; the natural world 8; stone 67
Whakarara Range 64
Whakarewarewa 53, 54, 95
Whakatāne 60, 63, 82, 87
Whakatāne River 60, 81
Whakatū (Nelson) 65
whalebone 82, 166, 167
whales 78–83; as taniwha 87 *see also* individual species
Whanawhana 134
Whangaehu River 64
Whāngaiariki 63
Whangamatā, near Taupō 66
Whangamoa, above Nelson 66
Whanganui 9, 47, 92, 108, 120, 133
Whanganui River 62, 64, 87, 90, 91, 164, 167
Whanganui tribes 112
Whangaokeno Island (also Whanga-o-keno Island, East Island) by East Cape 96, 129
Whangaparāoa (Auckland) 57, 82
Whangaparāoa (East Coast) 57, 82, 83
Whāngarā 46
Whangaroa 141
whangewhange (plant) 158
Whānui (Vega) 16, 22, 130, 175
Wharekauri *see* Chatham Islands
Whātaitai 63, 86–87
Whātonga 59, 180
Wheketoro 96, 129
wheki, wheki-ponga *see* tree ferns
whelk (kawari) 144, 145
whenua *see* land, placenta
Whiro (god of the underworld) 97, 126, 127
white heron *see* kōtuku
White Island *see* Whakaari
white rock shell (hopetea) 144, 145
white slipper shell 144
whitebait 140, 147
whitehead (pōpokotea) 120
Whiting, Cliff 13
Wiki, Jim 14
wild Spainard (taramea) 114
Williams, William 161
winds 26–34
women and land 42–43
wood 139

Y
yam *see* uwhi
yellow-eyed mullet 20
yellow-eyed penguin (hoiho) 125
Young Nick's Head 58